WRITING
WIDOWHOOD

WRITING
WIDOWHOOD

THE LANDSCAPES OF BEREAVEMENT

JEFFREY BERMAN

Published by State University of New York Press, Albany

For information, contact State University of New York Press, Albany, NY
www.sunypress.edu

Production, Jenn Bennett
Marketing, Fran Keneston

Library of Congress Cataloging-in-Publication Data

Berman, Jeffrey, 1945–
    Writing widowhood : the landscapes of bereavement / Jeffrey Berman.
        pages cm
    Includes bibliographical references and index.
    ISBN 978-1-4384-5819-9 (hc : alk. paper)—978-1-4384-5820-5 (pb : alk. paper)
    ISBN 978-1-4384-5821-2 (e-book)
    1. American literature—Women authors—History and criticism. 2. Widows in
literature. 3. Bereavement in literature. 4. Widows' writings. 5. Widowhood—
Psychological aspects. 6. Autobiography—Authorship. I. Title.

PS152.B47 2015
810.9'9287—dc23   2014045579

10 9 8 7 6 5 4 3 2 1

By the Same Author

Joseph Conrad: Writing as Rescue

The Talking Cure: Literary Representations of Psychoanalysis

Narcissism and the Novel

Diaries to an English Professor: Pain and Growth in the Classroom

Surviving Literary Suicide

Risky Writing: Self-Disclosure and Self-Transformation in the Classroom

Empathic Teaching: Education for Life

Dying to Teach: A Memoir of Love, Loss, and Learning

Cutting and the Pedagogy of Self-Disclosure (with Patricia Hatch Wallace)

Death in the Classroom: Writing about Love and Loss

Companionship in Grief: Love and Loss in the Memoirs of C. S. Lewis, John Bayley, Donald Hall, Joan Didion, and Calvin Trillin

Death Education in the Writing Classroom

Dying in Character: Memoirs on the End of Life

Confidentiality and Its Discontents: Dilemmas of Privacy in Psychotherapy (with Paul Mosher)

To the Memory of My Brother, Elliot

People in grief become more like themselves.

—Roger Rosenblatt

Contents

Acknowledgments

Just as caring for a dying spouse is a sacred duty, an act of love and devotion, so is writing a book about the landscapes of bereavement. I have done my best to do justice to the five memoirists here: Joyce Carol Oates, Sandra Gilbert, Gail Godwin, Joan Didion, and Kay Redfield Jamison. Their memoirs are deft tutors to the landscapes of bereavement awaiting widows and widowers.

Of all the truths I discovered while researching and writing this book, none was greater than Eleanor Bergstein's prescient observation to the newly widowed Joyce Carol Oates: though you loved your spouse deeply and could not imagine life without him, you may fall in love again with another person, though you might not think so now. That observation came true for me. I am grateful for my wife, Julie, who has tolerated good-naturedly my decade-long preoccupation with writing about love and loss. Julie has helped me maintain a continuing bond with the past and forge a new bond with the present and future, allowing companionship in grief to transform mysteriously to companionship in joy.

I am deeply grateful for the help of James Peltz, co-director of SUNY Press, whose support and enthusiasm for this project never wavered. James patiently stood by my side as this manuscript slowly evolved to its present form. Special thanks to Jenn Bennett, who supervised the production of the manuscript, and to Laura Tendler, for her superb copyediting skills. I am also grateful for the perceptive criticisms and generosity of spirit of three of the SUNY Press anonymous evaluators who revealed their identities to me after the manuscript was accepted for publication: Dawn Skorczewski, Linda Wagner-Martin, and Virginia Blum. Their suggestions for revision immeasurably strengthened the manuscript; I am alone responsible for lingering weaknesses.

Special thanks to Chris Mangini for designing the striking book cover.

"Widows' Stories of Love After Loss" was given at the 29th International Conference on Psychology and the Arts in Ghent, Belgium, on July 8, 2012.

Finally, I dedicate this book to the memory of my brother, Elliot. Rated one of Connecticut's best dentists, he was loved and admired by his family, friends, and patients. No one enjoyed life more than Elliot did; his courage, humor, and kindness were inspirational. He was fearless in the face of approaching death.

Introduction

"The Most Life-Changing Event"

The death of a spouse, Thomas Holmes and Richard Rahe report, is the most life-changing event that one is likely to experience. A life-changing event may not necessarily be the most devastating event: there is no hierarchy or calculus of loss, and the death of a child or parent may awaken in some people the most intense grief. Nevertheless, most researchers believe that the death of a spouse—the person with whom one has lived for a lifetime and whom one knows (and is known by) better than anyone else—is the most life-altering event. No matter how independent one is, living with a beloved spouse for many decades is like living with the better part of one's self. Life without that other becomes unimaginable. When the unimaginable occurs, one may not wish to remain alive—that's why widowhood is so harrowing and destabilizing. Robert C. DiGiulio, a professor of education whose wife, oldest daughter, and in-laws were killed in a car accident, agrees with Holmes and Rahe, adding that spousal loss is "more stressful than serious personal illness, separation, or divorce; being sentenced to prison; or living through the death of a parent or child" (57). The shock of widowhood is greater when the loss is sudden and unexpected. People are now living longer than decades ago, but the shock of widowhood remains.

There is no shortage of self-help books to assist widows and widowers with their grief. These books often serve a valuable if limited role—limited in that they sometimes dispense formulaic advice that fails to capture the complexity of grief and the difficulty if not impossibility of recovery. In their desire to be helpful, therapists sometimes speak about the resolution of grief, or "closure," to which some readers may find themselves resistant. Laura A. Tanner observes, for example, that in the years following

1

her father's death she turned to "theories of mourning" but came away feeling "unsatisfied" (84). As Amy Katerini Prodromou observes about what she calls "memoirs of textured recovery," "grief is not an event that we must 'get over' quickly, though neither must it last forever" (personal communication, August 19, 2014).

To understand the reality of bereavement and the authenticity of lived experience, one may turn to widowhood memoirs written by many of the finest writers of our age. These stories dramatize love and loss in ways that compel the reader's sympathy and identification. Widowhood memoirs, a term synonymous with spousal loss memoirs, appeal to a large audience, particularly to an ever-widening community of mourners. These stories demonstrate that bereavement is largely a function of the personality of the bereaved and the specific nature of the relationship lost. Unless an elderly couple dies at the same time, as Ovid describes in his touching story of Baucis and Philemon, two devoted lovers who are granted their wish by the gods to die simultaneously and are transformed into trees entwined in each other's branches, one partner will almost always predecease the other—and usually it is the widow.

Spousal deaths vary greatly, ranging from the sudden and unexpected, on the one hand, to the expected and protracted, on the other hand. But even the agonizingly slow death of a spouse is a shock, resulting in a startling shift from presence to absence of the beloved. As Virginia Blum remarked when reading an early draft of this manuscript, "the marriage-plot novel might end in marriage, but long marriages end in death, one before the other. Someone is always left behind to grieve." Widowhood memoirs avoid sugarcoating the truth but hold out the possibility of hope, not that one's deceased spouse will magically return to life, but that life will sooner or later become meaningful again.

The Shock of Widowhood

Nowhere is the shock of sudden widowhood more apparent than in Joyce Carol Oates's *A Widow's Story*, published in 2011, which chronicles the death of her husband, Raymond Smith, on February 18, 2008, at age seventy-seven. Smith appeared to be recovering from pneumonia at the Princeton Medical Center when he developed a virulent secondary infection in his "good" lung that did not respond to medication and quickly became deadly. *A Widow's Story* describes Oates's forty-eight-year marriage and her panic, confusion, and despair following his death. The real shock for the reader of *A Widow's Story* arises not from sudden spousal loss but from Oates's almost unrecognizable self-portrait: that of a distraught, masochistic woman who cannot stop torturing herself over her husband's death, though in no way does she deserve blame or criticism. One can certainly imagine a widow so grief stricken that she seems out of control, scarcely able to get out of bed, and yearning to die, but the image of Oates as self-blaming, self-lacerating, and self-loathing is so different from the one she has cultivated in her many scholarly books and articles, where she always seems composed and detached, that readers suddenly wonder whether they have been transported into one of her trademark Gothic horror stories.

Sandra M. Gilbert is an eminent feminist literary critic and poet, not a memoirist, but when her husband and fellow literary critic, Elliot Gilbert, died suddenly at the age of sixty following routine prostate surgery on February 11, 1991, she wrote a gripping memoir, *Wrongful Death* (1995), which honors his memory. Like Oates, Gilbert writes about widowhood decades before losing her husband, almost as if she is rehearsing death. Like Oates, she associates sudden widowhood with shock and horror, though she does not believe, as Oates does, that the widow "deserves" punishment. Nor does she believe, as Oates does, that the dead are betrayed by the living. Unlike Oates, Gilbert consults several "grief books" for help and finds much wisdom in reading them. Gilbert cannot "right the wrong" of her husband's death, but she is an author who, in her need to bear witness to traumatic loss, is compelled to "write wrong" in her widowhood memoir and in her later books. Gilbert is one of the few authors of a widowhood narrative who writes extensively about being in love again, and for this reason alone her books on bereavement are significant.

Widowhood also compelled the distinguished novelist Gail Godwin to write the largely autobiographical *Evenings at Five* (2004), which memorializes her lifelong companion, the composer Robert Starer, who died on April 22, 2001, at the age of seventy-seven. Godwin's two-volume journal, *The Making of a Writer*, casts light on her early life, including the suicides of her father and half-brother. She explores in her journal her struggle with depression, part of her paternal legacy; her two failed marriages; and her search for fulfillment in love and work. We also see her passion for writing and her development as a novelist. The two characters in *Evenings at Five*, Christina and Rudy, are based closely on Godwin and Starer. Godwin reveals little about Starer's life before she met him, but we learn a great deal about his personal and professional lives in his two books: his memoir, *Continuo: A Life in Music*, and his only novel, *The Music Teacher*. Reading these books deepens our understanding and appreciation of *Evenings at Five*. A widowhood memoir as well as a "ghost story," *Evenings at Five* portrays Rudy as a powerful presence in Godwin's life; paradoxically, in some ways she is more attuned to him in death than in life.

Life can change in an instant. The sentence comes from Joan Didion's *The Year of Magical Thinking* (2005), her iconic memoir about the sudden death of her husband, the writer John Gregory Dunne, to whom she had been married for nearly forty years. In *Companionship in Grief*, I discuss Didion's reaction to her husband's death, which represented, consistent with clinical theory, the most transformative event in her life up until that time. Dunne died on December 30, 2003, at the age of seventy-one, but the death of their thirty-nine-year-old daughter, Quintana Roo Dunne Michael, on August 26, 2005, from acute pancreatitis may have been more cataclysmic for Didion. After completing *The Year of Magical Living*, Didion was confronted with an almost unimaginable challenge: writing about the loss of her only child. The result is a poignant companion memoir, *Blue Nights*, published in 2011. Didion has a catastrophic imagination, imagining in her novels the worst coming true, but in her case the worst did come true.

A mother's loss of her daughter has been one of Didion's lifelong fears, appearing in her earliest novels, *Play It as It Lays* and *A Book of Common Prayer*. These novels eerily foreshadow *Blue Nights*. Few readers will fail to be moved by *Blue Nights*, but the memoir raises troubling ethical questions about Didion's decision to reveal her daughter's psychiatric diagnosis as "borderline personality disorder." There are no ethical problems for a writer to reveal her own psychiatric profile, as Didion did at the beginning of her writing career in *The White Album*, but it's ethically questionable for a writer to reveal the psychiatric diagnosis of another person who would be deeply embarrassed over this self-disclosure if she were still alive. *Blue Nights* is unsettling for many reasons, and though it focuses mainly on a mother's grief over her deceased child, it reads like an end-of-life memoir, with the author waiting stoically for the end.

Unlike Oates, Gilbert, Didion, and Godwin, Kay Redfield Jamison is not a literary writer or English professor but a professor of psychiatry at Johns Hopkins University. She is also a pioneering researcher on the relationship between mood disorders and creativity. Jamison's memoir *Nothing Was the Same* (2009) honors the memory of her husband, Richard Wyatt, a physician who made important contributions to our understanding of schizophrenia. *Nothing Was the Same* is the only widowhood memoir in which we see protracted death. It's also the only memoir to portray grief as generative and transformative. Richard Wyatt developed life-threatening Hodgkin's disease in 1973, when he was thirty-three, and he was treated with chemotherapy and radiation therapy, both of which cured the cancer. But the aggressive therapy was responsible for creating two later cancers, Burkitt's lymphoma, which he developed when he was sixty, and lung cancer, to which he succumbed in 2002 at age sixty-three. Throughout *Nothing Was the Same*, Jamison expresses gratitude for her nearly twenty-year relationship with Wyatt. Her memoir emphasizes the importance of positive emotions, including gratitude; she shows how caring for a loved one is a gift that makes possible recovery after loss.

"People in Grief Become More Like Themselves"

"People in grief become more like themselves," Roger Rosenblatt remarks in *Kayak Morning* (128), his memoir about his daughter's death. Rosenblatt doesn't elaborate on the meaning of this provocative statement, but he implies that grief somehow exposes the bedrock of one's character, the core self or identity that embodies an inner sense of sameness and continuity. Do widows in grief become more like themselves? Despite the growing body of research on trauma studies, bereavement studies, and literary studies, clinicians and theorists seldom discuss whether novelists and memoirists grieve in ways that are consistent with their pre- and post-widowhood lives. Just as we can understand our life only backward but must live it forward, as the Danish philosopher Kierkegaard remarked, the only way to determine whether writers in grief "become more like themselves" is to look at the entirety of their work.

To see how authors respond to love and loss, we must look closely at their writings both before and after they became widows. For this reason, a biographical approach is valuable. "Biography can deceive, of course," Elliot Gilbert points out in *The Good Kipling*, "but it can also, by increasing the critic's confidence in his intuitions, by offering him, as it were, another avenue of approach to his subject's always ingeniously guarded secret, reinforce an insight already established by careful textual analysis, or at least offer a metaphor for that insight" (205).

Clinical theory also helps us to understand how widows write about widowhood—how they portray the various landscapes of bereavement. We must recognize, however, that there is often a tension if not suspicion between creative writers, on the one hand, and psychotherapists, on the other. Indeed, one of the most striking differences that we encounter in our study of widowhood is the extent to which psychotherapy is valuable to the grieving widow. Two memorists, Oates and Didion, reveal a lifelong antipathy toward psychotherapy; a third, Gilbert, creates a sympathetic psychotherapist who helps a grief-stricken character in the novel *The Good Husband* achieve emotional intelligence; a fourth, Gilbert, is indebted to the authors of "grief books"; and a fifth, Jamison, is herself a clinical psychologist though wary of colleagues who are judgmental of those who suffer from mood disorders.

Oates, Gilbert, Godwin, Didion, and Jamison find their lives changing irrevocably after their spouses' deaths, but significantly, they struggle to recreate themselves in ways that are consistent with their earlier lives. Their widows' stories complement, supplement, and complicate each other's. In each chapter I give an overview of the writer's life and art before widowhood, including her early preoccupation with love, loss, and death. I then discuss the writer's life as a bereft widow, the aesthetic and psychological richness of each memoir, and the ways in which penning a spousal loss memoir contributes to her recovery.

Is the grief arising from spousal loss a form of derangement, resulting in the widow's near collapse, or is it a condition that ends sooner or later? I return to this question, implicit throughout my study, in the Conclusion. I also discuss why widows write spousal loss memoirs, why we read them, the parallels between morning sickness and mourning sickness, and the similarities between widowhood memoirs and end-of-life memoirs, including Susan Gubar's searing account of ovarian cancer, *Memoir of a Debulked Woman*.

Continuing Bonds

Widowhood memoirs and end-of-life memoirs demonstrate what bereavement clinicians call the "continuing bonds" theory of mourning, which argues, contrary to Freud, that the mourner does not shatter the relational bond with the deceased—does not, to use Freudian language, decathect from the lost love object. "We now know," writes J. William Worden, "that people do not decathect from the dead but find ways to develop 'continuing bonds' with the deceased" (35). One of the tasks of mourning, Worden explains, "is to find a place for the deceased that will enable the mourner to be connected with the deceased but in a way that will not preclude him or her from getting on with life. We need to find ways to memorialize the dead, that is, to remember the dead loved one—keeping them with us but still going on with life" (35). In *Widow to Widow*, Phyllis R. Silverman suggests a central paradox of bereavement: "We cannot live in the past or carry on as if the deceased is still a part of our life, but we cannot let go of the relationship, either—in a sense trying to act as if the past did not exist. The bereaved find ways to construct connections to their dead loved ones that are both comforting and sustaining" (38). Dennis Klass, Phyllis R. Silverman, and Steven L. Nickman argue that "survivors hold the deceased in loving memory for long periods, often forever." Maintaining an inner representation of the deceased is "normal rather than abnormal" (349). They quote a statement made by the playwright Robert Anderson after his wife's death: "death ends a life, but it does not end a relationship, which struggles toward some resolution which it never finds" (17). Widowhood memoirists continue their bonds with the deceased while simultaneously forging new bonds with the living.

Life changes instantly after a spouse's death, as every widow and widower knows. Widowhood memoirs offer us probing insights into the most life-changing event anyone is likely to encounter. The stories are, predictably, wrenching to read. How could they not be? They are filled with the symptoms of grief: shock, sadness, confusion, anger, denial, yearning for the dead, anxiety, and uncertainty. Oates, Gilbert, Godwin, Didion, and Jamison acknowledge losing the most important people in their lives—losing, indeed, the desire for life itself.

And yet the stories reveal that life goes on after calamitous loss and that, as often as not, new love emerges. The widows' stories reveal courage amid adversity, unexpected resilience, and the crucial role of writing and reading in recovery. Oates, Gilbert, Godwin, Didion, and Jamison have different attitudes toward religion and spirituality, but they would all agree that writing about their deceased spouses became a sacred death ritual for them, one that was necessary for their own survival. Spousal loss may have shattered their assumptions about life and themselves, but writing helped them re-create their worlds. Writing also provided them with comfort and consolation. Writing gave them something to do during a time of bereavement and emptiness when they felt they couldn't do anything else. Writing reminded them of their losses but forced them to think about new life emerging from death. Writing was, in short, a solace and a lifeline, a form of grief work that led from loss to recovery.

1

———∿∿———

Joyce Carol Oates

A Widow's Story

Joyce Carol Oates is the most prolific major American author of the last half-century and among the least autobiographical novelists, but the appearance of two books within four years, her *Journal* and *A Widow's Story*, gives us unprecedented insight into her life. These two texts are in many ways bookends. The publication of *The Journal of Joyce Carol Oates: 1973–1982* in 2007, when she was sixty-nine, reveals a young woman deeply in love with her husband and even more deeply in love with writing, her life's greatest passion. There are, to be sure, a few entries in the 509-page journal where she allows herself momentarily to imagine what life would be like without her beloved husband, but she cannot bring herself to consider this possibility. And why should she? Little on the horizon in the 1970s and 1980s seemed ominous. But when disaster struck, Oates responded in the way she knew best: by writing about it.

A Widow's Story is longer, more detailed, and more emotionally charged than any other memoir written by a widow or widower. It's also darker in tone, mood, and characterization than any other spousal loss memoir, presenting us with a stunning taxonomy of grief. The memoir offers us a radically different view of Oates: a portrait of a woman deranged by grief and fixated on suicide. The story abounds in surprises, contradictions, ironies, and paradoxes that have captivated the public's attention in a way that is unprecedented in Oates's career. *A Widow's Story* is not a traditional memoir; only after its publication did she admit in several interviews that she based it on her journal. The journalistic form of *A Widow's Story* makes possible the use of the historical present, giving the story a dramatic intensity and spontaneity that might otherwise be impossible.

Oates's *Journal* and *A Widow's Story* offer us a unique opportunity to see the continuities and discontinuities between a major writer's early life and her "posthumous" life. Few authors have claimed a more radical split between their private and public lives than Oates. And few writers have created such an aura of invisibility in their private life while at the same time commanding so strong a public identity. This split, apparent in her early journal entries, has become more pronounced over the years. Oates asserts repeatedly that as a novelist she has no fixed identity; instead, she takes on the lives of her fictional characters. She thus regards herself, more seriously than not, as a multiple personality, a writer whose ability to imagine a myriad of male and female speakers creates a vast cast of characters. Yet despite the fact that she is a master of impersonation and compartmentalization, Oates is the same person who wrote *Journal* and *A Widow's Story*, books that have more in common than may first appear evident. Of the many intriguing characters Oates has imagined in scores of novels, none is more fascinating than the one she creates in *A Widow's Story*. Oates's self-portrait as a widow becomes even more complex when we compare it with the writer who emerges from the pages of the *Journal*.

Oates's *Journal* covers the years when she had already achieved early fame from her 1969 novel *them*, which won the National Book Award. The *Journal* is only a small fraction of the more than 4,000 single-spaced pages (as of 2007, and growing every day) housed in the Joyce Carol Oates Archive at Syracuse University, where she did her undergraduate work. Presumably, other volumes of her *Journal* will appear, constituting one of the most comprehensive records of any major writer.

The Motives Behind Journal Writing

In the introduction, Oates points out the ironies and paradoxes of undertaking such a project. One of the reasons she keeps a journal is to preserve the past, though she rarely rereads her entries because it's "excruciating" to revisit the past. "I haven't the words to guess why" (xii), she confesses, a startling statement from someone who is seldom defeated by language. She then wonders, parenthetically—many of her most important statements are expressed in parentheses—whether the "uncensored" journal may reveal too much about herself or, alternatively, reveal a self "with which I can't any longer identify or, perversely, identify too strongly" (xiii). She makes no effort to conceal the risks of personal writing or her ambivalence about self-disclosure.

Oates offers other explanations for keeping a journal. "Is the keeping of a journal primarily a means of providing solace to the self, through a 'speaking' voice that is one's own voice subtly transformed? A way of dispelling loneliness, a way of comfort?" (xiii). She concludes that homesickness, which involves both "mourning and memorialization," is a powerful motive behind much literature. She recognizes a major paradox: "the more we are hurt, the more we are likely to take refuge in the imagination, and in creating a 'text' that has assimilated this hurt; perversely, if we choose to publish this text, the more likely we are to invite more hurt in the way of critical or public opprobrium" (xiii). She admits that writing a journal is the "very antithesis of writing for others." She doesn't entirely reject the idea, advanced by a "skeptic," that the writer of a journal is creating a "journal-self, like a fictitious character," but she insists that it would be impossible to maintain such a pose for several years. Like "our fingerprints and voice 'prints,' our journal-selves are distinctly our own" (xiv). The implication is that Oates's *Journal* represents her inner self, the self with which she most strongly identifies, at least during the time when she wrote a particular entry. Her views, values, and perceptions are remarkably consistent throughout the ten-year period covered by her journal, suggesting the stability of her character and identity. Her decision to use her journal entries as the basis for *A Widow's Story* highlights her desire to represent her inner, core self.

Throughout her journal, Oates is relentlessly self-analytical, questioning everything, including the process of self-interrogation. She makes a statement, then immediately qualifies it, exploring the ambiguities of both statement and counterstatement. She never mentions John Keats, but she would wholeheartedly concur with his belief in negative capability: "That is when man is capable of being in uncertainties, Mysteries, doubts, without any irritable reaching after fact & reason" (261). Committed to both her inner and outer lives, she nevertheless realizes that the private nature of journal writing encourages a subjectivity that may fail to capture the writer's intense involvement with the world.

Oates admits, without defensiveness, that journal writing encourages narcissism. All people, she asserts on May 13, 1977, are narcissists, including the journal writer. "But the journal-keeper, unlike other people, confronts his or her narcissism daily. And—it's to be hoped—conquers it by way of laughing at it" (194). Keeping a journal is not always pleasurable, but Oates's sense of order, obligation, and curiosity compels her to keep writing regularly even when she is tempted to skip an entry. Greg Johnson's observation in his biography *Invisible Writer* has proven uncannily prescient: "One key to Joyce's intense productivity had always been her ability to continue writing even in times of exhaustion, illness, or depression" (291). It would be hard to imagine a more prophetic statement in light of *A Widow's Story*.

Reading Oates's *Journal*, one is struck by the intelligence, fairness, and compassion of her judgments and perceptions. Her journal sometimes has a gnomic quality, as when she writes on February 28, 1980: "I oscillate between thinking I am crazy and thinking I am not crazy enough" (358). Nearly always a reliable narrator, she is less reliable when she refers repeatedly, without irony, to her "idleness," "laziness," and "unworthiness." She claims she is "inclined toward laziness" (99), "haunted by a sense of laziness or unworthiness" (171), struggling against a "profound feeling of unworthiness" (194), and "astounded" at her "laziness" (362). She contends her "true self is staggeringly indolent . . . for which I sometimes feel genuine shame, & sometimes amusement, bemusement" (454). Readers will shake their heads in disbelief, for only in terms of godlike perfection are these merciless self-accusations true. In *Conversations with Joyce Carol Oates*, she admits to her "laughably Balzacian ambition to get the whole world into a book" (5), but this has been a lifelong aim about which she has been deadly serious.

For whom does Oates write her *Journal*? She never directly confronts this question, but she implies she writes mainly for herself. She feels no obligation to maintain the *reader's* attention. "The value of this journal for me," she writes on July 26, 1978, "is that, strictly speaking, it makes no pretensions about being 'interesting'" (264). And yet Oates also writes for posterity, for readers who will be interested in her growth and development as a writer. She may not have known, when she first began keeping a diary, that it would one day be housed in a university library, but she certainly realized this at some point, probably sooner rather than later. It is unlikely Oates would spend so much time writing her journal if she didn't imagine eventual publication. In *Where I've Been, and Where I'm Going*, she takes a dim view of the possibility of achieving biographical truth, but she makes one important qualification: "Unless the subject is a fanatic diarist, the greater part of his or her inner life will be lost, not simply to the biographer but to the very subject" (231). Oates is herself a "fanatic" diarist whose daily and weekly entries provide an indispensable account of her inner life. Writing a daily journal entry kept her anchored even during those crises when she found herself unmoored.

Anorexia

Oates writes guardedly about anorexia, a conflict she has struggled with for much of her life, including during her widowhood. The first time she implies having an eating disorder occurs on September 18, 1976, when she gazes at recent photographs of herself appearing in *People* magazine: "I came to the conclusion that I am awfully thin . . . though when I look at myself in the mirror it doesn't seem so, I seem merely normal" (145). On March 4, 1977, she refers to Simone Weil's suicidal self-starvation. "She successfully *killed* her body. Which she would have interpreted as 'triumphing' over it and achieving union with 'God.' Having felt such temptations . . . having been visited by them . . . I understand what they are from the inside. And they are terrible. Terrible" (177).

In an entry written on April 5, 1979, Oates, who is five feet nine inches, recalls how in 1970–1971 she experienced the "early stages of what was probably anorexia . . . when I weighed 95–98 pounds for a while, and had no appetite: or, rather, what should have been an appetite for food went into an 'appetite' for other things," adding, in a significant parenthesis, "(I say *for a while* but it was a considerable period of time. And I'm not free of the old psychological aspects of that experience . . . about which I can't talk altogether freely)" (297–298). She then offers a psychologically astute interpretation of the "appeal" of anorexia: "A way of controlling and even mortifying the flesh; a way of 'eluding' people who pursue too closely; a way of channeling off energy in other directions. The mystic 'certainty' that fasting gives . . . a 'certainty' that isn't always and inevitably wrongheaded." In another entry penned on the same day, she suggests that anorexia is a "controlled and protracted form of suicide, literally. But figuratively & symbolically it means much more. No one wants to be dead—! But there is the appeal of Death. The romantic, wispy, murky, indefinable incalculable appeal . . . which seems to me now rather silly; but I remember *then*" (298).

Most clinicians would agree with Oates that underlying anorexia is the need for control, though they would also suggest the related need for perfectionism. Oates refers in a September 29, 1981, entry to her own perfectionism, though she doesn't use this word. "I have wanted to be a model wife; and a model daughter; and a model professor; and a model friend (this, in limited doses); and a model writer (in the sense that my writing doesn't drive me mad, or turn me away from others, or become the very means by which I am laid waste). I wanted all along to lead a model life by my own standards of fairly conventional morality" (*Journal* 436).

Perhaps one of the reasons Oates judges herself so harshly in *A Widow's Story* is because she wants to be a model widow, a goal that no one can achieve, not even a perfectionist. There are only a few references to eating (or not eating) in *A Widow's Story*, but they suggest that Oates had little appetite for food—or for life. "So long as I have one meal a day with people—at an actual table—with the social protocol of courses—the logic of 'eating' make perfect sense," she writes to Richard Ford and Kristina Ford on February 22, 2008; "alone, with no spouse, with no wish to sit at the familiar table, it seems faintly repellent. . . . My favorite time now is sleeping—but it doesn't last long enough" (116). At the end of the month, she visits her physician and describes her anxiety over being weighed. She refuses to watch the scale as he adjusts the little weight. Consulting his notes in her folder, the physician observes that she has lost eight pounds since her last visit a year earlier.

Literary historians have explored in detail the pervasiveness of eating disorders in fictional female characters and their female authors. In *The Madwoman in the Attic*, Sandra M. Gilbert and Susan Gubar note the many thematic parallels between Catherine Earnshaw's speeches in *Wuthering Heights* and Sylvia Plath's poetry. Gilbert and Gubar point out how masochistic or suicidal behavior, especially among adolescent girls and young women, is symptomatic of powerlessness, an interpretation with which Oates would almost certainly agree.

Raymond Smith

Based on the extensive evidence of her journal—and there is no contradictory evidence anywhere—Oates's marriage to Raymond Smith was close to idyllic for both wife and husband. The dozens of references to her husband portray the marriage as warm, close, trusting, and respectful—in short, an excellent match for both of them. In a November 15, 1974, entry, she writes about the balance between "private, personal fulfillment (marriage, friendship, work at the University) and 'public' life, the commitment to writing," adding that the "artist must find an environment, a pattern of living, that will protect his or her energies: the art must be cultivated, must be given priority" (*Journal* 31). Oates never worried about finding the right balance between love and work, and there is little evidence that her husband resented her fierce commitment to writing. She often quotes approvingly Flaubert's insistence that "you must live like a bourgeois so that you save all your violence for your art." No artist has taken these words more to heart than Oates—and few serious writers have surpassed her legendary productivity.

Domestic harmony is what Oates wanted, and domestic harmony is what she received throughout her forty-eight-year marriage to Smith. On her sixteenth wedding anniversary, January 23, 1977, she notes that she and her husband "are so close that I suspect neither of us can guess how utterly dependent we are upon each other" (*Journal* 166). Not being married, she adds, is unfathomable. Thinking like a writer, she knows she cannot adequately convey marital happiness in literature because fiction demands conflict. In one of her most candid descriptions of married life, she observes on August 2, 1978, that because there is "nothing dramatic" about "marital happiness," it rarely finds its way into literature. "One takes a happy relationship for granted. There is no need, really, to comment on it. Like the air we breathe: only when it's contaminated do we notice it" (266–267).

Raymond Smith was eight years older than Oates and, like her, an academic. He sensed early in their marriage her prodigious talent and spartan self-discipline, and he prided himself on helping to nurture that talent by taking care of most of the domestic chores. In many ways he resembled Virginia Woolf's husband, Leonard Woolf, also a distinguished editor and publisher. But whereas Woolf was dependent both financially and psychologically on her husband, Oates's salary as a Princeton professor and best-selling novelist makes her financially dependent on no one.

Raymond Smith was also a writer, at least during the beginning of his career, authoring a scholarly monograph in 1977 on the highly prolific eighteenth-century British satirist Charles Churchill. Smith's decision to give up academic writing and a promising university career to devote himself to editing the *Ontario Review* may have been not only because of his loss of interest in scholarly writing, as Oates implies, but also because of his effort to forge a career that would complement rather than compete with her genius. Reading Smith's book on Churchill, one recognizes that it is thoughtful and persuasive, a solid contribution to academic scholarship, but not one that heralds the arrival of a major new literary critic, as Oates's books demonstrate.

Oates enjoyed a deeply fulfilling, nearly conflict-free marriage, but she knew the limits of marital understanding. On May 30, 1976, she writes about personality as a mask, observing, "Might it be a fact that not even my husband knows me since in his particular presence I *am* . . . that which his presence evokes?" (117). She never wonders whether there are aspects of her husband's life and personality that remain hidden from her—a question she raises, unsettlingly, in *A Widow's Story*.

Depression and Suicide

Oates's *Journal* shows that her interest in death and dying began early in her career. Part of this interest focused on suicide and its link to depression. On November 17, 1974, she mentions finding a letter Anne Sexton mailed to her a year earlier. Sexton's suicide in 1974 distressed Oates, particularly because she had not taken seriously certain remarks in Sexton's letter that were "very, very sad, in a helpless way" (34). On February 11, 1975, she fears reading Sexton's *The Awful Rowing Toward God*, which she is reviewing for the *New York Times*. "I am afraid to read the poems because I am afraid of missing her too much and more than that (to be honest) I am afraid of the death in the poetry, the death-knowledge" (68). It is one of the few times anywhere in Oates's writings that she fears being infected by a poem or story's dark meaning. She empathizes with Sexton's and Woolf's struggles with suicide and praises their efforts to remain alive.

Oates came close to suffering from depression in 1971. As she relates in an entry written on December 2, 1974, two of her friends had recently died, and she was being stalked by a Detroit resident referred to as "A. K.," who demanded that she write a positive review of his novel. When she refused, he became angry and threatened to kill himself. During this time, she was "at the very nadir of my psychological life, the closest to depression I have ever been, damaged by the deaths back home (one in July, and we left for England about six weeks later . . .) which I had no idea how to deal with, how to mourn, and then the astonishing trouble with A. K." (48). A physician prescribed barbiturates for her when she couldn't sleep. "Enormous dosage, so powerful I could barely wake for hours the following day, and did he care?" (49). She took the sleeping pills for months and one day flushed them down the toilet, thanks to "an instinct for survival—tremendous relief afterward, feeling I had escaped something dangerous. Hence my knowledge of, sympathy for, those who are addicted . . . but my ultimate disapproval . . . for this sort of thing is truly suicidal, as those of us who've been there can testify" (49). Like Woolf, Oates speaks disparagingly of physicians, especially male physicians who treat female patients. She also speaks deprecatingly of medication, describing in *The Tattooed Girl* pharmacological poisoning as a "kind of genocide afflicted upon free souls by the rest of shocked mankind" (118).

Psychoanalysis, Psychiatry, and Psychotherapy

Oates has long been suspicious of psychoanalysis, psychiatry, and psychotherapy. Her scathing portrayal of mental health professionals has remained consistent throughout her fiction. "I can't begin to imagine going to a psychotherapist," she remarks in a *Playboy* interview published in *Conversations 1970–2006*. "You're going to another person who has some dogmatic ideas and his or her own agenda. Why go to somebody else, anyway? Theoretically they're listening, but in fact they're not, they're looking at the clock, thinking, How can I bend this person to my own theories? Go for a long walk or go jogging, take a retreat and meditate and think. Or read Walt Whitman" (160).

Oates's fictional universe is vast enough to find exceptions to nearly every generalization, but I'm not aware of any stories where she considers the value of medication for someone suffering from a serious mood disorder like clinical depression or manic-depressive (bipolar) disease or a thought disorder like schizophrenia. Kay Redfield Jamison presents a powerful counterargument that psychiatrists who do not prescribe drugs like lithium for patients suffering from manic-depressive disease may be guilty of malpractice. Oates is part of a long tradition of writers, which includes novelists as different from each other as Ken Kesey and Vladimir Nabokov, for whom psychotherapy and psychopharmacology are unmitigated evils. We see much more positive views of both psychotherapy and medication in Gilbert's *Wrongful Death*, Godwin's *Evenings at Five*, and Jamison's *Nothing Was the Same*.

Oates's experience with depression taught her that the "psyche can't be manipulated, dreams should not be altered, consciousness itself not altered any more than is necessary" (*Journal* 50). She reaches the same conclusion in *A Widow's Story*, where she rejects psychopharmacological drugs that alter her consciousness and instead embraces her therapy of choice, writing, to help her emerge from deep depression and suicidal ideation.

In her journal, Oates begins to formulate her own psychological theory of depression. "There's no doubt in my mind that depression is suppressed anger," she declares on July 31, 1976. "Perhaps there is no such thing as 'depression' at all. One feels profoundly and deeply wounded, threatened, paralyzed . . . simply because the natural emotion, anger, has been blocked" (133). She reaches this conclusion partly as a result of receiving a letter that depressed her at first and then made her angry. Her dark emotions lift when she responds, firmly and politely, to the letter writer. "This is the therapeutic value of expressing oneself either in person or by way of writing. It cannot be over-estimated" (133).

The Writing Cure

It is not the talking cure that Oates affirms but the writing cure—though she would never imply that writing is a cure for the inevitable wounds incurred in life. At best, writing is a way to live with one's wounds, physical and psychological; a way to prevent the wounds from festering. Writing has been the driving force in Oates's life, the activity around which she structures her day and which she dreams about at night. Writing remains the center of her life, and she feels idle when she does not write. "I find that my mind moves on to the work I've done, the writing I've done, and that everything else is peripheral," she observes on July 22, 1977. "The phenomenal world and its great temptations, its beauties, its privileges, the endless drama of human relationships . . . appear to fade, or at any rate to lose their authority, set beside art" (202). The "irresistible force" in her life, she admits on January 6, 1980, is her "eagerness to work" (349).

Oates/Smith

Perhaps Oates's most striking revelation in her journal is her belief in a radical split between her public and private selves, her "Joyce Carol Oates" and "Joyce Carol Smith" identities. Most writers will concede that they have a public and private self, but what is unusual about Oates—or Oates/Smith—is her insistence that these selves are radically different and discontinuous. She claims that the distance between art and life is absolute, as she makes clear on January 8, 1976. "The artist's essential nature—whether easy-going or difficult—should not have much to do with the art itself. 'Joyce Carol Smith': the process of living with as much pleasure as possible. 'Joyce Carol Oates': the process that exists in and through and because of the books. No reason that 'Joyce Smith' should feel obligated to 'Joyce Carol Oates' in any way—to be 'intellectual' or 'mysterious' or 'artistic.' One's life is one's own business" (94).

What does Oates/Smith gain by splitting art and life, her public and private selves? To begin with, the split allows her to subordinate life to art and gain productivity. She knows that art depends upon conflict. To create art, "one must deal with conflict; to create serious art one must deal with serious subjects; drama arises out of tragic actions and misunderstandings, not out of serendipity." By contrast, one tries to avoid conflict in one's personal life. It "doesn't necessarily follow," she avers, that one "believes that unrest is the basic law of the universe" (98). The writer Joyce Carol Oates searches for conflict to power her stories; the person Joyce Carol Smith is content to avoid conflict in her private life. From this point of view, the less conflict one experiences in life, the more conflict one transmutes into art.

The art/life split permits Oates to distance herself from painful criticism of her writings. "Someone once told me that I was the 'most hated' of contemporary writers," she admits ruefully on April 1, 1976. "I can't believe this. I don't even know very many people." She concludes the entry by stating that the "resentment that others feel toward me is an exaggeration, surely" (100). If she cannot change her image as the most hated of contemporary writers, the most prodigious writer of the century, she can at least project this image onto her public self, leaving her private self immune from such criticism. "Oates" becomes the split-off part of the self, the fiercely ambitious writer who has an existence apart from the quiet, unassuming Mrs. Smith.

The Oates/Smith split enables the writer to imagine points of view vastly different from her own while maintaining a stable identity. "I can be anyone, I can say anything, I can believe literally anything," she writes on March 26, 1976, which gives her an almost godlike freedom. The writer encompasses the world, limited not by her personal life or identity but only by her capacious imagination.

Additionally, the art/life split allows Oates to separate herself from statements she has made in published writings or interviews that she now wishes to qualify or repudiate. She declares on May 30, 1976, that she no longer believes in the remarks she made years earlier in an interview titled "The Dark Lady of American Letters." Rereading the interview, she is now struck by the "hypothetical" nature of her Joyce Carol Oates identity. Dissociating herself from her writerly persona means that she doesn't need to accept credit for her literary successes or blame for her failures.

Oates also achieves a degree of safety from the art/life split that would otherwise be impossible. "The self is protected by the persona, but the persona also protects other people from the self," she records in a

September 24, 1977, entry. She then makes a statement that remains true until the publication of *A Widow's Story* thirty-four years later: "This journal comes as close as I care to go in terms of laying 'bare' my heart" (214).

Oates never comments on the irony that in her journal her two selves are inextricably fused, perhaps for the first time. Joyce Carol Oates the writer and Joyce Carol Smith the person were both necessary for each other's existence and well-being. Neither could live or write without the other. Her "normal" life as Joyce Carol Smith makes possible her wildly imaginative life as Joyce Carol Oates. She passes effortlessly from one world to another. "Does a normal, ordered, tidy life compensate an interior life of the bizarre, the flamboyantly imaginative?" she asks on December 5, 1976. "Perhaps, perhaps. Who can tell. We inhabit a world of ostensibly closed surfaces which, nevertheless, can slide open at any moment, like panels in a wall. We can't anticipate the sliding-open, the revelation, but we can have faith in it" (*Journal* 150).

Oates cannot imagine that a new and frightening world will slide open thirty-two years later, when her husband dies. How can one imagine this when one is young? It is easy to forget while reading her journal that for the most part she is still a young person. While writing her journal, Oates knows that her four main values in life remain intact, as she records on May 28, 1978: "Love. Friendship. Art. Work" (*Journal* 253). Most of her statements in her journal reflect the optimism and hopefulness of a person whose world remains whole, as when she says on August 6, 1977, musing on Anne Sexton's suicide, "But why die, why take one's self so seriously?" She then adds, in a statement fraught with irony, "Some of us are too normal, too healthy, to comprehend—that is, to *really* comprehend, for as a novelist I haven't any difficulty—the despair that drags one to death" (206–207). She was not yet forty when she penned this entry, and she could not yet imagine feeling the despair that drags one to death. Decades later, she could imagine it, and when she did, she compelled Joyce Carol Oates the memoirist to write about Joyce Carol Smith the person.

A Widow's Story

Oates opens *A Widow's Story* with an incident titled "The Message" that sardonically foreshadows the nightmarish mood of the next year of her life. Rushing to her car, which she has parked "haphazardly" on a narrow street near the Princeton Medical Center, where she is visiting her stricken husband, she sees what looks like a parking ticket beneath her windshield wiper. At once her heart "clenches in dismay, guilty apprehension—a ticket?" (3). It turns out to be both better and worse—not a traffic summons but a note scribbled on an ordinary piece of paper: "LEARN TO PARK STUPPID BITCH" (4). She then switches from first-person narration, the dominant voice in the story, her "Joyce Carol Smith" voice, to third-person, her "Joyce Carol Oates" voice, and compares her story of the widow-to-be to a Kafka parable *"in which the most profound and devastating truth of the individual's life is revealed to him by a passer-by in the street"* (4).

"This Can't Be Happening"

Oates may not be an expert at parking an automobile in a crisis—who is?—but she is an expert writer, and part 1 of *A Widow's Story* describes in abundant detail her husband's sudden illness and death. She wakes up on February 11, 2008, to discover him hunched over the *New York Times*. He admits feeling "strange" when she asks him apprehensively if something is wrong. He tells her this in a "matter-of-fact voice," but she knows he is not his usual self. A "cautious, caring, and hyper-vigilant spouse" (13), she insists calmly but forcefully that they go immediately to the ER and, despite his objections, she drives him there, where he is soon diagnosed as having pneumonia. She feels relief: "Pneumonia! The mystery is solved. The solution is a good one. Pneumonia is both commonplace and treatable—isn't it?" (20).

Oates returns home. A few hours later, as she is about to drive to the hospital, she receives an urgent phone call informing her that her husband's heartbeat has accelerated and cannot be stabilized: *"in the event that his heart stops do you want extraordinary measures to be used to keep him alive?"* (21). Stunned, as anyone would be, she cannot understand the question. *"Yes anything you can do! Save him! I will be right there*—for this is the first unmistakable sign of horror, helplessness—impending doom" (21). She then finds herself lying on the kitchen hardwood floor, astonished she has just fainted. "Six o'clock in the evening of February 11, 2008. The Siege—not yet identified, not yet named, nor even suspected—has begun" (22).

What follows is a harrowing story filled with concrete details and piercing emotions. Medical tests determine that Raymond Smith's right lung has been infected by *E. coli*, and he is immediately given an IV antibiotic. During the next five days, specialists monitor his condition, and for a time he appears to feel better. Oates quotes several of her e-mails to friends and acquaintances to document his progress. Ominously, a "second-ary infection" of "mysterious origin" appears in his left lung—"nothing to worry about" (50), she is told. But worry she does, and for good reason. A telephone call awakens her at 12:38 a.m. on February 18 with the alarming news that her husband is now in critical condition. *"This can't be happening"* (55), she says to herself. By the time she arrives at the hospital, he is dead.

Self-Blame and Guilt

Everyone would be horrified to be in Oates's situation, but not everyone would be as overwhelmed by self-blame and guilt as she is. No one can fault her behavior—her insistence on driving her husband to the ER, her daily visits to him, her efforts to cheer him up when he is awake and to anticipate his every need, her willingness to speak with his physicians about his condition. Nevertheless, she criticizes herself for everything, beginning with her parking. She blames herself for angering the chattery hospital aide whom she has hired to help her husband. She blames herself for being asleep when he died. She blames herself for driving him to the Princeton Medical Center rather than to New York City or Philadelphia, where, her friends tell her, the hospitals are better. She blames herself for not execut-ing perfectly the flurry of "death-duties" that arise from a spouse's death. She blames herself when her grocery bags overturn in her car, spilling everything on the floor. And she blames herself for not being with him when he died. *"I have come too late. I too abandoned him"* (187).

Nor is this all. Oates blames herself for being too scared to read her husband's unpublished novel, *Black Mass*, which he abandoned forty years earlier. *"You are terrified of reading Ray's novel because you are terrified of discovering something in it that will upset you"* (242). She blames herself for surviving her husband. "The widow feels in her heart, she should not be *still alive*" (278). She blames herself when she forgets to bring in her cat and he freezes to death. And she blames herself when she rereads one of her prize-winning short stories, "In the Region of Ice," later made into an Academy Award–winning film, based on a former student who had shot and killed his rabbi in a temple and then turned the gun on himself: "I am stricken with sympathy, sorrow, guilt. *I could have done more. I could have done—something*" (348).

How do we feel about the relentless torrent of blame, guilt, self-condemnation, and failure that dominates *A Widow's Story*? Surely Oates knows, on some level, that she cannot be reproached for the disastrous events that unfold in the story. Nothing she did or did not do could have prevented her husband's death. Only those who believe a person can be omniscient and omnipotent will judge her guilty of being "stupid, selfish, neglectful" (72), as she judges herself after forgetting to bring her husband a large Valentine card signed by their friends. In her desire to document all her emotions during the first year of widowhood, she exposes the darkest side of Joyce Carol Smith's life, the nightmarish side that believes, as the officer in Kafka's "In the Penal Colony" discovers, when he jumps onto a torture-and-execution machine, "guilt is never to be doubted." There are moments when Oates tries to universalize her experience, as when she learns that "a widow is one who *makes mistakes*" (72), but she always assumes more than a reasonable degree of responsibility for events beyond her control. *"It is wrong to have outlived Ray,"* she repeats to herself, a mantra symptomatic of her posthumous life. Dark emotions flood the memoir, and we watch in dismay as the brutal current nearly sweeps the widow away.

Suicide

Oates's self-blame is the most shocking revelation in *A Widow's Story*, followed closely by her obsession with suicide. Thoughts of suicide recur throughout *A Widow's Story*; indeed, apart from the irrational hope that her husband will miraculously return to life, the longing for death is her most powerful and recurrent fantasy. There are dozens of references to suicide, particularly during the months immediately following his death. She wishes she had died with him to escape from the grief and loneliness of widowhood. She thinks about nineteenth-century Indian widows who immolated themselves on their husbands' funeral pyres in the Hindu practice of suttee. She tells us that neither she nor her husband had wished to outlive the other, though she is quick to point out his horror of suicide and rejection of it as a romantic option. She doesn't regard suicide as a realistic possibility, but that doesn't make the fantasy less tempting to her.

There are many reasons people attempt or commit suicide, and it is important to understand the reasons behind Oates's fantasy. She does not believe in the possibility of life after death, and she never imagines reuniting with her deceased husband in another realm. She feels anger, even rage, toward the man who has "abandoned" her, but she knows he didn't want to die. She doesn't regard suicide as a way of revenging herself on the dead, as Sylvia Plath suggests in her poem "Daddy," where the speaker attempts to get "back at" her father for dying. One of the main predictors of suicide is hopelessness, but Oates is never so despairing that she believes life is not worth living. She is aware of the devastating consequences of suicide, its dark legacy, or illegacy, for family and friends, and for this reason alone she is careful not to advocate suicide as a realistic option for the bereft.

Nevertheless, Oates sees suicide as a way to escape from intolerable suffering, and she cannot stop thinking about it. She recalls her father saying, with "masculine bravado," when he was middle-aged: "*If I ever get bad as*—[referring to an elderly chronically ill and complaining relative]—*put me out of my misery!*" (67). Some people might be frightened by the thought of suicide, but she regards it as a consolation. "For suicide promises *A good night's sleep—with no interruptions! And no next-day*" (94). The yearning for death is such a potent fantasy that she decides any action a widow takes, no matter how naive, foolish, or futile, is a positive alternative to suicide. On two separate occasions she quotes Nietzsche's wry aphorism: "The thought of suicide can get one through many a long night" (117, 212). Two other Nietzschean statements, the first from *Human, All Too Human*, which she had quoted in *The Profane Art*, and the second from *Thus Spake Zarathustra*, run "like electric shocks" through her mind in *A Widow's Story*: "*If you stare too long into an abyss, the abyss will gaze back into you*," and "*Many die too late, and some die too early. Yet strange soundeth the precept: Die at the right time*" (212–213). Both statements prove relevant to her situation. The more she gazes into the abyss, the more it stares back at her; and, like Nietzsche, who died ten years too late, she believes her life should have ended with her husband's death.

Along with existential guilt, another source of Oates's suicidal feeling is the masochistic need to punish herself. *A Widow's Story* abounds in masochistic fantasies, which appear to have *preceded* her husband's death rather than developed as a response to it. She hints at this when she suggests how "masochism masks fear, horror, terror—how frequently in the past I had consoled myself that, should *something happen to Ray*, I would not want to outlive him" (67). She then wonders how common this fantasy is. "It's a consolation to wives-not-yet widows. It's a way of stating *I love him so much, I am one who loves so very much*" (67).

The problem with this "consolation," however, is that masochism generally arises from the fear that one has *not* loved (or been loved) enough—in this case, loved neither one's spouse nor oneself enough. It makes more sense to believe that a person who is overwhelmed by self-blame and guilt after her husband's death and who fantasizes about suicide day and night is worried not about having loved too much but about having loved too little. This is what clinicians call pathological or "complicated" grief, the "intensification of grief to the level where the person is overwhelmed, resorts to maladaptive behavior, or remains interminably in the state of grief without progression of the mourning process towards completion" (Horowitz et al. 1157). Yet if Oates's need to punish herself preceded her husband's death, she is not willing to explore this question. Readers of *A Widow's Story* are thus left in a quandary about what to believe. The strong and convincing love that lasted throughout her forty-eight-year marriage is hard to reconcile with the severity of the masochistic fantasies that push her toward suicide.

Are Oates's masochistic fantasies related to the impulse toward perfectionism that we see in her *Journal*, where she acknowledges the need to be a model wife and to lead a model life? She is amazed in her *Journal* that she seems to have succeeded in these goals, or at least not to have failed in them, but then she reminds herself that "so much of life lies ahead to be lived, and to be explored" (*Journal* 436). By all accounts, Oates had an excellent marriage, but no marriage is conflict free. Her relentless hyper–self-criticism, held in check during her husband's life, appears to have been released by his death, producing lacerating self-blame.

In her journal, Oates is seldom judgmental of those writers who have committed suicide, and in *A Widow's Story* her sympathy toward them is only heightened. She remarks on the number of undergraduate students in her fiction workshops who turn in stories about suicide based on their relatives' or friends' attempted or completed suicides. She never reveals to her students anything personal about herself. "My intention as a teacher is to refine my own personality out of existence, or nearly—my own 'self' is never a factor in my teaching, still less my career; I like to think that most of my students haven't read my writing" (174). There are two ironies here, only one of which is intentional. After her husband's death, Oates prides herself on teaching her undergraduate fiction workshop as if nothing in her life has changed. After one class, however, two students from the preceding semester visit her to offer their condolences. "When they leave, I shut my office door. I am shaking, I am so deeply moved. But mostly shocked. Thinking *They must have known all along today. They must all know*" (174). The other irony, on which she never comments, is that her students will be even more shocked when they read *A Widow's Story*, for the teacher/student relationship will be forever changed.

Oates is aware of the ways in which gender shapes how men and women regard themselves, but she doesn't explore how gender plays a decisive role in suicide. Three times as many women as men attempt suicide, but three times as many men complete suicide, mainly because men choose more violent and therefore more successful methods to kill themselves. Women tend to overdose on drugs or, as in the case of Sylvia Plath and Anne Sexton, asphyxiate themselves, while men use guns. Oates imagines overdosing, "hoarding" her prescription painkillers so that, in an emergency, she can "put myself out of my misery" (211). One of the reasons she looks forward to lectures, readings, and book signings out of town is that she would never harm herself away from home. Despite her large pill cache, she admits she doesn't have a concrete suicide plan, which she knows would heighten the risk of danger. She elaborates on the various ways of committing suicide, including accumulating pills, shooting oneself in the brain, and inhaling carbon monoxide, but then she concludes that there is no foolproof method. She shatters the taboo of silence surrounding suicide by spending many pages writing about her death wish, but she then tries to distance herself from her ruminations by making two disclaimers: *"Of course I don't mean it! I mean very little of what I say. Of course, I am a fantasist . . . You can't possibly take me seriously"* (233).

Oates may be a fantasist, but that doesn't mean we fail to take her words seriously. Her prose becomes hypnotic when she writes about how methodically she counts her pills. The fantasy and ever-present reality of suicide are as strong in *A Widow's Story* as they are in the novels and poems of Virginia Woolf, Ernest Hemingway, Sylvia Plath, and Anne Sexton. Sexton speaks of the wish to die, Oates reminds us, as *"the almost unnamable lust"* (344), and, if anything, the lust is named more fully in *A Widow's Story*. Nor is Oates averse to sharing her suicidal ideation with friends, even if it means worrying them about her state of mind. Later, after commenting on the "strange lethargy" that prevents her from answering condolence letters from friends like Philip Roth, she ponders the futility of language and mentions the suicide note scrolling in her head much of the time. She never shares the suicide note with the reader, perhaps fearful that it will sound melodramatic.

The Basilisk

Oates describes the thought of suicide as a comfort, consolation, and longing, something devoutly to be wished, yet she personifies suicide as a repulsive-looking basilisk that stares at her abysmally, compelling her horrified counterstare. Whether we interpret the basilisk as the Christian Satan, the Nietzschean abyss, or the Freudian superego, it represents the hideous reality of suicide. To those who argue that the alluring descriptions in *A Widow's Story* glorify suicide and thus may pose a danger to certain readers already at risk—the well-documented contagion theory of suicide—Oates might counterargue that the opposite is true, for she tells us repeatedly, if not always convincingly, that suicide is a temptation that must be resisted.

"The Most Seductive of Literary Genres"

Three-quarters of the way through *A Widow's Story*, Oates, still immersed in grief and despairing of recovery, reports a friend's suggestion to see a therapist or grief counselor or join a self-help group for people who have lost a spouse. Given her lifelong mistrust of all forms of psychotherapy and psychopharmacology, it is not surprising that the recommendation evokes Oates's anger and mistrust. She offers a different objection, however, from the ones she generally expresses in her journal and fictional writings. Living in the "age of memoir," she cannot trust mental health professionals to maintain confidentiality. Oates has in mind Anne Sexton's psychiatrist, Martin Orne, who, with the permission of the poet's daughter Linda Gray Sexton, gave to biographer Diane Wood Middlebrook three hundred hours of audiotapes of Anne Sexton's therapy sessions. Oates then elaborates on the meaning of living in an era of full disclosure. "The memoirist excoriates him-/herself, as in a parody of public penitence, assuming then that the excoriation, exposure, humiliation of others is justified" (300). She characterizes the memoir as the "most seductive" and "most dangerous" of genres, because it claims to be a "repository of truths" when, in fact, the truth of a widow's grief is too vast to be perceived in a single gaze—or captured in a single book.

Coincidentally or not, Oates referred often to memoirs in the years immediately preceding *A Widow's Story*. In *Uncensored*, she divides the contemporary memoir into two types, the "coming-of-age memoir," which reads like an " 'authentic' version of the autobiographical novel," and the "memoir of crisis," which "focuses upon a single season or dramatic event in the memoirist's life" (109). She cites William Styron's *Darkness Visible* as an example of a memoir of crisis. Both types of memoir, she adds, can be rewarding or disappointing, "depending upon that elusive factor we call 'style'—'voice.' " Oates admits that a "mediocre memoir may be easier to compose than a mediocre novel since, presumably, one need not invent much, but memoirs of distinction surely rank with novels of distinction, for no literary genre is by definition inferior to any other" (109–110). She could not possibly imagine that six years after she made these observations in *Uncensored* she would write her own distinguished memoir of crisis.

Oates reports in *A Widow's Story* that three friends and a fourth person gave her contradictory and unsolicited advice about writing a memoir. One friend urged her to write a memoir about her husband's death; a second friend warned her not to write, at least not yet; a third friend angered her by declaring, "with evident seriousness," that she probably had already written one or two novels about her deceased husband; and a fourth person, a Princeton University acquaintance, exclaimed, with "an air of hearty reproach—'Writing up a storm, eh, Joyce?" (300), a comment that infuriates her.

This moment in *A Widow's Story* is fraught with irony, not all of which is intentional. Appalled by unnamed sensationalistic memoirs, Oates writes a self-revealing story that is more self-excoriating than any other spousal loss memoir. Her characterization of herself as a woman deranged by grief, filled with guilt and shame, longing for death, and scarcely able to remain in control in public will shock those familiar with the way she presents herself in her *Journal*, scholarly books, and interviews. Oates has no patience for those who imagine her soon writing about the death of her husband—indeed, she is exasperated by how others assume she is sturdy enough to begin writing. Yet she publishes her 417-page story exactly three years after her husband's death, a length of time that most other memoirists would consider miraculously short.

Memoir or Journal?

A Widow's Story is subtitled *A Memoir*, but Oates never tells us that what we are reading is, in fact, based on her journal. Only in interviews given after the publication of *A Widow's Story* does she explain how the book came into existence. In an online interview with Louise McCready on February 16, 2011, the week in which *A Widow's Story* was released, Oates observes that the memoir was "assembled rather than 'written,' as it is composed of journal entries from Feb. 11, 2008 onward." "Its form," she notes, except for several chapters that are clearly set in the past, "is that of a quilt or a mosaic." Unable to write fiction in the summer of 2009, she "turned to the journal notes and assembled a sort of memoir out of them; but it wasn't until late in this process that I came to realize that the effort of creating the memoir was a kind of 'pilgrimage'—its destination unknown when I'd set off." Writing a memoir, in her view, is "to look back coolly and calmly and begin with a date, a time, perhaps years ago." Such writing, she tells McCready, "is both seductive and dangerous because it allows for so much misremembering, selection of memories, distortions both intentional and unintentional. The journal/diary is much different—it unfolds in present time, breathless, and filled with the humiliating, small details that comprise our lives, and not given a more elevated or elegiac shape."

It is not a shock to learn that Oates is unable to read her published journal, which explores an idyllic time in her life when her husband was alive. It *is* a shock to learn, after the publication of *A Widow's Story*, that she continued to write daily journal entries immediately before, during, and following her husband's illness and death. One can understand why she called *A Widow's Story* a memoir rather than a journal, a distinction she makes in *Uncensored*: "The memoir is to be distinguished from the diary, a presumably day-by-day chronicling of life *in medias res*, for the root of 'memoir' is after all 'memory,' and its vision is retrospective" (110). Despite this distinction, it is still puzzling that Oates did not call *A Widow's Story* a "journal" or perhaps a "memoir-journal." Why does Oates omit in *A Widow's Story* any reference to the daily journal entries that form the basis for the memoir? Perhaps because it would suggest a greater resilience than she wished to acknowledge during her darkest despair. And perhaps because we might conclude that Joyce Carol Oates was never as bereft as Joyce Carol Smith.

Oates declares in a letter published in the May 26, 2011, issue of the *New York Review of Books* that *A Widow's Story* consists of "perhaps 98 percent" journal entries. She gains much by using daily journal entries as the basis for the memoir. She is able to write in the historic present, using "real time," which allows her to recall feelings and experiences that are only a few hours old. She thus captures the white-hot flame of grief and melancholy before it cools. Journals are, by their nature, fragmented, discontinuous, disconnected; sudden widowhood produces the same broken feelings. The other 2 percent of *A Widow's Story* consists of material that helps to structure and unify the story, including brief discussions of writer-friends who are also widows.

There are few dated journal entries in *A Widow's Story*, which explains why it doesn't resemble a traditional journal. Oates tells us in the chapter titled "The Nest" that she is working on "short things—reviews, essays, stories" (136), but she omits any reference to keeping a journal. There are eighty-six sections in the book, some as short as a half-page, others as long as twelve pages. Two of the longest sections are also the darkest, one titled "Fury," the other "Sinkholes." The one section in which Oates explicitly acknowledges she is writing a memoir is called "Pilgrimage," where she declares that "You begin at X, and you will end at Z. You *will end*—in some way" (368). This would seem to be the appropriate place to acknowledge that she is not writing a traditional memoir but "assembling" a book based on journal entries, yet she remains silent about this. *A Widow's Story* is organized around five chapters: "The Vigil," in which her husband is still alive; "Free Fall," the weeks immediately following his death; "The Basilisk," when her suicidal thoughts intensify; "Purgatory, Hell," a Dantesque account of the depth of her despair; and "You Looked So Happy," an account of her earlier life. The epilogue consists of three brief events occurring in August 2008 and a one-sentence conclusion, "The Widow's Handbook," which marks the first anniversary of her husband's death.

The main reason *A Widow's Story* doesn't read like a journal is that it contains two distinct voices, the first-person journalistic voice of Joyce Carol Smith, the grief-stricken woman who has lost her husband and is almost paralyzed with fear, and the third-person professorial voice of Joyce Carol Oates, JCO, her ironic, detached, analytical, writerly self. These two separate voices give us both subjective and objective views of a widow's experience. The "I" of the story is immersed in grief and despair, unable to see an end to widowhood except, perhaps, in death. The "she" of the story, sometimes "you," looks back from the vantage point of three years, observing the beginning, middle, and end of widowhood. The "she" uses flashbacks and flashforwards that gain added significance during later rereadings. After revealing in her Joyce Carol Smith voice that for months following her husband's death she telephoned her home number to hear his voice on the answering machine, she speaks directly to the reader in her Joyce Carol Oates voice: *"As you will too, one day. If you are the survivor"* (205). These two voices are countervoices, working like counterpoint in a Baroque fugue.

There is another reason why Oates calls *A Widow's Story* a memoir instead of a journal. "A motive for a memoir of someone who has died," she remarks in her interview with McCready, "is very obvious as the survivor is compelled to talk about the lost loved one, to keep his or her name in the air, 'alive'—so to speak. The survivor is drawn to write about the person and the experience of loss. Much of literature is *memorialization*—a way we have of assuaging our homesickness. When you lose someone close to you, the loss is perhaps a kind of homesickness. I thought of *A Widow's*

Story as a way of keeping Ray alive, and preventing him from being forgotten." Ironically, Oates had first propounded the idea of memorialization in her journal! In an interview with Craig Wilson published in *USA Today* on February 14, 2011, Oates said that she didn't know how *A Widow's Story* would end. "It's typical of a pilgrimage—how you're always moving on."

The Nest

Oates writes in her "nest," suggesting that artistic expression is not only a comfort to her but also essential to her health and recovery. Writing in the nest also links artistic creativity with the mystery of birth and renewal. It is understandable for a writer who has spent her entire adolescence and adulthood writing to return to that activity, but now, for the first time in her life, writing takes on, literally, a life-or-death urgency. She has many reasons to continue living, but writing remains, both before and after her husband's death, her greatest passion. One suspects that, as grief stricken as she is by her husband's death, the loss of the ability to write would be a greater calamity.

Oates is quick to admit that writing becomes unusually difficult for her after her husband's death. She can hardly write a two-sentence note to readers of *Ontario Review* informing them that the journal will cease publication after the May 2008 issue. "It's a measure of my fractured concentration at the time—my reputation for prolificacy notwithstanding—that numerous drafts were required to compose this melancholy rejection slip" (193). Her words strike her as melodramatic, self-pitying, subjective. Revising her sentences involves nothing less than revising her emotions—no easy feat. Throughout April it remains nearly impossible for her to write fiction; she compares herself to a "drunken woman staggering, colliding with walls, stunned" (355), though she finally does complete a short story. Writing a longer work of fiction is still out of the question. "No more could I plan a new novel than I could trek across the Sahara or Antarctica" (356).

The Writer's Woundedness

The presentation Oates gives less than a month after her husband's death— "The Writer's 'Secret' Life: Woundedness, Rejection, and Inspiration"— testifies to her belief that art often arises from trauma. "The writers of whom I speak—Samuel Beckett, the Brontës, Emily Dickinson, Ernest

Hemingway, Sam Clemens, Eugene O'Neill among others—are brilliant examples of individuals who rendered *woundedness* into art; they are not writers of genius because they were *wounded* but because, being *wounded*, they were capable of transmuting their experience in to something rich and strange and new and beautiful" (*A Widow's Story* 220–221).

Oates belongs on the list. *A Widow's Story* is a striking confirmation of the theory of the writer's woundedness, for she transmutes grief and loneliness into art, creating a memoir that is in its own way rich and strange and new and beautiful. Nowhere in *A Widow's Story* does she mention writing the memoir or even a desire to write about the experience of widowhood—this is one of the story's most conspicuous omissions—but we can assume that the idea of writing a memoir came to her sooner rather than later, perhaps immediately after her husband's death. During her presentation she feels "buoyed aloft—as always—as if my particular *woundedness* has been left behind, in the wings of the stage" (221). Speaking about woundedness is thus, paradoxically, a healing experience for her, her version of the talking cure. The exhilaration is short-lived—returning to her hotel after the lecture and book signing, she is lonely again—but that does not invalidate the genuine pleasure, relief, and sense of control she experiences while talking about woundedness.

"A Solace and a Lifeline"

For many authors, writing and reading are forms of wounding, as Kafka observes in a 1904 letter: "the books we need are the kind that act upon us like a misfortune, that make us suffer like the death of someone we love more than ourselves, that make us feel as though we were on the verge of suicide, or lost in a forest remote from all human habitation—a book should serve as the ax for the frozen sea within us" (16). Oates would endorse this view of literature, yet at the same time she would also point out that writing is a solace and a lifeline. Of all the lifelines in *A Widow's Story*, writing is the one that she finds most effective in allowing her to escape from the glaring basilisk. She realizes, however, with wry irony, that most people are not writers. "There are those—a blessed lot—who can experience life without the slightest glimmer of a need to add anything to it—any sort of 'creative' effort; and there are those—an accursed lot—for whom the activities of their own brains and imaginations are paramount" (12). Ray Smith, though the author of a scholarly book and a prize-winning editor and publisher, was among the blessed non-writers. He did not have to worry about the often crushing pressure of bringing new fictional universes into existence. This explains the meaning of his droll observation that editors don't have to worry about killing themselves.

Oates rarely uses words like *therapeutic* or *cathartic* to describe the impact of writing on the writer, but she does use *solace* and *lifeline*. In an e-mail sent a week after her husband's death to Robert Silvers, the editor of the *New York Review of Books*, she writes about completing her review of a new book on the cultural history of boxing. The content of the review is less significant than her ability to remain engaged in life-saving work: "as Barbara Epstein [a founding editor of the *New York Review of Books* who died in 2006] felt also, in the end it is our work that matters, and our work that can be a solace and a lifeline" (*A Widow's Story* 116). A day earlier, she had sent an e-mail to Edmund White in which she admitted that "just typing this letter is satisfying somehow. We are addicted to language for its sanity-providing" (115). Oates cannot write fiction in the first few months following her husband's death, but she can turn to other types of writing, with salutary results. Immersed in work, "I can forget the circumstances of my life—almost!" (136). She doesn't cite the social scientist Mihaly Csikszentmihalyi, but she would identify with his theory of "flow," in which we become so immersed in certain activities that we lose all sense of time.

Friendship is another lifeline. She calls three friends immediately after her husband's death, and they arrive at her home shortly after 2 a.m. and remain with her until 4 a.m. She counts on her friends for advice and support, especially her women-writer friends. Friendship has always been important to Oates, as can be seen in her journal entries. She includes many emails to and from friends to demonstrate the survival value of friendship: *"for the widow, as for all who are grieving, there is no way to survive except through others"* (*A Widow's Story* 158).

Grief stricken though she is, Oates reaches out to others for comfort and support. Some of these friends are distinguished writers, such as Philip Roth, John Updike, E. L. Doctorow, Elaine Showalter, Gail Godwin, and Sandra Gilbert. These e-mails allow us to understand Oates's week-by-week progress in moving through grief during the first year of widowhood. She also quotes condolence letters from acquaintances, particularly widows. She reads these letters "avidly" because they are written in a "special language" she is beginning to understand. The widows offer her sound advice that is never platitudinous: "You will be grief-stricken for the rest of your life, but don't lose your sanity"; "Please be kind to yourself. Healing will come in its own good time" (309–310). Oates's conclusion is that words "may be 'helpless'—yet words are all we have to shore against our ruin, as we have only one another."

Teaching is another solace and lifeline for her, as well as a source of pleasure and relief after her husband's death. "Teaching is an act of communication, sympathy—a reaching-out—a wish to share knowledge, skills; a rapport with others, who are students; a way of allowing others into the solitariness of one's soul" (172). She then quotes Chaucer's statement about the young scholar in *The Canterbury Tales*: *"Gladly wolde he lerne and gladly teche"* (172).

JCO: "An Island, an Oasis"

What saves Oates after her husband's death is her "JCO" self. Most of the references to JCO in her journal are wry if not ambivalent, but in *A Widow's Story* she generally feels more sympathetic to her literary alter ego. Her initial references, however, are guarded and ironic. She admits that she and her husband tried not to share anything with each other that was "upsetting, depressing, demoralizing, tedious—unless it was unavoidable." She tried to shield him from her writing self. "In this way I walled off from my husband the part of my life that is 'Joyce Carol Oates'—which is to say, my writing career" (123). Two pages later she observes dryly that she, Joyce Carol Smith, has walled off herself from Joyce Carol Oates as well. She confesses in *A Widow's Story*, just as she does in her journal, that it is her "task to impersonate 'Joyce Carol Oates,'" though now she describes JCO not as a person but as an "author-identification" (171).

Suddenly Oates casts aside her ironic tone in *A Widow's Story* to acknowledge that JCO has become an "island, an oasis" to which she can row. Defining JCO to include her professorial as well as her fiction-writing self, she admits that a "shivery sort of elation enters my veins" as soon as she arrives at the university. Impersonating JCO helps her to elude the basilisk. On the eve of her husband's birthday, March 11, when he would have been seventy-eight years old, she remarks on an exhibition of her books in the Powell Library at UCLA under the title JOYCE CAROL OATES—THE WONDER WOMAN OF AMERICAN LITERATURE. She does not find either the title or timing amusing: "What the widow has lost—it would seem a trifling loss, to others—is the possibility of being *teased*" (237). Nevertheless, there is no doubt that JCO gives her strength and purpose in a time of weakness and meaninglessness. Feeling too fragile and unfocused to impersonate her alter ego, she writes, *"I am not a writer now. I am not anything now"* (243). The paradox is that only a writer can write that she is not writing.

Dark Humor

Oates reveals her characteristic dark humor when writing about widowhood. She finds herself in situations that unexpectedly challenge her patience and good will. She is grateful for the gestures of kindness extended to her. She appreciates the expensive floral displays, crates of fruit, gigantic plants and trees in massive ceramic containers, and sympathy gift baskets, many sent by the specialty company Harry & David, which arrive every day by UPS and FedEx. The gift baskets are filled with exotic nuts, chocolate, cakes, cheese, smoked salmon, and Russian caviar—enough for a feast. Her gratitude soon gives way first to dismay, then to anger, and finally to guilt and shame as the elaborate gourmet baskets fill up her home, and she is forced to dispose of them, unopened. No thought or emotion, however dark, is too painful or shameful for Oates to ignore; as angry as she is at others, she is always angrier at herself. She never hesitates to portray herself in the least sympathetic light. The irony surrounding these lavish gift baskets is that she has little if any appetite for any food.

Another incident she conveys through wry humor is the dinner party of "heroic proportions" that a friend tries to arrange for her. Disregarding Oates's request for a small dinner party, the friend keeps adding new guests to the dinner list, but as the list grows, it becomes impossible to find a convenient night for everyone to attend. She concludes that although the friend and her husband claim they want to see Oates, they probably regard the widow as a "leper" (181). Oates never mentions C. S. Lewis's iconic *A Grief Observed*, the most famous of all spousal-loss memoirs, but he too refers to the stigma of death. "Perhaps the bereaved ought to be isolated in special settlements like lepers" (10).

Oates's sardonic humor and ironic wit give *A Widow's Story* the style and voice that make it a memoir of distinction. Of all the characters she has imagined in her scores of novels and hundreds of short stories, none is as intriguing or complex as Oates herself. The Dark Lady of American Letters reveals a Hamletesque lacerating self-mockery. Like Henry James, she is a writer on whom nothing is lost.

The Shattered Self

Raymond Smith's death shatters Oates's "assumptive world," a term Colin Murray Parkes uses to describe a "strongly held set of assumptions about the world and the self which is confidently maintained and used as a means of recognizing, planning and acting. . . . Assumptions such as these are learned and confirmed by the experience of many years" (132). Ronnie Janoff-Bulman identifies three fundamental assumptions that are at the " 'core' of one's assumptive world": the belief that the world is benevolent, the belief that the world is meaningful, and the belief that the self is worthy (6).

Oates never believed that the world is benevolent, for her fictional world is a frightening and violent one where the innocent are often victimized. It is doubtful whether she believed that the world is meaningful. Each person creates his or her own meaning, she would say, a meaning that shifts according to one's life experiences. But she did believe that the self is worthy—worthy in the sense that she believed it is possible for a person to live a good, fulfilling life, as she herself did while her husband was alive. His death shattered this most fundamental assumption. She is now a self-blaming, guilt-ridden widow who regrets she is still alive.

Throughout *A Widow's Story*, Oates struggles to re-create and maintain her identity. It is important for her to resume as much of her everyday life as possible, if only to prove to herself that she can still function. She wants to behave professionally. "I did not want to betray myself as weak, 'feminine' " (26). The smallest details, such as hauling trash cans to the street and hauling them back, emptied, take on the greatest significance. She discovers what most people who lose a beloved spouse discover, namely, that life is changed irrevocably. Paradoxically, she is both the same and different. Fearful that her "frail 'personality' could shatter into pieces" (154) and that she will break down in public, she remains remarkably composed in the classroom, on the lecture circuit, and in her daily encounters with people. Despite feeling overwhelmed by all the "death-duties" that follow spousal loss, she functions efficiently in her dealings with funeral directors, lawyers, and probate court officers.

Oates has always believed that the self is forever elusive, mysterious, and unknowable. As close as she was to her husband throughout their forty-eight-year marriage, there was in him a "hidden chamber, a region to which he might retreat, to which I don't have access" (*A Widow's Story* 65). In death, he becomes even more mysterious to her, and she wonders whether she really knew him. She concedes that there was a "side of Ray unknowable to me—kept at a little distance from me. As—I suppose—there was a side of myself kept at a distance from Ray, who knew so little of my writing" (96). She reaches the "frightening" conclusion that perhaps she has never really known her husband, a conclusion that only adds to her self-blame.

The Mystery of Black Mass

As a writer—she never stops being a writer even when she doesn't write—Oates deepens the mystery surrounding her husband's identity by referring to his unpublished novel, *Black Mass*, which she has never read, and which she assumes he wrote before they met. She sustains this mystery by referring several times to *Black Mass*. The unread manuscript becomes one of the major revelations in *A Widow's Story* and the main plot device she uses to create and sustain suspense. At first she looks forward to reading all his writings, published and unpublished, thinking, hopefully, *"I will get to know my husband better. It isn't too late!"* (*A Widow's Story* 126). But when she looks at the old, worn manuscript, she becomes afraid. She begins imagining the manuscript will contain a fearful secret that will call into question his love and devotion for her. She then breaks off the thought and doesn't return to the manuscript for seventy-five pages.

While being introduced by E. L. Doctorow at New York University, where she has been invited to speak, Oates suddenly has a "wild fear" that "something will happen to Ray's uncompleted manuscript *Black Mass*—something will happen to the house in my absence" (*A Widow's Story* 225). Forty pages pass before she reminds herself to read *Black Mass*, which rests on her bedside table. The novel "is a secret document, I am thinking; as my own writing, in a kind of code, is a secret writing; as all writing is secret, even as it is made public—'published' " (265). More than one hundred pages pass before she returns briefly to *Black Mass*, reminding us that she is afraid to read it. *"Will I regret this? Would it be better for me to put the manuscript away, and never look at it again? Is there a story of Ray's secret life that he'd have wanted to keep secret?"* (371).

The partial answers to these questions appear in two chapters, "Black Mass I" and "Black Mass II," near the end of the memoir. Oates finds herself reading the story in a "trance," feeling the way she did when she was a young girl "wandering onto rural property posted NO TRESPASSING" (380). One hundred typed pages long, the novel describes a protagonist, Paul, who is similar to the young man Oates met in graduate school at the

University of Wisconsin in 1960. Like her future husband, Paul comes from a devout Catholic family. Highly intellectual but also insecure, Paul is both a professor and a priest. He finds himself falling in love with a student, Vanessa, who is eight years younger, the same age difference between Ray Smith and Oates. Paul and Vanessa meet for the first time at a university-sponsored Christmas party—again, similar to the way Smith and Oates met (not at Christmas but in October). The conflict in *Black Mass* arises when Paul finds himself caught between his commitment to the Church, on the one hand, and his romantic involvement with his student, on the other. The "crux of the novel," as Oates describes it, "is Paul's rejection of Vanessa, and Vanessa's subsequent suicide; not immediately but several years later" (382).

Black Mass is unnerving to Oates for several reasons. She is heart-broken that her husband worked so hard on a novel he finally abandoned, wondering whether her prodigious literary output may have intimidated him into silence. When she reads her husband's notes to the novel, she discovers he never confided in her key details about his life before they met in graduate school. One sentence in particular haunts her. "Paul is an alter ego—he is how I would have been had I entered the Jesuits at 19 instead of having a nervous breakdown" (*A Widow's Story* 384). Oates is stunned to learn about her husband's breakdown, though as she muses over this discovery, she vaguely remembers him telling her about this early in their relationship. As she continues to read her husband's notes to *Black Mass*, she is astonished to come across a passage that explains how he was able to recover from the breakdown: " 'Love'—'affair' with young woman at the sanitarium—this gave me reason to live, gave me something to think of—a new obsession, as it were. Psychiatrist had referred to me being 'Love-starved.' (Would Paul be love-starved)" (385). Ray Smith had never told Oates about this affair, and though it ended long before they met, she finds herself feeling "belated jealousy—on a May morning in 2008, reading of a love affair that had occurred in 1949" (386). Some of the details of *Black Mass* indicate that, contrary to what her husband told her, much of the novel was completed *after* the two of them met. She then wonders whether her husband thought of himself as a celibate priest in his marriage to her—an idea that would be jarring to anyone. Reading her husband's novel for the first time, three months after his death, she now knows what it feels like to be love starved.

If reading about *Black Mass* fills Oates with guilt, writing about his story—and the sinkholes and minefields that threatened him, particularly his conflicted relationship with his family—produces even more guilt. "In writing this, I feel that I am betraying Ray. Yet in not writing it, I am not being altogether honest" (361). There is no purpose in writing a memoir, she adds, if it isn't honest. The memoirist must navigate between discretion and good taste, on the one hand, and truthfulness, no matter how painful or cruel it may be, on the other. The journey becomes more perilous for a writer who feels uncomfortable about revealing anything personal about herself or her family. She knows that she may be exposing his deepest wounds and secrets to the public. She doesn't dwell on the "betrayal" of art, the ways in which writers reveal and sometimes exploit the vulnerability of their relatives and friends.

Yet there is little about Oates's depiction of Raymond Smith that is likely to have embarrassed him. The portrait that emerges is loving and respectful, and he comes across as an unusually thoughtful and kind man with many talents and interests. He was an expert gardener—"an editor of living things" (11), in Oates's felicitous words. She singles out his capacity for enjoying life, his common sense and good cheer, his unfailing modesty. His willingness to take on most of the domestic and financial responsibilities made it possible for her to devote herself entirely to her writing. Without being patronizing or chauvinistic, he shielded her from many problems that would have taken her away from her work. Though Oates generalizes that men are elusive to women—the "male is the *other*, the one to be *domesticated*; the female *is* domestication" (196)—Raymond Smith seems the more domestic of the two, willing to subordinate his own career to hers. They enjoy an egalitarian marriage, each connected to but not dependent on the other. Honoring her husband, she is also honoring their long and happy marriage.

Oates reaches several important conclusions about *Black Mass* that offer insight into her husband's life and her own. Those who have taught writing, and who are themselves writers, will agree with her observation that it is necessary to finish a writing project to be free of it. Many great writers ended their careers dejected and defeated because of their inability to complete a novel on which they were working for years or decades. To cite one example, Alexandra Styron discloses in her memoir, *Reading My Father*, how William Styron's failure to finish his World War II novel *The Way of the Warrior* was one of the major causes of his severe clinical depression that almost culminated in suicide, and from which he never entirely recovered.

Oates knows from experience that "It's a terrible thing to be devoured by one's work—you must learn to leap free of it as one might leap free of a raging fire" (388). Her husband apparently did not have this ability.

Reading *Black Mass*, Oates must have felt torn between wanting to admire it because it was written by her husband and judging it from the perspectives of a professor of creative writing and a seasoned novelist. Her professionalism is never in doubt. "*Black Mass* is fascinating to me, to read yet would probably be impenetrable to someone else" (388)—an editorial judgment that would result in a publisher's prompt rejection of the manuscript. She momentarily considers completing the novel herself but then rejects the idea, for lack of time. "For my own writing moves with such excruciating slowness" (388), an explanation that is hard to believe because of her legendary productivity.

Dedicatory Grief

Oates rejects the idea of completing her husband's novel, but in writing *A Widow's Story*, she not only brings him to life verbally but also endows him with literary immortality or, more accurately, the *illusion* of immortality. Admittedly, she would find this statement cold comfort. She remarks ruefully that centuries ago writers hoped to attain "a kind of immortality through their writing." She refers to Shakespeare's sonnets and the last lines of Ovid's *Metamorphoses*, which are "suffused with this hope." She then argues that such a claim with regard to contemporary writers "has an ironical/comical ring to it" (236). "It's a sad comfort—far more sad than comforting," she continues, "to know that one's books are being translated, sold, and presumably read in many countries, even as one's life lies in tatters" (237). She quotes Hemingway's statement to George Plimpton that if writers create something that is true and alive "you give it immortality" and then responds: "The ringing idealism is at odds with Hemingway's deeply wounded if not mutilated self—his twisted soul, his embittered and grudging spirit—yet, how powerful" (221). She wishes she could agree with the assertion that art compensates for the disappointments of life. "Philip Roth's claim is that 'print on paper' endures in a way that life can't endure, and maybe this is so, in a manner of speaking—(at least, for those writers whose work isn't permanently out of print)—and yet, what chill, meager comfort!" (283).

In an unpublished essay quoted by Robert C. Solomon in his book *In Defense of Sentimentality*, Janet McCracken uses the term "dedicatory grief" to describe the ways in which grief may compel us to honor our lost loved ones. "When someone we love has died, we desire to *do honor to, to show appreciation for*, that life as a whole, differently from and more importantly than the honors or rewards she may have received for particular accomplishments during her life" (92). Oates's dedicatory grief shows up in her loving descriptions of Ray Smith as a husband, scholar, editor, and publisher. There is never any question in her mind that he was "worth" the intense suffering she now experiences.

Oates creates for her husband what I call in *Dying in Character* a posterity self, a writer's published, or, in this case, unpublished writings that become part of his or her legacy. Seeking to "immortalize *oneself* by writing a memoir is not necessarily a noble endeavor," G. Thomas Couser states, but conferring "unexpected immortality on a hitherto anonymous, but noteworthy, person . . . can be an important and generous gift" (*Memoir* 179). Ray Smith was not exactly anonymous, though few people had heard of him outside the world of the *Ontario Review*. Oates endows her husband with a posterity self that is one of the accomplishments of *A Widow's Story*.

"In the early days, weeks, months of her new posthumous life," Oates observes near the end of *A Widow's Story*, "the widow must live *without meaning*" (368). Writing a book about her new posthumous life compels her to create a new meaning, a new assumptive world. Writing a memoir about widowhood helps her to author a new posthumous life. But Oates's preferred genre is fiction, not memoir; in fiction she can create imaginary counterworlds where she can project herself into characters, plots, and situations without worrying about violating too much of her private life.

How does Oates feel about a widow falling in love again? About the need for a companion? About the desire for sexual fulfillment? The memoirist conspicuously avoids raising these questions in *A Widow's Story*, but the fiction writer confronts these questions and others in three stories, one titled "The Widows," appearing in her 1977 collection of short stories, *Night-Side;* and the other two, "Probate" and the title story, published in her 2010 collection, *Sourland*. These three fictional stories help us understand what Oates's memoir conceals about the nature of widowhood.

"The Widows"

Oates was in her late thirties when *Night-Side* was published, and as her journal entries indicate, the future looked bright to her and her husband. Widowhood was more than thirty years away, a subject she could hardly imagine. And yet "The Widows," one of eighteen stories in *Night-Side*, anticipates with startling accuracy the shock, horror, grief, and depression she later writes about in *A Widow's Story*. It's as if, looking deeply into her imagination, Oates could foresee a situation she would not allow herself to contemplate in her journal.

Two women in their late twenties, Beatrice Kern and Moira Greaney, live in a university city in New Hampshire called Manitock. Both have recently lost their academic husbands: Wallace Kern was killed instantly in a car accident when a young driver crashed into him broadside, and Edgar Greaney succumbed after a long battle with throat cancer. Beatrice and Moira did not know each other before their husbands' deaths, but because Manitock is such a small community, they hear about each other's loss and soon meet. "They fell into each other's lives as if, all along, they had known about each other. Parallel lives, parallel habits" (*Night-Side* 50). But not parallel personalities. Beatrice is angry, bitter, hostile, while Moira is warm, open, trusting.

Beatrice is burdened with guilt that the story dramatizes but never clarifies—an existential guilt for surviving her husband's death. But it is more than existential guilt. Though we know little about Beatrice's life before the story opens, we learn that her brutal self-judgment was held in check while her husband was alive. She and her husband were married only for five years, but his death shocks her and calls into question every aspect of her life.

The tone in "The Widows," as in *A Widow's Story*, hovers between tragedy and absurdity. Angry and self-pitying, Beatrice doesn't know what to feel or how to act. Her response to grief seems at times normal; at other times, abnormal. Grief cannot be described in normative words; there is no "normal" response to profound loss. Nor is there only one way to grieve. And words like *rationality* and *irrationality* do little to understand the grief stricken, who exist in a world that defies intellectual analysis.

"The Widows" implies that the bereft are guilty of nothing they have done but of what they represent to others—the presence of death. In Oates's world, widowhood is a story of crime and self-punishment. Beatrice feels "contaminated by death" (*Night-Side* 38). Moira also regards herself as a criminal, though her crime is receding into the past.

Both widows know why their situations are frightening to others. Oates offers a sociological interpretation of bereavement that psychologists often miss in their emphasis only on the individual. Moira is acutely perceptive about the ways in which cancer patients and their caregivers are stigmatized. "They dreaded the very word *cancer*. They dreaded me. . . . But now that he's dead, people can see I'm still alive. I'm not a leper, I'm not contaminated with his disease. After all, death isn't contagious" (*Night-Side* 37). Unlike Beatrice, who is still in retreat from society and from herself, Moira has returned to life, and she helps the other widow resume hers.

"The Widows" precedes *A Widow's Story* by thirty-four years, but there are many uncanny similarities: the paralyzing nature of spousal loss, the yearning for death, the inability to sleep, the stigma of widowhood, the withdrawal from the world, and the frightening alteration of consciousness caused by prescription medication, "being in the thrall of psychotropic medication" (*A Widow's Story* 371). Anticipating Oates's response to her husband's death, Beatrice is deranged by grief and feels alienated from others and herself. Her posthumous life resembles a dark night of the soul. Grief has its own mysterious ebb and flow, and its force is most violent immediately following spousal loss. Both widows, Beatrice and Oates, "went down into the grave" with their husbands, in Moira's words, and the journey back to life is fraught with pain and uncertainty. Both Beatrice and Oates react in the same physical way to suffering, becoming pale, ill, and losing weight. Both stories explore widowhood as a period of transgression that can be eased through the passing of time and a network of devoted friends. Both stories affirm the importance of interconnection in female identity—women feeling connected with other women. The bond between Beatrice and Moira is dynamic and at times ambivalent, but there is nothing ambiguous about the need for friendship during the time of bereavement. Like Oates in *A Widow's Story*, in the beginning of the story Beatrice wants to die, but by the end she feels alive and well. Affirming an ethics of care, "The Widows" and *A Widow's Story* show how friendship can develop out of deep loss and, along with the passage of time, allow the bereft to find new meaning in life. Avoiding didacticism, both stories suggest that there is only one death duty that matters for the widow: keeping herself alive.

The striking similarities between "The Widow" and *A Widow's Story* raise an intriguing question. How could Oates have foreseen, decades before the loss of her husband, how she would react to his death? Reflecting on the intersections between her fictional and real selves, we see that art is sometimes a projection screen for a future reality that may not come into existence for several decades. Additionally, Oates's account of her own widowhood may borrow from her earlier fictional account, suggesting the inseparability of the writer's art and life.

"Probate"

The first book Oates completed after her husband's death was *In Rough Country* (2010), a collection of essays and reviews. She admits in the preface that the title, taken from Yeats's apocalyptic poem "The Second Coming," has a double meaning: the "treacherous geographical/psychological terrains" of her subjects and the emotional terrain of her own life as a widow. After completing *In Rough Country*, Oates wrote a collection of fictional stories called *Sourland*, also published in 2010, which dramatizes the plight of distraught widows who struggle with sudden loss and bereavement. Of the sixteen stories, the most intriguing, biographically and psychologically, is "Probate." As *A Widow's Story* reveals, "Probate" arose from Oates's own experience when a probate court officer instructed her to write to all of her husband's relatives, informing them of his death, so that they could see his will and determine whether they "had claims to make against the will" (*A Widow's Story* 363). It was a nuisance for Oates to fulfill this onerous death duty, but the court's demand gave rise to one of her most psychologically harrowing short stories. Before taking a bizarre twist near the end of the story, "Probate" could be viewed as Oates's portrait of the artist as a widow.

Adrienne Myer was married for thirty-two years to a Princeton history professor who had been in excellent health, like Oates's husband. Tracy Emmet Myer's brief illness and unexpected death closely parallel Raymond Smith's. More importantly, Adrienne Myer's response to her husband's death is identical to Oates's. Adrienne experiences intense anxiety and dread along with a feeling of dislocation, derealization, and depersonalization. She appears in a dazed-zombie state, and her frail personality threatens to shatter into pieces. She cannot stop brooding over her husband's death and funeral, reliving every detail, including his cremated remains. She values education but is too fatalistic to believe that knowledge is power. She thinks about committing suttee, the ancient Hindu custom of burning the widow alive on her husband's funeral pyre, the same fantasy that Oates discusses in *A Widow's Story*.

Oates begins "Probate" with a protagonist whose personality and situation resemble her own, but she then complicates the plot with the addition of a black teenaged mother, Leisha, who is also at the Mercer County Courthouse, trying to deliver a message to her children's father, who has been arrested for domestic abuse. The two women develop an improbable bond based on grievance. Through a series of bizarre plot twists, Adrienne discovers to her horror not only that there is an irregularity in her husband's last will and testament, but also that there is a possibility he was not divorced from his first wife, making his marriage to Adrienne, his "second wife," not fully legal. She has been so dependent on her husband that she doesn't know how to live without him. The fear that she has never known him makes her posthumous life more wrenching. How will the widow continue to live? How can she free herself from the yearning for death? What will she do with her new life? Oates answers these questions with the most startling metaphor in the story, indeed, one of the most powerful metaphors of widowhood found in any story or memoir. "She was a tree whose roots had become entwined with the roots of an adjacent tree, a seemingly taller and stronger tree, and these roots had become entwined inextricably. To free the living tree from the dead tree would require an act of violence that would damage the living tree. It would require an act of imagination. Easier to imagine *suttee*. Easier to imagine swallowing handfuls of barbiturates, old painkiller medications in the medicine cabinet. *I can't do this. I can't be expected to do this. I am not strong enough*" (*Sourland* 234).

Oates and Adrienne have been inextricably entwined until this moment in the story, but what happens next in "Probate" is purely an act of imagination—and signature Oates. Adrienne's interview with the judge ends with "shocking abruptness," and the distraught widow is taken away by a security guard to a vast Kafkaesque waiting room, where another woman in a bailiff's uniform orders her to take off her clothes and slip into a paper smock and paper slippers. Adrienne undresses "like one in a trance" and then submits to a degrading physical examination that is depicted as a sexual violation. Her silent cry, *"This is not possible,"* soon changes to *"This is what is possible."*

At the end of "Probate," Adrienne and Leisha are mysteriously drawn to each other and recognize a bond of kinship based on grievance and victimization. Both women are connected by Leisha's two-year-old daughter, Lilith. Leaving the courthouse, Adrienne hears the toddler's faint cry outside the building, assumes she has been abandoned, scoops her up, carries her to her car, and then speeds home, believing she and Lilith are embarking on a new life together.

Adrienne sheds her former cautious, diligent, responsible self and emerges through an act of violence into a new woman, ready to seize an opportunity that she believes will transform her life. No longer depressed, emotionally withdrawn, and suicidal, she has finally become engaged with the world. Having separated herself for the first time from her deceased husband, she is now an independent woman. She believes, with justification, that she can provide Lilith with a better home than can her biological mother or the county welfare system. Adrienne acts recklessly, completely out of character, but that is Oates's theme in the story. The widow must imagine herself into a new person if she is to survive.

The ending of "Probate" is tinged with irony. The "geological cataclysm" of Trenton described at the beginning of the story, a corroded slum with barricaded streets and deafening jackhammers, all demonstrating a city under construction, has its counterpart in Adrienne's psychic cataclysm at the end. She cannot probate her husband's will without further legal documentation, but she can probate her will to live by becoming a new person, one who is willing to break the law to act communally and nurture another life. The toddler's name heightens the irony of the situation. In Jewish folklore, Lilith is believed to be Adam's first wife, who left her husband to assert her independence and take on a new identity as baby stealer and mother of demons. In literature, Lilith often represents the dark side of women; Jung identified her with the *anima* in men, the repressed female within. In Oates's story, Adrienne is the baby stealer, the woman who asserts for the first time the desire for equality and independence. Not quite a demon, Adrienne speeds away from probate court with a new life and a new purpose, achieving hard-won freedom through an act of imagination. Writing the story demanded an act of imagination from Oates as well, and surely it is significant that she ends "Probate" with the belief that in the morning all that is confusing in Adrienne's life will become clear. "She had faith" (*Sourland* 247).

"Sourland"

Not all of Oates's widows, however, can look forward to a promising future. Sophie Quinn, the protagonist in the title story in *Sourland*, has much in common with Moira Greaney, Beatrice Kern, Adrienne Myer, and Oates herself. That's what makes the story of her widowhood so terrifying. Fifty-nine pages long, the longest story in the volume, "Sourland" is Oates's most haunting portrait of the way in which a widow's sexual longing leads to a situation beyond anything she can imagine.

Sophie's life replays Oates's in many ways. Sophie and Matthew Quinn meet in graduate school at the University of Wisconsin, Madison, in the 1960s. He is a doctoral student in American constitutional law; she a master's student in nineteenth-century American literature. They marry not long after meeting. He is thirty when they marry, she twenty-two, the same age difference that separates Oates and her husband. Their close marriage of nearly twenty-six years comes to an end not as a result of pneumonia or a staph infection but a sudden heart attack.

Oates projects many of her feelings and experiences of sudden widowhood onto her fictional character. Widowhood brings a posthumous life that Sophie has never imagined, and she feels distraught, bereft, heartsick. Dependence on her husband leaves her feeling bewildered and lost. Many of the experiences Oates writes about in *A Widow's Story* appear in "Sourland." Sophie is overwhelmed by the ringing telephone immediately after the funeral and by the many floral displays, potted plants, gift boxes of fruit, and gourmet foods she receives from her husband's friends and business associates, all sent "as for a lavish if macabre celebration" (315). She nearly faints when she goes to probate court. A slender woman, Sophie has lost fifteen pounds since her husband's death. She moves "in a kind of spell of self-laceration" (318), walking around in a "haze of anesthetized grief" (329). She performs all of the necessary death duties, including having her husband's body cremated and ordering a double cemetery plot. Despite being practical, competent, and conscientious, fearful of embarrassing, upsetting, or annoying others, she suffers from "demented" grief, as "slovenly and smelly as something leaking through a cracked cellar wall" (329).

Sophie has few resources to rely upon after her husband's death. Religion provides no consolation to her, and though she thinks she hears her deceased husband's voice and even talks to him on one occasion, she never believes in the possibility of reunion in another world. Like Oates's other widows, Sophie has had a good marriage, but that knowledge does little to sustain the present or provide hope for the future. Resources that are sometimes helpful to other widows, such as psychotherapy or support groups, are never a good option in Oates's world. Nor is volunteer work or community service helpful. Reading or writing does little to alleviate the widows' loneliness. Nor are they interested in learning how other widows have coped with their losses. Childless—it was her husband's decision not to have children—Sophie has neither relatives nor friends to rely on for support. She has been employed for years at a university press, but she is now on a leave of absence, thus depriving her of the lifeline of work.

Like Oates's other widows, Sophie feels guilty for surviving her husband. Thinking about the decision to have her husband's body cremated, presumably a decision he would have wanted, she had "signed the document, for the cremation. And yet, she'd gone unpunished. No one seemed to realize" (*Sourland* 354). That is, she goes unpunished not for the decision to cremate his body but for her willingness, however reluctant, to remain alive.

Marriage provides Oates's four fictional wives, Moira, Beatrice, Adrienne, and Sophie, with stability, structure, and safety, a social net they all need. When their marriages end in their husbands' deaths, the widows find their social net is torn, threatening to plunge them into an abyss. Without their husbands, the widows feel isolated, even imprisoned, thrown back upon the solitary self, deprived of the social contact necessary for their own identity. *"We have no personalities unless there are people who know us,"* Oates remarks in *A Widow's Story*. *"Unless there are people we hope to convince that we deserve to exist"* (20). Widowhood obliterates their identities, shatters all of their assumptions, and forces them to create new assumptive worlds, new identities.

The words *surviving spouse* appear fourteen times in "Sourland," contributing to the story's hypnotic power. It's as if Sophie cannot break free from the terrible condition of widowhood, unable to see herself from any other perspective or subject position. Oates's strong identification with her protagonist creates an equally strong counteridentification that results from the writer's need for distance and detachment. As in *A Widow's Story*, Oates suggests that her protagonist's reaction to the loss of her spouse is representative of all surviving spouses. She tells us what Sophie is thinking and feeling while at the same time evoking the extent of her confusion, dread, and uncertainty. Knowledge and reason have limited value to Sophie, and her husband's death thrusts her into a dark new world for which she is entirely unprepared.

A widow is "one who *makes mistakes*," Oates declares in *A Widow's Story* (72), but she never describes any serious mistakes she makes. "Sourland" dramatizes a widow's fatal mistake, one that Sophie seems to know, unconsciously, she is bound to make. She can hear her husband cautioning her to be careful when she blindly follows her instinct and responds to a series of mysterious photographs and letters she receives in a manila folder postmarked Sourland MINN from an old acquaintance they had known in graduate school decades earlier.

The acquaintance, Jeremiah Kolk, a classics graduate student caught up in the violence and radical politics of the 1960s, poses a grave danger to Sophie. One of Oates's most menacing characters, Kolk has long been presumed dead, killed in an accidental detonation of a "nail bomb" in a Milwaukee warehouse. There was "something monkish and intolerant" in Kolk's manner (*Sourland* 330), and after her husband's death, when she begins receiving photographs and letters from Kolk, Sophie recalls an incident at Madison, before getting married, when the two men argued at a party and Kolk called Matt a "fink, scab." Sophie tried to comfort the aggrieved Kolk on a staircase, reaching out to touch his arm, but he angrily pushed her away. That was the last time they saw each other. Sophie cannot stop replaying this incident. *"So long ago,"* she thinks. *"Who would remember. No one!"* (331).

Sophie remembers even after more than a quarter of a century. She recalls this incident when she and Kolk begin corresponding, and she cannot help fantasizing over a romantic relationship when he invites her to visit him in his isolated cabin in remote northern Minnesota. "They would fall in love, Sophie reasoned. She would never leave Sourland" (334). Sophie is Oates's only widow who imagines falling in love again after her husband's death, the only widow who feels a sexual reawakening, the only widow who is ready to embark on a new love relationship.

And yet there is something doomed about their relationship from the beginning, partly because of the sinister nature of Kolk's character and history; partly because of the uncompromising part of the country in which he lives, the foothills of the Sourland Mountains; and partly because of the darker motives behind Sophie's decision to meet Kolk. Her greatest similarity to Oates lies in her belief that a widow deserves punishment. Before flying from Newark to Sourland, Sophie visits her husband's cemetery and promises him that she will be back, adding, "I need to do this. Kolk needs me." Feeling the "rebuke of the dead, their resentment of the living" (*Sourland* 336), she acknowledges her overwhelming desperation and thinks, *"Maybe you should kill yourself instead"* (336), a wish that turns out to be self-fulfilling.

Greg Johnson's recognition that the "drive toward anorexia" in Oates's fiction "is often coupled with a portrayal of female sexual experience in wholly negative and destructive terms" uncannily characterizes Sophie Quinn. So, too, does his observation that "the vast majority" of Oates's women "experience sex as degrading and even horrific" characterize Sophie; "rarely do lovers in Joyce's fiction experience genuine tenderness and communion in the sexual act" (173). We don't know anything about Sophie's sexual relationship with her husband, but her sexual desire after his death compels her to make the worst possible choice in selecting a new mate.

A central assumption in Oates's world, including the autobiographical *A Widow's Story* and the fictional widows' stories in *Night-Side* and *Sourland*, is that the dead resent the living. "It's a taboo subject," Oates asserts in *A Widow's Story.* "How *the dead* are betrayed by the living" (332). The idea of betrayal, however, originates from the living, not from the dead.

And surely not all people believe that the dead resent the living. To believe that the dead resent the living, moreover, is to believe in a supernatural world, one in which the dead are capable of feeling and thinking.

In Oates's world, widows do not believe that their deceased husbands would want them to enjoy the remaining years of their lives. Nowhere in *A Widow's Story*, "The Widows," "Probate," or "Sourland" does a husband tell his wife that he wants her to go on living after his own death. It's true that four of the five husbands die unexpectedly, but most are middle-aged or older, and such discussions often take place during marriage. Nor do the wives imagine the opposite situation in which, while dying, they encourage their bereft husbands to remarry after their wives' deaths. A husband or wife's desire for the surviving spouse's happiness is a gift that can ease the pain of widowhood, but it is a gift that is never given in Oates's fictional world.

Oates states repeatedly in her memoir that widows deserve to suffer. *"Widowhood is the punishment for having been a good wife"* (*A Widow's Story* 102). And yet one must make a crucial distinction, as Oates does not, between the feeling of punishment that arises from lost love and the belief that one should punish oneself for the rest of one's life. Lost love is inevitable, producing grief that may be experienced as punishment. But grief changes over time, and widows may discover joy reentering their lives. Moira, Beatrice, and Adrienne re-create their lives and find new meaning to sustain them. Sophie does not. She knows, unconsciously, that her pilgrimage to Kolk is a journey to disaster.

From the beginning, Sophie's relationship with Kolk is charged with ambiguity. Does she reach out and touch him on the arm in Madison, following his bitter quarrel with Matt, because of a desire to comfort him or because she is attracted to him? Does she decide to visit him in Sourland because she wishes to comfort him again, because he needs her, as she plaintively tries to explain to her husband, or because she is deranged by grief? Is she hoping to find happiness with another man or seeking to punish herself for betraying a dead man?

There are moments when Sophie believes she is following an instinct for survival, but mostly she believes that nothing good will come from her pursuit of Kolk. Arriving at the small, "grim" airport in Grand Rapids, she thinks, *"My punishment has begun"* (*Sourland* 337). Nor is she reassured when she sees Kolk. He looks like a figure from a gothic horror story: the left side of his face is badly disfigured; a part of his lower jaw is missing; and a "double row of teeth [was] exposed as in a ghastly fixed smile" (337). When she arrives at his cabin after a grueling three-hour drive in his jeep, she confronts a vicious bulldog mix aptly called Cerberus, named after the three-headed dog of Hades. And when she pulls back the worn comforter and bedsheets in the "guest room" and picks up a set of bedclothes with a musty odor, she thinks about the last woman who slept there. *"She has died there. My predecessor. Allowed to starve to death, to die and become mummified"* (349).

Sophie immediately realizes she has made a terrible mistake. Seeing Kolk's ravaged face, which in the shifting firelight looks like that of a devil, she thinks, *"This is what the surviving spouse deserves. A demon missing half his face"* (*Sourland* 356). Kolk claims he is a new person, a person who is *"being born only now, in these words to you,"* but he is the same old person, brutal and antisocial, and while he calls himself a *"pilgrim in perpetual quest"* (333), he is perpetually paranoid, a radical outlaw who despises people. She has no choice but to have sex with him, but she is terrified the entire time, for she knows he is a "predator, ravenous for prey" (363). Hours later, when she wakes up, bruised and terror stricken, she tells him she wants to leave, but he pushes her back into the room and locks the door. That night she escapes through a window and starts to run, though she is hopelessly lost. He finds her easily and drags her back to the cabin, where the story ends. She too will be allowed to starve to death, to die and become mummified.

"Sourland" is a gothic horror story not only because of the menacing Kolk, who is even more demonic than Arnold Friend in Oates's classic story "Where Are You Going, Where Have You Been," but also because of the mood and imagery of the story. "Sourland" opens with the new widow gazing in horror at an infestation of spiders in her house. The image recalls the end of *A Widow's Story*, when Oates writes about her horror of spiders, which evokes painful memories of when she and her husband lived in Beaumont, Texas, filled with flying palmetto bugs. Sophie destroys the spider webs, her fingers "clenched like claws, transfixed with rage" (314), but the spiders are ubiquitous. A spider bite in Kolk's cabin develops into a rash that "pulsed and flamed" (355). The lurid bites throb with heat, one more torment to endure.

Oates is one of the masters of gothic fiction, and "Sourland" demonstrates her belief that widowhood is a state of medieval horror. The gothic, to which her imagination is repeatedly drawn, emphasizes the night side of human existence, the terror and violence associated with darkness. Fantasy predominates over reality in gothic fiction, just as irrationality overwhelms rationality. The lonely, sinister, remote setting of Sourland is the perfect place for gothic horror. The demented, demonic Kolk preys on unsuspecting victims like Sophie, who, contrary to the meaning of her name, Greek for "wisdom," has cast aside prudence and common sense.

"Sourland" begins in November, when Sophie's husband dies, and ends in April, the month of rebirth, but there is nothing hopeful or affirmative about the end of the story. Her posthumous life turns out to be no life at all, and she ends a captive to her worst fears that have all come true.

Love, Loss, and Recovery

Oates ends her memoir with "The Widow's Handbook," only one sentence long: "Of the widow's countless death-duties there is really just one that matters: on the first anniversary of her husband's death the widow should think *I kept myself alive*" (416). Long suspicious of sensationalistic memoirs, psychiatric textbooks, clinical guides, and self-help books, she refuses to offer advice to widows beyond stating what helped her. Changing King Lear's "ripeness is all" to "survival is all," she allows her story to speak for itself.

But Joyce Carol Smith the bereft widow and Joyce Carol Oates the indomitable writer have not simply endured the dangerous aftermath of spousal loss. *A Widow's Story* teaches us much about love, loss, and recovery. No spousal loss memoir has gone into more excruciating detail in exploring the dark emotions of widowhood, and no memoir has been more successful in *dramatizing* these emotions. Joan Didion describes in her memoir the process of magical thinking that accompanies spousal loss, but Joyce Carol Oates implicates the reader in the derangement of widowhood, and in doing so, she greatly expands the notion of "normal" grief. Oates examines nearly every aspect of widowhood, and there is little that escapes her writer's eye.

There is, however, one subject about which Oates remains nearly silent. Thirteen months after her husband's death she remarried. Nothing in *A Widow's Story* prepares us for this startling event except for a veiled passage on the penultimate page in which she remarks on having hosted a small dinner party at her home the previous night, August 29, 2008, and invited a guest who was a stranger to her, a Princeton neuroscientist. "I could not have guessed," the paragraph-long sentence ends, enveloped with Jamesian ambiguity, "how another time so purely by chance, as years ago in Madison, Wisconsin, it was purely chance that Ray had come to sit beside me, my life would be altered—*You must not forget it is a gift freely given you could not deserve*" (415).

What makes the revelation, or anti-revelation, more astonishing is that there is not a single moment in *A Widow's Story* when Oates imagines falling in love with another man. Nor does she even question whether she wants to be in love again. Throughout *A Widow's Story* her yearning is to die, not to find another man. There is no mention of romantic love or the need for male companionship except for an odd moment when, speaking at the Sanibel Island Public Library, on the Gulf Coast, she finds herself looking at older, white-haired men in the audience, men of her husband's age. A "bizarre fantasy" comes over her that she will meet an older man, in a wheelchair, and that she will have a "second chance" with this man who will need a nurse/female companion. "What could be more ridiculous," she asks, "casting an envious eye on strangers in wheelchairs! No one can believe what compulsive fantasist the widow is, even the widow herself" (244).

What's hard to believe, however, is not that Oates would wish to imagine that her husband is alive and home again, in need of rehabilitation, but that she has never had a single thought or fantasy during the time she was writing *A Widow's Story* of falling in love again with another man. Surely many if not most widows happily married for nearly half a century would entertain this thought. Falling in love again is one of the most complicated parts of widowhood, raising vexing psychological, existential, familial, and legal questions. How can a spousal loss memoir studiously avoid raising these questions if it ends with an impending marriage? This is the part of *A Widow's Story* that is not ridiculous but certainly curious.

Rereading *A Widow's Story* with the knowledge of Oates's speedy remarriage, one wonders whether some of the existential guilt and lacerating self-blame she describes in the memoir arise from falling in love again. She tells us during the early stage of widowhood that she and her husband had "fantasized" that "neither of us wished to outlive the other" (64), explaining that this fantasy is a "consolation to wives not-yet-widows" (67). The fear of abandoning her husband after his death makes more sense in the context of remarriage. So, too, does her "Advice to the Widow" become more understandable in light of a widow's swift remarriage: "Do not think that grief is pure, solemn, austere and 'elevated'—this is not Mozart's Requiem Mass" (111). It is unlikely that guilt is ever "pure," certainly not when a widow or widower remarries and experiences a new set of emotions that includes both grief and joy.

In the chapter titled "Taboo," Oates remarks that "How *the dead* are betrayed by the living" is a "taboo subject," elaborating: "We who are living—we who have survived—understand that our guilt is what links us to the dead. At all times we can hear them calling to us, a growing incredulity in their voices *You will not forget me—will you? How can you forget me? I have no one but you*" (332). This guilt becomes more understandable in light of a widow's speedy remarriage. There is no "correct" time to wait before a widow or widower begins dating, but it's reasonable to assume that falling in love again becomes more complicated for those still burdened by existential guilt or self-blame. Describing her suicidal depression, Oates quotes Hamlet's lines, "How weary, stale, flat and unprofitable, / Seem to me [all] the uses of this world!" She might have quoted, a few lines further in the play, the main reason for Hamlet's melancholy: his mother's "o'er hasty marriage": "Thrift, thrift, Horatio! The funeral-baked meats / Did coldly furnish forth the marriage tables" (I. ii. 180–181).

Readers of *A Widow's Story* are likely to be sympathetic to Oates's decision to remarry. She reveals on two different occasions her "indescribable terror of aloneness" (110), her inability to "bear to live alone" (291). She does not want the life that Philip Roth had after the end of his marriage with Claire Bloom, a "life so focused upon writing and reading; a life of isolation in the interstices of which there are evenings with friends, and (seemingly short-lived) liaisons with younger women" (291). Roth's life may be a "brave life," she suggests, a "stoic life," but not the kind she desires.

There are many moments in *A Widow's Story* when it would have been appropriate for Oates to tell us she had met another man. Midway through the memoir, in a chapter titled "Morbidity Studies," she recalls having dinner earlier in the evening at an "elegant house in Princeton" with her friend E., "whose domestic/marital life, too, has collapsed" (268), not because of death but divorce. After discussing friends and acquaintances who have been abandoned by their spouses, Oates then mentions that "Ray was the first man in my life, the last man, the only man" (269). This observation could segue easily into her feelings about meeting another man. Another moment occurs at the beginning of chapter 5, "You Looked So Happy," when she quotes her friend Eleanor Bergstein's perceptive remark: *"Though you loved Ray, very much, and could not imagine living without him, you will begin to discover that you are doing things that Ray would not have been interested in doing, and you are meeting people you would not have met when Ray was alive, and all this will change your life for the better, though you might not think so now"* (273). This would have been a perfect opportunity to comment on the many prophetic ironies in this statement, ironies that Oates may not have seen immediately but came to realize over time.

In the same chapter, Oates recalls reading to her husband one of Nietzsche's aphorisms that she had used as an epigraph to her 1964 novel *With Shuddering Fall*: "Whatever is done out of love always takes place beyond good and evil" (317). She adds wryly that her Jesuit-trained husband, the "shrewdest of editors," identified the word *always* as problematic. Regardless of whether what is done out of love *always* or only *sometimes* takes place beyond good and evil, falling in love again after the death of one's beloved spouse affirms both the living and the dead. Throughout *A Widow's Story*, Oates recalls the comforting advice offered to her by her close friend Gail Godwin: "Suffer, Joyce! Ray was worth it." A happy and long first marriage that ends in widowhood is motive enough for a second marriage.

Just as Oates was shocked when she came across her husband's secret "love affair" with another woman, an experience he fictionalized lightly in *Black Mass*, so are readers shocked when they discover that she began dating six months after her husband's death, two-and-a-half years before the publication of *A Widow's Story*. Why the secrecy? She has long felt that happiness is antithetical to literature. She may have felt that writing about a joyful experience in the context of a heartrending spousal loss memoir would be inappropriate, out of character, and unnecessary. "Most of my writing is preoccupied with 'the imagination of pain,'" she told an interviewer in 1989, "and this is simply because people need help with pain, never with joy. There's no need to write about happy people, happy problems; there's only the moral need to instruct readers concerning the direction to take, in order to achieve happiness" (*Conversations with Joyce Carol Oates* 54). It is easier for Oates to write about love lost, widowhood as victimhood, than love regained, widowhood as an opportunity for growth.

Love regained, however, in the context of love recently lost is a fascinating and instructive story, one that is much more challenging to write about than the story of love lost. For love regained in the aftermath of devastating loss is not pure happiness because it is inevitably tinged by the sadness of love lost as well as by existential guilt. Love regained following spousal loss is a greater taboo than the subject of how the dead are betrayed by the living. Indeed, often it is the same taboo! To lose the love of one's life and then fall in love again may seem like a betrayal. One can understand Oates's reluctance to write autobiographically about the experience of falling in love again, and yet, paradoxically, no one is a greater master of the "imagination of pain" than she is. The story of falling in love again after a spouse's death is a part of the story of widowhood that almost always remains untold.

As I discuss in *Companionship in Grief*, only a few spousal loss memoirists have been willing to narrate the story of love regained. John Bayley, the distinguished British literary critic, wrote three memoirs about his novelist-wife, Iris Murdoch, who developed and eventually succumbed to Alzheimer's disease: *Elegy for Iris* (1999), *Iris and Her Friends* (2000), and *Widower's House* (2001), the last of which is a hilarious account following his wife's death of his sexual misadventures with two younger women whom he calls Margot and Mella. Bayley makes a statement in *Widower's House* that Oates would wholeheartedly endorse: "I could not escape back into my old self, because my old self no longer existed. In widowhood you lose not only your loved one but much of yourself. And there is no new one to take its place" (3–4). At the end of *Widower's House* he tells us about the beginning of his new life with an old friend, Audhild (Audi) Villers, whom he married in 2000, one year after Iris Murdoch's death.

Donald Hall, the former US poet laureate, also writes about falling in love after the death of his wife, the poet Jane Kenyon. In "Postscript 2005," the last section of his memoir *The Best Day the Worst Day*, Hall writes about being incapacitated by grief after her death. Oates would certainly understand the depth of his despair and his obsession with his wife's death. At the end of *The Best Day the Worst Day*, written a decade after Kenyon's death, he mentions being in love with a woman named "L. K.," to whom he dedicates the memoir. He then elaborates on his relationship with Linda Kunhardt in "Grief's House," the penultimate chapter of his 2008 memoir *Unpacking the Boxes*.

Much wisdom resides in C. S. Lewis's *A Grief Observed*, published in 1961, shortly after the death of his wife, Joy Davidman, who succumbed to bone cancer in 1960 at the age of forty-five. He survived her by only three years, dying in 1963 at the age of sixty-five. Oates might not have identified with Lewis's struggle with religious faith following the death of his wife, to whom he was married only for four years; his "muscular Christianity" was not something that preoccupied Oates. But she would have been intrigued by the insights into love and loss he reaches at the end of *A Grief Observed*. Lewis discovers that "passionate grief does not link us with the dead but cuts us off from them" (54). Oates would surely agree with him that the Victorian tendency toward "mummification" makes "the dead far more dead" (55). She would endorse his conclusion that grief "is like a long valley, a winding valley where any bend may reveal a totally new landscape" (60). And she would understand his statement that insofar as writing a book about love, loss, and widowhood "was a defence against total collapse, a safety-valve, it had done some good" (59). Or, as Oates observes in *Uncensored*, "The act of writing a memoir can be seen, ideally, as an act of reclaiming the victim's very nerves" (129).

"Breach of Narrative Promise"

Oates never anticipated the firestorm of criticism that arose from her failure to disclose her remarriage at the end of *A Widow's Story*. And yet she must have suspected, when referring in *A Widow's Story* to living in the "era of 'full disclosure'" (300), that readers would expect her to be forthcoming about major new life events. What could be more momentous than her remarriage, which occurred while she was writing her memoir? The harshest criticism came from Janet Maslin, who in a February 13, 2011, review in the *New York Times* complained about the omission. "A book long and rambling enough to contemplate an answering-machine recording could have found time to mention a whole new spouse."

Oates often reacts swiftly and publicly, not always to her advantage, to negative reviews of her work. In a long letter appearing in the May 26, 2011, issue of *The New York Review of Books*, she replies to Julian Barnes, who published a review in the same fortnightly magazine suggesting that Oates's omission in *A Widow's Story* of her remarriage has created for some readers a "breach of narrative promise." Oates defends her decision to exclude this information, arguing that *A Widow's Story* is "perhaps 98 percent journal entries with only two or three conventionally composed chapters, to provide marital background." She didn't intend to write an "autobiographical work," she continues, which would require the addition of many more chapters. Rather, she hoped to write a memoir that emphasizes the first six months of widowhood, a memoir that "might find some resonance with other widows in the first half-year or so of widowhood."

Nevertheless, Oates concedes in the opening and closing paragraphs of the letter that she should have included this information. "In retrospect I can see that I should have added something like an appendix, to bring my personal history up to date; yet—(I hope this doesn't sound disingenuous!)—I would not have thought that my personal history in the aftermath of early widowhood was so very relevant to the subject."

Disingenuous or not, Oates's justification for omitting crucial information from *A Widow's Story* raises more questions than it resolves. She tells us at the end of *A Widow's Story* that the small dinner party in which she meets for the first time the Princeton neuroscientist occurs on August 29, 2008, six months and eleven days after the death of her husband. Even thirteen months after the death of one's lifelong spouse is still *early* widowhood, and a widow's remarriage is an essential part of the story of love, loss, and recovery. Oates's long literary discussion of *Black Mass*, presumably among the "two or three conventionally composed chapters" in *A Widow's Story* to which she refers in the letter, is not simply "marital background" but material that explains her belated jealousy upon learning that her husband was in love with another woman. Writing about the process of falling in love again and remarriage would help to explain her belief that the living betray the dead. Such material, written by one of the world's greatest authors, would certainly find "some resonance with other widows in the first half-year or so of widowhood"—and, one might add, without limiting the audience of Oates's memoir, the first thirteen months of widowhood.

Oates's statement that she plans to add an appendix to future editions of *A Widow's Story* came as an unwelcome surprise to her editor, Daniel Halpern, the president and publisher of Ecco Press. "I completely disagree," he was quoted as saying to Charles McGrath in the ArtsBeat section of the *New York Times*. " 'I thought I had talked her out of that,' he said. 'She wrote a book about what it's like to be in limbo—about what it was like to lose the man she had been married to all her life. Why include the next husband?' " (May 10, 2011).

McGrath is right that the inclusion of this information "breaks the spell of the book," but Oates herself breaks the spell by telling us at the end that she has survived the first year of widowhood. The dark spell of *A Widow's Story* needs to be broken, Oates implies on the last page, so that other wives-to-be widows can learn from her experience. In an interview appearing in the online journal *SocialSquawk* on May 5, 2011, Oates referred to *A Widow's Story* as a "practical, darkly funny guide—a widow's handbook—with advice, for instance, on how to pick a grave plot and coping with the death duties, such as having to produce copies of the death certificate ad nauseam until you want to scream." What can be better practical advice for wives-to-be-widows than the possibility that one can fall in love again after a devastating loss?

Joyce Carol Gross

The contrast between Oates's portrayal of widowhood in her memoir and fiction and her own post-widowed life could not be more stunning.

In interviews she has spoken glowingly about being remarried and has expressed no conflict between honoring the memory of her first husband and revealing delight with her present husband, Charles R. Gross. "Ray would love Charlie," she told Louise McCready in the online newspaper *Huffington Post*. "Charlie is very, very funny and has great enthusiasm for life. He is tireless, always planning new projects, and over-commits himself. I think that Charlie would like Ray—who was quiet, thoughtful, just slightly shy or reticent at times." Unlike her first husband, Oates's second husband reads all her writings, and he is not afraid to express criticism of her work. In an interview with Amy Ellis Nutt published in the New Jersey *Star-Ledger* on March 15, 2010, Oates stated that her new husband is an avid hiker and that the first hike he took her on was to Sourland Mountain in Hillsborough, New Jersey—not the Sourland Mountains in Minnesota where Oates's less fortunate widow, Sophie Quinn, meets her new paramour.

Neuroscientist and Storyteller

Charles G. Gross is also a writer, the coeditor of *Readings in Physiological Psychology* and the author of two books published by MIT Press, *Brain, Vision, Memory: Tales in the History of Neuroscience* and *A Hole in the Head: More Tales in the History of Neuroscience*, the latter of which he dedicated to Oates. (She dedicated *Sourland* and her 2010 novel *Little Bird of Heaven* to him.) As the subtitles of his two books suggest, he is also a storyteller, fascinated with the history of science and the cultural and personal clashes that have characterized the long simmering tension between science and religion.

In 2004, Gross received the American Psychological Association Distinguished Scientific Contribution Award. An article published the following year in *American Psychologist* offers a lively portrait of him. He comes across as an iconoclastic thinker who combines scientific thinking with a love for the humanities. Devoted to his research and teaching, he knows how to have fun, whether it is through hiking, traveling, or photography. Born in Brooklyn in 1936 to secular Jewish parents who were "Communist intellectuals," he wanted to major in history at Harvard but "soon found that his politics were inconsistent with getting A's, so he majored in biology" (753). Receiving his PhD at Cambridge in 1961, he began teaching at Princeton in 1970, where he made noteworthy discoveries on the role of the cerebral cortex in perception and behavior. Throughout his long career, the article suggests, Gross has been "extraordinarily fortunate" in three main ways: his outstanding graduate students and postdoctoral fellows; his association with enthusiastic MIT, Harvard, and Princeton undergraduates; and his support from the three universities that have funded his research. Were a professional organization to honor Oates's long career at Princeton, where she began teaching in 1978 and where she has continued her prodigious literary productivity, one suspects that she would express similar gratitude.

Life after Widowhood

Of all the statements in *A Widow's Story*, the one that foreshadows most accurately Oates's current life, as well as those of many others who find themselves in her situation, comes from Eleanor Bergstein: widows and widowers may find themselves meeting people they would not have met if their spouses were still alive. Life is a tragedy filled with joy, and no one can predict when love will unexpectedly reenter his or her life, shattering, once again, assumptions about the future. Oates's happy second marriage would seem unbelievable—especially if it appeared in a fictional story by Oates herself, the master of the imagination of pain.

How, Oates's readers may ask, can a person so heartbroken and grief stricken while writing *A Widow's Story* enter into a new relationship so easily and quickly? How does one free oneself from crushing existential guilt and self-blame associated with the loss of a spouse? How does one come to terms with the belief that the living betray the dead and that the dead resent the living? How does one transform companionship in grief into companionship in joy? Throughout *A Widow's Story*, we fear that Oates has become one of her ill-fated fictional widows, deranged by grief. It is with relief, then, that we discover she has been able to separate her art from her life.

Oates is not alone in re-creating her life during widowhood. DiGiulio reports from his own and others' research that 40 percent of widows experience relief following the deaths of their husbands and that a majority of women characterized changes following the deaths of their spouses as "positive or at least as a mixture of positive and negative changes" (34). Although fewer than 5 percent of widows over the age fifty-five remarried—Oates is the exception here—many form long-lasting and fulfilling relationships. DiGiulio, whose family perished in a car accident, declares that, eight years after their deaths, he has discovered life is still good. "This book is no 'song' or tribute to widowhood," he writes in the preface, "but it is my clear statement that within the experience of losing one's spouse is the beginning of hope. For most widowed, it gets better" (xv).

Oates never tells us in *A Widow's Story* whether she believes her deceased husband would want her to find a companion after his death, but she refers to this question briefly in her article "Why We Write about Grief," cowritten with Meghan O'Rourke, appearing in the *New York Times* on February 26, 2011. "Often it's said that survivors must 'move on'— 'make a new life' for themselves. It's impossible to say if this is only just wishful thinking, or has some basis in human psychology. But surely those who have been magnanimous in life can be imagined as magnanimous in death. We want to believe that the deceased whom we loved would love us enough to wish us well, in what remains of our lives." Readers will be happy to know that although Oates's fictional widows do not receive permission from their husbands to remarry, the writer imagines her own beloved deceased husband to be magnanimous to her.

2

———～～———

Sandra M. Gilbert

Wrongful Death

"I was thinking of you, and your wonderful lost husband," Joyce Carol Oates writes to Sandra M. Gilbert in a brief e-mail on February 19, 2008, adding that Raymond Smith's demise "was something similar—though not a 'wrongful death' I'm sure" (*A Widow's Story* 83). Lest the allusion remain obscure, Oates explains to her readers a few pages later that [Gilbert's husband] "Eliot [sic] had died a *wrongful death* at the U. C. Davis Medical Center, as a result of negligent nursing care" (102). Suddenly Oates questions whether her own husband's death from a secondary infection was also due to medical malpractice, though she never returns to this possibility. It's unlikely she would have decided to pursue a lawsuit against the Princeton Medical Center had she reread Gilbert's 1995 memoir *Wrongful Death: A Memoir*, based on Elliot Gilbert's sudden death at the age of sixty following routine prostate surgery on February 11, 1991. Nevertheless, Oates would have learned much from her friend and former Princeton colleague about the trauma of sudden widowhood and the urgent need to bear witness to spousal loss while still in the throes of sorrow.

Gilbert is best known for her pioneering studies of feminist literary criticism and formation of a female literary canon. With her longtime collaborator and friend Susan Gubar, Gilbert published in 1979 the groundbreaking *The Madwoman in the Attic*, which perhaps more than any other single American literary study helped to define and create the emerging field of feminist literary criticism. A few years later, Gilbert and Gubar published the influential *The Norton Anthology of Literature by Women*, which sought to recover a long, rich, and neglected female literary tradition. Continuing their fruitful collaboration, Gilbert and Gubar then published their three-volume work *No Man's Land: The Place of the Woman Writer in the Twentieth Century*. Gilbert is also a prize-winning poet, having authored nine critically acclaimed volumes of poetry.

After the death of her husband, Gilbert turned her attention to bereavement and became an expert on the literature of loss, as can be seen in *Death's Door*, a magisterial study of death from a literary and cultural studies point of view. *Wrongful Death* and *Death's Door* are complementary texts, the former focusing on the mystery surrounding Elliot Gilbert's unexpected death and the ways in which physicians and hospital administrators engaged in a cover-up, the latter exploring the memoirist's grief and efforts to interpret and theorize the representation of death in literature. Both works represent the continuing bond with her deceased husband.

"Why Must Your Poems Be So Morbid?"

Gilbert's preoccupation with death may be seen in her earliest poems, as she acknowledges at the beginning of her autobiographical *On Burning Ground* (2009). "You had a happy childhood, dear," her mother would sometimes exclaim after attending one of her readings. "Why must your poems be so morbid?" (ix). Richard Eberhart makes a similar observation in the introduction to *In the Fourth World* (1979), her first volume of poetry. "She is probably the most outspoken fear-poet of the times. The actual world is threatened repeatedly by dark forces behind appearance." In *On Burning Ground*, Gilbert muses on how she might not have suffered a miscarriage had what lawyers call the "hypotheticals" been slightly different. " 'What if you hadn't gone on that roadtrip across Europe when you were twenty years old and six months pregnant? Would the baby have come to term—and lived?' " (x).

The loss of Gilbert's first child was so devastating that she has never been able to write a publishable poem about the death, "perhaps a measure of the intensity of that early shock," as she admits in *On Burning Ground* (x). But throughout *In the Fourth World* she depicts other personal losses, including in the first poem, titled "Getting Fired, or Not Being Retained," the loss of her first teaching job at California State College. This poem, in retrospect, is stunningly ironic, given her spectacular academic career at a number of leading universities, including Indiana University; the University of California, Davis; and, in the middle 1980s, Princeton. She recalls in "The Fear of the Night" her dread of the unknown when, imagining herself pursued by a swooping predator, she pretends to "play dead" (9). In "Accident" she reveals an imagination like Oates's, attuned to the catastrophic element in life. In "After a Death," dedicated to the memory of her father, she is "astonished by my calm. / Have you really left me no pain?" (15). In "The Dream of the Sun" she contemplates a dialogue with her father, now dead for seven years. " 'I've been reading Nietzsche, Tom Paine, Gautama Buddha,' / he says. 'I think I've found the answer.' " As the poet awakens, she hears her father sob, "Sandra, Sandra, don't leave me here!" (42).

Gilbert remarks in "Five Meditations on One Who Is Dead" that the deceased are never entirely gone, if only because they invade the living's thoughts and dreams. The epigraph to part 2 of *In the Fourth World* comes from George Eliot's memorable observation in *Middlemarch*: "If we had a keen vision and feeling of all ordinary human life, it would be like hearing the grass grow and the squirrel's heart beat, and we should die of that roar which lies on the other side of silence." The other side of silence becomes the theme of many of Gilbert's poems in her first collection, including a ten-line poem presciently titled "Widow" in which she associates widowhood with numbness and darkness.

"I'm a Widow"

The story of Gilbert's widowhood began with the early widowhood of her own mother, Angela Caruso Mortola. Gilbert recounts in *Death's Door* the phone call she and her husband received on April 21, 1964, at 2:00 a.m. when her mother announced bluntly, "Well, I'm a widow" (19). The death became more real to Gilbert a day later when she saw her father's body in a coffin at the funeral home. As her mother kept repeating, "I wasn't ready," "I'm a widow," her daughter, an only child, thought, "Why did she keep reiterating the fate of the *I* who was doing the lamenting rather than the sorrowful end of the *he* who was the subject of the lamentation?" (22). Gilbert found herself "utterly alienated" from her mother's grief. Only after she became a widow herself did she understand her mother's situation.

Gilbert pays tribute to her two literary foremothers, Emily Dickinson and Emily Brontë, in her poem "Daguerreotype: Widow" in *Emily's Bread*. The widow in the poem has lived for thirty years in a little village where language is "heavy with shutters and ruined walls" (40). Each day the widow walks to the mountains, where she collects a basket of pebbles that she fashions into "talisman rings / for the women in the soft valleys, / the children, the mourners." The speaker in the poem is sensitive to the widow's loneliness, admiring her stoical courage and patience while recognizing the joylessness of her daily existence. Bereavement has defined the widow's identity, rendering her into a cautionary tale for the villagers. Accepting her fate, at dawn she "paces / the small square in the center of her village, / alert as any sentry." Yet if the widow is on guard, as the sentry image suggests, for what is she waiting? The answer seems to be death, though she does nothing to hasten—or delay—its arrival. The speaker wonders at the end of the poem what will happen if the widow's "pebble harvest" should vanish.

Many of the poems in *Emily's Bread* are mournful, none more so than "Elegy," one of Gilbert's most suggestive statements about the power of writing to connect the living with the dead. "Elegy" begins with a vivid metaphor: "The pages of history are open. The dead enter. / It is winter in the spine of the book / where they land, inexplicable texts" (49). "Elegy" only hints at the theme of textual resurrection that Gilbert develops years later, but already we see her interest in how the living and dead struggle to remain in touch with each other. Poems like "Elegy" become a form of communion with the dead. Reading cannot bring the dead back to life, but elegiac poetry helps us imagine their words.

Marital Happiness

Many of the poems in *Emily's Bread* memorialize the dead, but other poems honor the living, particularly the two that Gilbert dedicates to her husband, "Parachutist" and "Simplicity." "Parachutist" opens with the speaker, a "tigress / purring along the highway" (80), driving away from the Indiana cornfields that have walled her in, a reference to the years she spent teaching at Indiana University while separated from her husband and three children, who were living in California. Suddenly a white parachute comes drifting down with a man "swaying / on the silky cord, / swaying, bumping, bubbling / back to me." His expected presence energizes both the speaker and the poem. And yet even as the parachutist's smile cheers the speaker, she wonders how long his visit will last. Gilbert's hope in "Simplicity" is that she and her husband will have as much time together and happiness as the "sixty-year-olds" in her poem. The speaker observes the couple as they stroll together, perhaps after finishing jogging. "Over their mild / gray heads the air / is pink with blossoms / accomplishing themselves" (89). She watches, enthralled, as the woman turns to her life partner and speaks "a word / that fills and falls like another petal, / easy, simple: / a word of thirst?—*milk? Wine?*— / a word of love?—*good run?*— (89). Neither here nor elsewhere does Gilbert sentimentalize marriage or aging. The speaker tries to overhear the elderly couple's conversation, hoping to learn from them the secret of a long, fulfilling relationship. Gilbert was in her mid-forties when she wrote "Simplicity," and she imagined the sixties as a period of fruition, the gray-haired woman turning to a tree and inhaling the "lucid perfume / of a blossom that promises / ripeness, night, the sweetness / of the plum" (90). Belying its title, "Simplicity" takes on poignant biographical significance when we realize that Gilbert became a widow in her mid-fifties.

Blood Pressure, the last volume of poems Gilbert published before her husband's death, evokes domestic bliss. "Marriage" conjures up the music of Mozart and Beethoven, which the Gilberts both loved. She implies that when their relationship began, he was the rakish Don Giovanni; she the "tender ear" he nibbled. Years later, they perform similar roles, he still Giovanni; she the lively and flirtatious Zerlinda to whom he remains attracted: a *faithful* Don Giovanni! They have now become at the end of the poem "ghostly chords, archaic harmonies" (*Blood Pressure* 103), still in love, still married.

They continue to be madly in love in "Anniversary Waltz," so much so that the poet fears everyone must stare at them, saying, "*Look at that crazy lady, muttering / Love, Love, like a lunatic!*" (*Blood Pressure* 104). The poet delights in their life together, he looking "Satanic, magisterial, Jewish!" (104). The poem momentarily darkens as it recalls the death of their firstborn child, twenty-one years earlier, but life has been good to them: "More children, more kitchens, better partitions. / Typewriters, studies, weeping in the pantry. / Making love like adolescents on the sly" (104). Growing old together, "we smile wryly, / we fatten, we grow dumb," with the poet gratefully concluding, "I cannot imagine who else / we might have become" (104–105). Gilbert read "Anniversary Waltz" at her husband's memorial service, where it took on an entirely different meaning. "When I wrote it," she remarks dolefully in *Wrongful Death*, "it was about our life. Now it was about how we *once* were alive together" (131).

Unlike Oates, Gilbert has never published a journal, and we thus lack a systematic record of her trajectory as a writer. But *On Burning Ground* and *Rereading Women* reveal her efforts to fulfill herself in love and work, a quest that eluded so many women in the 1950s. She began her career following the path blazed by Sylvia Plath, who had not yet become well known in the literary world. (Gilbert has written much about Plath, revealing more sympathy for her than have other critics, including Oates.) In 1957, Sandra Mortola was selected to serve as guest managing editor at *Mademoiselle*, working with Cyrilly Abels, the managing editor whom Plath mercilessly caricatured in *The Bell Jar*. Asked by the editor of Knopf to read her collection of poems recommended by one of her Cornell professors, Mortola modestly refused. "Oh I don't know. No. I don't think I'm really ready to show that manuscript to anyone. I don't think it's really good enough" (*On Burning Ground* xi). She stopped writing poetry for five years and didn't publish her first collection of poems for twenty-two years.

Oates met Raymond Smith, who was eight years older, in graduate school at the University of Wisconsin and soon married him; Mortola met Elliot Gilbert, who was six years older, when she was an undergraduate at Cornell and he a doctoral student and teaching fellow. They married when she was twenty, and she took his name. Unlike Oates, Gilbert has never viewed her identity as split between a private and professional self. Nor does she write about self-impersonation, as Oates often does. Gilbert did, however, subordinate her own career to her husband's, at least early in their marriage. Instead of accepting a fellowship to graduate school, she dutifully followed her husband to Germany when he was drafted into the army. It was at this time that she lost her first baby. Returning to the United States after his military service, she had three more children, Roger, Katherine, and Susanna; earned a PhD at Columbia in 1968, where she wrote her dissertation on D. H. Lawrence's poetry, which was later published; began writing poetry again; and once more followed her husband, this time to California, where he was hired in 1966 at the rapidly expanding UC Davis. Sandra Gilbert's male colleagues, unused to female academics, regarded her at the beginning of her career as a professor's wife, but once she began her collaboration with Susan Gubar, she soon eclipsed nearly everyone in the discipline, including her husband—a phenomenon that was also true of Oates. Sandra Gilbert's appointment at Princeton did not include a similar position for her husband, and after four years she gave up her Princeton professorship and returned to her old position at Davis because she disliked being in a commuter marriage.

Elliot Gilbert

Unlike Raymond Smith, Elliot Gilbert remained a professor and writer his entire life. According to a UC Davis obituary, Gilbert was a "charismatic teacher who presented literature within the widest possible cultural context of history and the arts." He helped create the UC Davis Creative Writing Program and founded and edited *The California Quarterly* in 1972. An authority on Victorian literature, he wrote a book on Rudyard Kipling and edited a volume of Kipling's letters to his children. He edited a 1978 anthology called *The World of Mystery Fiction*, a collection of twenty-four detective stories with a lively introduction about the history of the genre. He also wrote *The World of Mystery Fiction: A Guide*, using both books in a popular course he taught on mystery fiction for the UC Berkeley Extension Program. Gilbert enjoyed writing mystery fiction, and his own stories appeared in *Ellery Queen's Mystery Magazine* and *Best Detective Stories of the Year*.

The University of California obituary offers us an insight into Elliot Gilbert's teaching and scholarship. "He was concerned with preserving the concept of a scholarly and cultural community and directed his often acerbic wit toward a university that, as one colleague has written, 'was forgetting its whole past' and toward 'fashionable academics' who thought that it did not matter.' Students, staff, and colleagues alike loved his sometimes intimidating verbal brilliance while recognizing in him a great compassion and an essential kindness. When learning of his sudden death, students wept in classes and in faculty offices." At her husband's memorial service, Gilbert refers to his "sometimes combative—even curmudgeonly—commitment to his own ideas about education" (*Wrongful Death* 130). These ideas did not prevent him from being appointed chair of the UC Davis English Department six months before his death.

"How Mysteries Affect People"

In an eerie irony, *The World of Mystery Fiction* underscores the difficulty of resolving the mystery of Elliot Gilbert's unexpected death in 1991, a disastrous event that has never been completely explained. Reading *The World of Mystery Fiction*, one is struck by the number of prophetic observations that apply to his own death. "The best hard-boiled fiction," he writes in *The World of Mystery Fiction: A Guide*, "is not so much about mysteries as about how mysteries affect people, not so much about what detectives discover as about how they manage to survive their discoveries" (9). The insight is strikingly true of *Wrongful Death*. The memoir cannot solve the mystery of who was responsible for Elliot Gilbert's death, but it shows how his wife and children reacted to and survived the wrenching loss. Edgar Allan Poe's masterful detective C. Auguste Dupin recognizes, in Elliot Gilbert's words, that "when a thing is hidden it must be *concealed*, this being the meaning the word 'hidden' has always had for him. On the strength of this assumption, he conducts one of the most thorough searches in all of detective fiction, but without success" (*Guide* 32).

So, too, does the exact cause of Gilbert's own death remain hidden and, by implication, concealed. Despite the family's expert medical consultants and lawyers' impressive detective work, including aggressive questioning of the defendants and sifting of clues, no one can locate the exact person or persons responsible for Elliot Gilbert's death. The extraordinary detective, for Gilbert, sees the world as it really is and thus is like a "great scientist and / or a great poet," combining the "best features of an orderly Rationalism and a creative Romanticism while avoiding the pitfalls of each" (*Guide* 29–30). The legal and medical sleuths who investigate Gilbert's wrongful death struggle to outwit the physicians and administrators who use the formidable resources of the University of California to withhold the truth of what actually happened to him during and following routine surgery. Like *The Mystery of Edwin Drood*, which remains incomplete because of Dickens's death, there are some mysteries, Elliot Gilbert concludes, "for which no solutions are possible" (*Guide* 43)—including his own death.

No one was imprisoned as a result of Elliot Gilbert's wrongful death, nor was anyone indicted for a crime. Sandra Gilbert and her family reached an out-of-court settlement, the exact details of which she is not permitted to disclose, but she never has the satisfaction of knowing who was responsible for her husband's death. Nevertheless, in pursuing a lawsuit against UC Davis Medical Center and then writing a memoir detailing medical negligence, Gilbert was released from some of the anguish and horror surrounding the event.

Acknowledging Spousal Help

One learns a great deal about authors from the way in which they acknowledge help in writing a book, particularly when it comes to acknowledging their spouses' help. Sandra and Elliot Gilbert are exemplary in the way they express gratitude toward each other. Witness Sandra Gilbert's acknowledgment in *Acts of Attention* in 1972: "My debt of longest standing is to my husband, Elliot Gilbert, without whose faith nothing would have been possible. To him I owe a debt of gratitude that neither public nor private thanks can ever fully repay" (xxvi). In *The Madwoman in the Attic*, she and Susan Gubar acknowledge "what has been profoundly important to both of us: the revisionary advice and consent of our husbands" (xiv). One of the two dedicatees of *The Summer Kitchen* is "Elliot Gilbert, my partner in the garden" (the other dedicatee is the poet Ruth Stone). "Again, for Elliot" reads Sandra Gilbert's dedication of *Blood Pressure*. Gilbert and Gubar cite their husbands' professional and personal help in each of the three volumes of *No Man's Land*, referring to them in volume 2, *Sexchanges*, "for being two very different but equally important models of 'the masculine,' from whom we ceaselessly learned" (xviii). *Wrongful Death* is itself an extended tribute to Elliot Gilbert's life and work. After his death, Gilbert and Gubar dedicated *Masterpiece Theatre* to him. Gilbert also dedicates *Ghost Volcano*, a book-length elegy that forms a moving narrative of her stages of grief, to him.

Elliot Gilbert is no less generous in acknowledging his spouse's help, dedicating his first book, *The Good Kipling*, to her and offering "special thanks" in *The World of Mystery Fiction: A Guide* to "Sandra M. Gilbert, who was always willing to take time from her own busy writing schedule to read, advise, and support." He dedicates his 1983 edition of Kipling's correspondence, *"O Beloved Kids": Rudyard Kipling's Letters to His Children*, to his own children and cites, as his greatest debt, his wife "for generously taking time away from her own many literary projects to help me complete this one" (225).

Wrongful Death

In the introduction to the 1997 paperback edition of *Wrongful Death*, Gilbert honors her husband for their thirty-year marriage and for being her "teacher in so many literary matters—I've done what I could and thought I should to speak for my husband, and specifically to tell the story of the wrong and mystery of his death" (3). She describes briefly her motivation for writing the book. "I feel myself to have been indelibly marked by a shock I still haven't assimilated even while I also feel I must bear witness to the reality—and the fatality—of an experience against which my whole self still protests" (2). She and her family realize they can never "right the wrong" of her husband's death, but they want to hold those accountable for medical negligence. Her goal is to narrate the tragedy that befalls her husband and family. She knows that no outcome of her lawsuit will raise the dead or release her from anger or sadness. Nothing will change her grief, which is carved in stone—a metaphor that appears throughout the memoir. She admits in the introduction that, five and a half years after her husband's death, "the questioning continues" (7).

And yet, despite her frustration, she has learned as a result of writing *Wrongful Death* that "even if there is no closure there is a *modus vivendi* called 'survival,' a way of living through and with grief that seemed absolutely impossible to me for months, even years, after February 11, 1991" (10). She begins the introduction with lines from Elizabeth Barrett Browning's poem "Grief," which suggests that hopeless grief is passionless, "Most like a monumental statue set / In everlasting watch and moveless woe" (1). Gilbert develops the metaphor, insisting that her grief is "carved in stone" (2). She ends the introduction by suggesting that most of the time grief has the "impervious facticity of a marble monument," but sometimes it takes on the "terrifying beauty of a muse" (10)—a muse that animates the pages of *Wrongful Death*.

Gilbert recounts in the preface to *Wrongful Death* a conversation with her former Princeton colleague and Nobel laureate Toni Morrison, "a storyteller I respect more than any other," who tells her to "do all the mourning things" (11)—by which she means communing with her deceased husband. "He'll tell you," Morrison insists. "And she was right," Gilbert responds. "He did. In whatever strange way the dead communicate with the living—through our deep knowledge of them, through our intuitions and memories of their needs, their passions, their desires—my husband spoke to me and told me to write this book" (11). And so Gilbert not only speaks *for* her husband in *Wrongful Death* but also *with* him, engaging in a dialogue from both sides of the grave.

Sounding like Oates in *A Widow's Story*, Gilbert concedes that she was "in many ways a kind of zombie" when she began *Wrongful Death*, unable to grasp the "unanticipated grief" that overwhelmed her. And yet in the next paragraph she points out that "writing down some of the details of my loss forced me to define the trauma, if not to master it" (14). Writing becomes not only an attempt to right a wrong but also, for a scholar whose weapon of choice is the pen or word processor, the best way to understand and live with traumatic loss.

"An Adverse Event"

Part 1 of *Wrongful Death*, succinctly titled "Adverse Event," focuses on the details of Elliot Gilbert's prostate cancer, the difficult decision whether to have surgery (as opposed to less radical treatments, including no treatment at all), the postsurgical complications, and the family's reaction to his death. Shock, horror, and grief characterize the mood of part 1, the section of *Wrongful Death* that most resembles Oates's *A Widow's Story*. Much of the time Gilbert functions as if in a trance. Nothing has prepared her for the events that follow, and her challenge as a writer is to evoke the nightmare of her husband's death, along with her sudden widowhood, as it is happening while, at the same time, offering us a larger perspective that comes through detachment and the passing of time.

Part 1 begins on Sunday, February 10, 1991, the day before Elliot Gilbert's surgery. The story is generally chronological, moving forward in time with occasional flashbacks to late July and August 1990, when he was first diagnosed with prostate cancer. The title of the book eliminates any uncertainty about the outcome of his surgery; the only suspense arises from the reasons for his death and whether the family will win its lawsuit against UC Davis Medical Center. The main antagonist in the story is the chief of urology at UCDMC, Dr. Ralph W. deVere White, a jaunty Irish surgeon with a hearty laugh and a charming bedside manner, neither of which prepares us for his refusal to be forthcoming with the family over his patient's death.

We learn much in part 1 about the incidence of prostate cancer, which strikes one out of eleven men, making it almost as common as breast cancer, which strikes one out of nine women. We also learn about the different ways of treating prostate cancer, ranging from doing nothing ("watchful waiting"), on the one hand, which is sometimes the best approach for nonvirulent forms of prostate cancer, to radical prostatectomy, on the other hand, which often results in incontinence and impotence. (Gilbert also refers to an even more extreme treatment, orchiectomy, surgical removal of the testicles—castration.) The possible side effects of the surgery "struck terror" into her husband's heart: "a three-to-five percent chance of incontinence, and an almost one hundred percent likelihood of impotence" (*Wrongful Death* 29). The Gilberts have heard about a new "nerve-sparing" surgical procedure that preserves potency, but such a procedure, the urologist tells them, is not "radical" enough, meaning that it might not remove all the cancer surrounding the prostate.

Gilbert, a renowned theorist of female identity, is especially sensitive to her husband's masculine anxiety over impotence. Indeed, he's so distressed that he refuses to read any of the books or articles on prostate cancer that are easily available to him through UCDMC. His wife "plows through" them, however, though she has trouble understanding their technical language. She tells us that before deciding on deVere White, who was enthusiastic and upbeat about the effectiveness of surgery, they consulted with other urologists. A Stanford urologist who made no effort to "soften the blow" of the size of Gilbert's prostate cancer terrified them, "practically driving Elliot, ordinarily a cheerful and solidly sane human being, to the brink of a breakdown" (46). DeVere White's confidence and charm win over the Gilberts.

The urologist also appears open-minded and obliging, for when Sandra Gilbert shows him an article she has discovered touting the benefits of an experimental three-month course of preoperative combination hormone therapy that has proven successful in clinical trials in shrinking prostate cancer, making radical prostatectomy easier, he agrees: "It can't hurt and it might help" (34). She finds endearing his Irish brogue and Irishisms, such as "Safe home." DeVere White's humor, however, is not always reassuring. She recounts his description of penile implants and injections that induce a two-hour erection. He senses their tension and tries to alleviate it through dark humor. " 'Now what're ye worryin' about?' he demands, turning his back to me and fixing his eyes even more intently on my husband. He lowers his voice a little. 'Y'know,' he confides, 'even with the nerve-sparing ye'll be a stuffer instead of a poker. But in any case, after a radical, I can give ye the best erection of yer life' " (33).

Gilbert conveys her husband's humor as well, remarking that before surgery he joked mordantly that the "chair of Urology can't kill the chair of English" (47), a statement that takes on sinister irony after his death. She reports on some of the problems that arise before surgery. During a biopsy of one of Gilbert's ribs, for example, to which it is feared his prostate cancer may have spread, a physician has difficulty "intubating" him, that is, placing a breathing tube down his throat, which is essential for general anesthesia. The rib proves noncancerous, and the prostatectomy is rescheduled for January 30, but the surgery is postponed because a team of anesthesiologists had spent two-and-a-half hours trying unsuccessfully to intubate him and damaged his throat. He nearly died from lack of air, a fact that the family is not told at the time. Because of the failed intubation, Elliot Gilbert is given massive doses of steroids to reduce the swelling in his throat, and the surgery is once more delayed, until February 11.

The operation appears to go well but takes much longer than expected. In the early afternoon, deVere White emerges from the operating room and informs the family ambiguously that the surgery "went as well as it could" (44). Returning to the hospital in the early evening, when they were told they would be able to see the patient, Gilbert and the family encounter deVere White in the parking lot. His behavior seems odd to them, but he never implies there is a serious problem. Nevertheless, Sandra Gilbert and her daughters become alarmed and begin second guessing themselves, worrying that UCDMC is a "bad luck" hospital.

DeVere White breaks the news of Elliot Gilbert's death to his wife and daughters around 9:00 p.m., forty-five minutes after the event. The urologist's words prove evasive, confusing, and contradictory. "We've had a problem, luv, a *big* problem," he informs Sandra Gilbert "briskly" of her husband's death, adding that "Dad's had a heart attack," all the time "shaking his head with what seems to be a strange ruefulness" (21). As Gilbert begins to cross herself furiously and her daughters scream, they are led into a small reception room in the hospital where they see an unfamiliar woman wearing a name tag, "Carolyn, Office of Decedent Services" (22). When Susanna Gilbert demands to know what happened to her father, who never had a history of heart problems, the urologist "shrugs his shoulders, hangs his head," and replies, again using a term of endearment that now sounds condescending, "I don't know, luv" (37). Gone forever are deVere White's medical authority and trustworthiness. He then makes a statement to Sandra Gilbert that is as self-pitying as it is infuriating. " 'I know, I know, for you this is unpleasant, awful,' the doctor resumes clumsily, 'but believe me for me it's *shattering* (39)—a statement she cannot help repeating to herself through the rest of the story.

"I Couldn't Feel Worse if It Were Me Own Father"

Gilbert is not a novelist, and one of her challenges in *Wrongful Death* is to characterize the urologist who is at the center of a dark mystery. She surely knows while writing *Wrongful Death* that he and his legal counsel will scrutinize carefully every word of her book. Left implicit is the possibility that he might not hesitate to file a countersuit for defamation of character. DeVere White was a prominent urologist in the early 1990s, and, notwithstanding the publication of *Wrongful Death*, his reputation has grown since then. According to a UC Davis Health System Web site, he is currently associate dean for Cancer Programs at the School of Medicine and director of UC Davis Cancer Center. The author of more than 250 peer-reviewed scientific articles and book chapters, he serves on the editorial boards of six international scientific journals. Gilbert's task becomes more daunting because deVere White comes from a prominent literary family, his father a well-known novelist and his stepmother an even better-known feminist biographer whom Gilbert had recently met and admired.

Gilbert conveys deVere White's character mainly through dialogue. Instead of expressing sadness over his patient's death, he states hyperbolically, "I couldn't feel worse if it were me own father" (*Wrongful Death* 42). After Gilbert's death, his family tries to reconstruct the bewildering events of the day, observing that the urologist seemed "strange" when he saw the family immediately after surgery. Gilbert thought at the time that he looked "angry," an impression that gains conviction in retrospect. "DeVere White *had* seemed odd when he came down from the OR at 1:45. Sweating profusely, not taking our hands and looking us in the eye, as he ordinarily would. I *had* thought he might have been angry at us for some inexplicable reason" (44).

But why would deVere White be angry if the surgery had gone well, as he claimed at the time? The question remains unresolved. He also looks upset at 6:15 p.m., when he reports that following surgery Elliot Gilbert "said something like, 'I feel lousy' " (*Wrongful Death* 45). When asked whether the patient had been given the two units of the blood that he previously donated, deVere White responds "curtly" that he needed five units. Sandra Gilbert gasps in disbelief. "But isn't that bad, that much blood?" "It's neither bad nor good," he retorts evasively (45). This is the moment in the story when the reader withdraws all sympathy from the surgeon. Later, after Gilbert requests her husband's medical records from UCDMC, she learns to her horror that he had required a total of *twelve* units of blood, suggesting massive internal bleeding.

Throughout *Wrongful Death*, Gilbert has a formidable undertaking, both as plaintiff and memoirist: to undercut the credibility of a urologist who has an excellent reputation. As the story progresses, however, deVere White's credibility is systematically undermined. He telephones Gilbert at home to report smugly that a colleague has looked at the deceased patient's pelvic area and reported nothing amiss. "The operation was successful. As I told ye. We made the right decision" (78). He later repeats the statement when the pathology report comes back indicating that none of the removed nodes were cancerous. Why, then, did her husband die? " 'That I don't know, luv,' he replies in a conspiratorial tone" (78). There's much that deVere White doesn't know—and much he doesn't want to know.

In parts 2 and 3, deVere White stonewalls the plaintiff's lawyers; he cannot reconcile the information on the death certificate that the patient died of cardiac arrest due to liver failure with the later discovery that Elliot Gilbert required twelve units of blood. Without realizing he had agreed to Sandra Gilbert's request for preoperative hormone therapy to shrink the prostate cancer, deVere White later angrily blames the hormone therapy for making the surgery more difficult. He contradicts himself repeatedly during the deposition, declaring that the patient was not bleeding despite overwhelming evidence to the contrary. He insists that he doesn't know why Elliot Gilbert died when it's apparent to nearly everyone else that the amount of blood he required during and following surgery indicated internal hemorrhaging. Several times deVere White makes statements that are almost certainly impeachable. He comes across, finally, as incompetent, which explains the UCDMC attorneys' speedy decision to offer an out-of-court settlement to the Gilberts.

A Detective Mystery

Sandra Gilbert crafts *Wrongful Death* as a detective mystery, the genre on which her husband was an authority. Much of the story's aesthetic power as a grief memoir derives from its form as a murder mystery. Death is always a mystery, but Elliot Gilbert's death raises questions that can never be resolved. There is no evidence that anyone *intentionally* killed him; nevertheless, there is no doubt he was the victim of negligent care. Throughout the story, Gilbert ponders the meaning of certain assertions that may hold the clue to his death, quoting repeatedly her husband's comment in the recovery room, "I feel lousy." She also repeats her husband's droll statement, the "chair of Urology can't kill the chair of English," a line that functions as a Wagnerian leitmotif. In constructing the detective mystery, Gilbert analyzes closely several documents, including the hospital's medical and nursing notes, her husband's autopsy report, and, most importantly, deVere White's deposition, filled with glaring contradictions. At first she doesn't want to read these documents because they are so painful and infuriating, but she soon realizes that she must understand them if she is to write about the wrongful death. She also struggles to comprehend the instruction she receives before her deposition. "Again and again I strain to reread, to *analyze*, the judicial instructions. The scholar-critic in me evidently feels it's essential to master their secret meaning" (227).

Gilbert calls upon pathologist Dick Asofsky and her lawyer, Dan Kelly, to explain the secret meaning of the medical and legal documents that form the heart of the lawsuit. Reading deVere White's deposition, Gilbert doesn't hesitate to express her ignorance, making statements like "I don't *get* a lot of what's going on" (*Wrongful Death* 280). These statements allow Asofsky to explain patiently to her and the reader the medical and legal significance of the surgeon's testimony. The pathologist's dialogue, which could appear in any murder mystery novel, not only casts light on the mystery but also heightens the story's suspense. " 'Hang on, Sandy, hang on,' he says soothingly. 'It'll be best if we begin at the beginning and go through the whole thing one step at a time so you can get a sense of how your lawyer develops his argument. That is'—he casts a worried frown in my direction—'if you think you can take it' " (280). Gilbert knows how to maintain the reader's attention, and throughout deVere White's deposition, Asofsky provides her—and the reader—with a running commentary, making statements like "He's on the ropes here" (289), "Now he's getting nervous" (293), "He's waffling again" (296), and "His lawyer is worried. . . . He's trying to slow the pace of the questioning" (297). Will Gilbert be strong enough to read through the entire deposition? Will she be able to understand its significance? Will deVere White incriminate himself? These questions drive the story's plot.

DeVere White's deposition forms the climax of *Wrongful Death*. He comes across, finally, as an unreliable narrator, one who does his best to deny responsibility for his patient's death. He withholds crucial information from the family that he was obliged to offer, including facts about an urgent blood test taken at 3:05 that was misplaced for hours, and the startling number of blood transfusions the patient required. The urologist's response to the anesthesiologist's written entry over the cause of Elliot Gilbert's death, "acute posthemorrhagic anemia," in short, bleeding to death, is mind-numbingly evasive: "Not that I know that that's the sole cause of it" (306). The unintentional black humor in the surgeon's deposition becomes for Gilbert a "ghastly text," evoking the ending of Samuel Beckett's 1953 novel *The Unnamable*: "I can't go on. I must go on, I'll go on" (307). The black humor also reminds her of *MASH* and *Catch-22*, especially when during the deposition deVere White is shown a note from the anesthesia department indicating Elliot Gilbert was "stable" and "comfortable" on February 12—one day after his death.

Even before the deposition begins, Gilbert offers her own theory of her husband's death, speculating that the bleeding began in the recovery room, when he became agitated, angry that he had been left alone, as had happened after his biopsy weeks earlier. "And so he was tossing and turning and a suture came undone and he started to bleed, to hemorrhage, but they left him alone because they were mad at him—and—and so he died" (*Wrongful Death* 145). This remains conjectural, however, and once the family accepts the hospital's out-of-court settlement, which absolves the UCDMC of all responsibility for Elliot Gilbert's death, the case comes to an end without resolution of the mystery.

The end of litigation does not end the story. Unlike Oates, who never explains how she writes *A Widow's Story*, Gilbert tells us exactly when, where, and why she begins writing the memoir. She starts writing the book in Berkeley on July 23, 1991, the day of her first meeting with Dan Kelly. Her greatest fear is that the attorneys for the UCDMC will try to prevent her from writing about the exact details of the case. She begins writing at 3:00 a.m. when, as usual, she finds herself unable to sleep. "I went into the kitchen with a notebook, and began, weeping as I wrote, to try to write" (239).

From the opening of *Wrongful Death*, then, we can see the link between "righting" and "writing" a wrong. The pages multiply during Gilbert's stay at Yaddo, and her family and friends encourage her writing. "It'll probably be cathartic for you," exclaims Dick Asofsky's wife, Leah. "No, I tell her rather sullenly. It's awful reliving the whole thing over and over again. What's more, I add ironically, it's hard to write a book when you don't know the whole story" (240). Both women are right. The book is harrowing to write, but it proves therapeutic if not cathartic, though she seldom uses either clinical word. Writing the book for Gilbert is the major way she grieves her calamitous loss. It is a wrenching book to write and a wrenching one to read: Gilbert tells us parenthetically near the end of *Wrongful Death* that her daughter Susanna "at first only reluctantly read a portion of this manuscript because, she confessed, it was too painful to her" (340). And yet as painful as it was for Gilbert to write, it would have been more painful *not* to write. She completes the book in three years, and it's published a year later, four years after her husband's death.

A Reliable Narrator and a Sympathetic Character

Sandra Gilbert's credibility as the story's major narrator depends on her ability to characterize herself and others: her perceptions, both before and after her husband's death; her motivations for bringing a lawsuit; her disparate roles as wife, mother, widow, and researcher; her judgments of herself and others; and finally her language. She remains a reliable narrator and sympathetic character throughout the story. She doesn't hesitate to recall the shock and horror she experiences upon being told of her husband's death. She is as horror stricken as Oates and no less willing to portray herself as deranged by grief.

Unlike the nonreligious Oates, Gilbert finds herself enacting religious rituals from childhood that surprise the reader and herself, such as crossing herself when she learns the news of her husband's death. She crosses herself again when she gazes at his still-warm body. "I am still crossing myself compulsively, and out of some archaic, nearly forgotten impulse from my Catholic childhood, whispering fragments of the Our Father and the Hail Mary to myself" (*Wrongful Death* 36). Some writers might not have reported this detail, embarrassed, perhaps, by the "archaic" impulse, but Gilbert never shrinks from acknowledging feelings she didn't know existed. A few minutes later, her daughter Katherine hands her a "get well" balloon that a friend had sent for an anticipated postoperative celebration; Gilbert decides to release the balloon in the hospital parking lot, watching it rise until it disappears. "'Go, Elliot, on your dark journey,' I say to myself theatrically, meaninglessly. For of course there is no journey" (41). Most people act theatrically, if not melodramatically, at times like this, but only an experienced writer, attuned to the meaningful and meaningless gestures surrounding tragedy, is able and willing to report on them.

Gilbert also writes about the lingering traumatic effects of her loss. Near the second anniversary of her husband's death, on 2/11/91, she suffers a couple of related "mental glitches": every time she dates a letter or check, she begins with 2/, even if the month is not February. A week earlier, she reports having the opposite problem: she finds herself writing anything *but* 2/, even though the month is February. Once she begins teaching again, a course on modern poetry, she discovers to her horror that she cannot pronounce T. S. Eliot's last name because it reminds her of her husband's first name.

Gilbert is alert to other inner conflicts and surprises. Though she is a nonpracticing Catholic and her husband a nonpracticing Jew, she never minimizes the power of religion in secular life. She decides on an ecumenical funeral service, with the family deferring to his Jewish heritage by saying Kaddish for him. "Yet I also want something of my own inheritance represented," Gilbert admits. "So his coffin will be in the *schul* [temple], as it would be in the church at a Catholic mass, and the rabbi will say prayers over it as a priest would. I believe the dead one should be in a sacred place for the mourners' last farewells" (*Wrongful Death* 68). She is more comfortable selecting the music for her husband's funeral. The service opens with the "Cavatina" from Beethoven's Thirteenth String Quartet, which Elliot Gilbert regarded as the "most transcendent piece of music ever written" (68), and the three children each read a psalm. Sandra Gilbert decides to remain silent. "I can't imagine being able to speak" (68). Later she cannot stop speaking—and writing—about her husband's death. The preparations for the funeral service, and the service itself, are emotionally exhausting but an essential part of the grieving process. After the funeral, she and the mourners return to her home for food and drink. Like Oates, she quotes the same lines from *Hamlet*: "The funeral baked meats / Did coldly furnish forth the marriage tables" (95), lines that Elliot Gilbert had once set to music.

Unlike the childless Oates, Gilbert has the strength of her three children to rely on, and she allows them to make several decisions that Oates makes for herself. Gilbert's two daughters have been with her both before and during Elliot Gilbert's surgery; after his death she calls her son, who lives in Ithaca, New York, where he is an English professor at Cornell. The children help their mother with the practical details of her new posthumous life, such as deleting Elliot Gilbert's voice on the telephone answering machine. (By contrast, Oates keeps her husband's voice on the answering machine for several months.) Gilbert's children also select a coffin for their father, something their mother is unable to do. While choosing her clothes for the funeral, she begins to weep and scream, the first time she has done so since deVere White informed her of the death. She has no reluctance to characterize herself as barely functioning, even on the verge of collapse.

The Aftermath of Loss

Gilbert doesn't long for death the way Oates does throughout *A Widow's Story*, but she momentarily considers jumping into her husband's grave during the funeral. "As I look down, the hole in the earth seems to widen and deepen. I'm afraid for a minute that I'll topple in. Or do I mean that I *want* to?" (*Wrongful Death* 95). Indifferent to her health, she begins smoking cigarettes again, which she knows distresses her family. Like Oates, she wants to stay in bed, isolated from the world. The night before her husband's surgery, she lies in bed next to him in his hospital room, unwilling to leave the "safe nest" (82) of the bed. (Oates, we recall, has used the same metaphor.) After his death, she finds herself remaining motionless in a chair for hours, unable to get up. For months, she has difficulty swallowing.

In short, Gilbert's posthumous life is weary, stale, flat, and unprofitable. She begins quarreling with family and friends, including Susan Gubar, who has flown to California from Indiana to assist her. She loses her temper when trying to explain her theory of her husband's death to her collaborator. " 'You're being *stupid*,' I say irascibly. 'God, you're being so stupid' " (*Wrongful Death* 145). Uncharacteristically, the two friends begin fighting over nearly every word in *Masterpiece Theatre*, their latest collaboration and first in memoriam publication. In the end, it takes them nearly an hour to write a two-sentence acknowledgment of Elliot Gilbert's help.

Masterpiece Theater has a dark humor that may derive as much from Elliot Gilbert's recent death as from the grim mood of the culture wars besetting academia in the 1990s. Gilbert tells us in *Wrongful Death* that her husband "loved this little project, which actually summarized many of his own skeptical ideas about the state of literary criticism today" (141). The comment may help to explain his "sometimes combative—even curmudgeonly" commitment to his own vision of literature and teaching. In *Masterpiece Theatre*, Gilbert and Gubar inhabit what they call a "kind of intellectual 'excluded middle,' an academic silent majority that seeks to find a way out of the darkling plain on which the culture war's impassioned armies clash by night and day" (xviii–xix). They satirize not only the conservative "Back-to Basic's" movement, on the one hand, and the "radical "Forward into Instability" movement, on the other, but themselves as well, whom they name interchangeably SG1 and SG2, each making a statement that the other claims to have made first. SG1 and SG2 poke fun at each other and themselves. Gilbert and Gubar reserve some of their most trenchant satire for Joyce Carol Oates, who throughout the docudrama publicly expresses outrage over gossipy sensationalism while thinking about how she can exploit the trashy material in a new book. Gilbert and Gubar dedicate *Masterpiece Theatre* to "the late Elliot Gilbert—whose generosity and wit helped set this project going" (xxiv).

Gilbert's marriage, like Oates's, was long and happy. Unlike Oates, she never worried that her late husband kept a dark secret from her, even when she receives two harassing telephone calls on a late Saturday night around midnight, just moments after friends have left her home. A "breathy young female" identifies herself as "Lisa," Elliot's "girlfriend," asks to speak with him, then hangs up. "Lisa" calls back immediately and leaves a "long melodramatic message" on the answering machine: " 'Oh, Elliot, I guess I was just talking to your wife. Oh, Elliot, why did you do me like you did that last weekend?' 'Oh'—breaking down in theatrical sobs—'Oh, Elliot, I love you, love you, love you' " (*Wrongful Death* 119). She listens carefully to the message and hears in the background the muffled sounds of a male speaker. Gilbert instantly calls her daughter and screams "anxieties" into the receiver. Gilbert is understandably dismayed, fearing, first, that her house is being watched and, second, that someone is taunting her. Tellingly, she is *not* worried about the possibility of infidelity. "It never occurred to me that my husband might have actually had a girlfriend named 'Lisa.' Elliot was too bourgeois, too shy, and indeed too uxorious. And besides, we hadn't been apart on a weekend in almost a year" (120).

Oates would have ruminated over "Lisa" in *A Widow's Story* and perhaps written a short story in which she transmutes "Lisa" into a sexually aggressive female who plunges into a relationship with the wrong kind of man that leads to disaster. The incident over "Lisa" is one more indignity Gilbert experiences as a new widow, but she uses the material comically in her story. She telephones the police, and an officer comes over, listens to the message, and asks her whether her husband had a girlfriend, to which she responds indignantly, " 'Of course not, officer,' I replied without hesitation. 'Why, my husband was a *professor*!" (*Wrongful Death* 121). As upsetting as the experience was, Gilbert must have appreciated ruefully, if only in retrospect, the irony of her innocent reply to the officer: "Nor could I understand why everyone in the room began to laugh."

Magical Thinking

Without using the term *magical thinking* that Freud coined and Joan Didion would popularize twelve years later, Gilbert gives several examples of her belief that her husband is still alive even when she knows otherwise. She is told that those who file a lawsuit for wrongful death may believe unconsciously that if they win, their loved ones will return to life. "If we could get the doctors and nurses at the UCDMC to admit that they did something wrong, then maybe we could get them to go back and do the *right* thing. Like running the film of the Kennedy assassination again so that the fatal bullet *doesn't* hit the president" (*Wrongful Death* 148). The fantasy comforts her despite its illogicality. "I live with the illusion—only I don't think it's an illusion—that Elliot is really still alive" (148). Another example of magical thinking occurs when she hears old friends calling her "Sandy," which she imagines gives her a new identity, thus allowing her to turn the clock backward and undo her husband's death. Later she becomes indignant when others refer to her "dead husband." Her children, she adds, have the same feeling, especially when they mistakenly use the present tense to suggest that their father *wants* the family to sue the hospital. She talks to her husband throughout the story and, near the end, reports telling a friend that she must finish writing the book *"before Elliot dies"* (334).

Self-Blame

Gilbert is less self-blaming than Oates, but there are several moments when she holds herself responsible for her husband's death. She reproaches herself for choosing UCDMC instead of the medical centers in Berkeley, Stanford, or San Francisco that they had also visited. She recalls an argument with her husband, shortly before surgery, when she had quoted a sentence from Katherine Mansfield's short story "The Daughters of the Late Colonel" in which a father chides his children for burying him: "Buried, you girls had me buried." Elliot Gilbert doesn't find the statement amusing: "Shut up about that" (*Wrongful Death* 91). She relives other argument with him prior to surgery, when they were both on edge. She remembers their last weekend together, after the failed intubation, when she seemed, "if anything, inexplicably harsh" with him. "I scowled at him. Yes I did. I remember now with embarrassment, no, with pain, as I stare dry-eyed at the bright new butcher-block cabinet that he had just finished building for the kitchen" (59).

Gilbert sounds here like she is on trial, not deVere White, confessing her guilt over not being a perfect wife. Later she remembers a more serious argument when she fails to respond empathically to his fears over the prostatectomy. Oates's anger toward her husband is delayed; Gilbert's immediate. She returns to the theme of self-blame in *Death's Door*, declaring that she feels responsible for her husband's death and, moreover, certain that "something secretly wrong in *me* had finally been exposed" (261).

Gilbert's blame shifts back and forth between her husband and herself before she finally realizes where the blame truly lies, with UCDMC. In some ways, she is more fortunate than Oates. Gilbert is able to focus her intense anger—and her no less intense powers of concentration— on waging a battle with an external adversary. The lawsuit, in all of its complexity, occupies nearly all of her attention during the remainder of *Wrongful Death*. In writing the memoir, she declares simply, without boasting, she has become a "minor expert on medical malpractice" (*Wrongful Death* 328).

Grief Books

Gilbert also becomes an expert on bereavement and loss. One of the most striking intellectual differences between Gilbert and Oates lies in their attitude toward psychotherapy. Oates's opposition to the mental health profession appears in dozens of her novels. She would agree with Nabokov's mordant observation in *Lolita* that the difference between therapist and the rapist is a matter of spacing. Unlike Oates, Gilbert refers often, always positively, to the many "grief books" that have helped her understand and cope with spousal loss.

Gilbert's first reference to her grief books occurs early in part 2 of *Wrongful Death*, "In Discovery," when she mentions that she hardly ever dreams of her husband, unlike many widows who regularly encounter their lost husbands in dreams. "I'm just as glad I haven't seen him much," she admits. "The two times he did show up were frightening" (115). The first dream occurred a few days after his funeral, when he complained that "It's cold here, . . . so cold." The dream is so terrifying that she wakes up trembling, her heart racing as rapidly as when she once had an episode of tachycardia. The second dream, less scary but almost as sad, occurred when he walked into her room and said, reassuringly, "Always here for *you*, babe" (116). Gilbert complains often about her dread of reading the medical records of her husband's hospitalization and death, along with the difficulty of understanding the legal and medical books and articles on malpractice. She never complains, however, about reading her grief books. At the end of March 1991, she refers to staying up half the night reading grief books and then not being able to wake up in the morning.

At the beginning of part 3, Gilbert reports on finally having "The Dream—the dream I never had before, the dream of closure and farewell that all my grief books talk about" (*Wrongful Death* 207). She writes down the details of the dream so she doesn't forget them—a dream that is nearly one and a half pages long in her published book. The dream ends with husband and wife hugging each other, Elliot telling her that he is fine and that he still loves her. He feels real and solid to her, like always. She can feel the warmth of his body and the prickliness of his beard. When she says, "let's get out of here," he brings her back to reality, reminding her, "I'm sorry, darling, but I can't come with you" (209). Gilbert interprets the dream, which she has read about in at least three different grief books, as the classic one in which the lost loved one says good-bye.

As the first Thanksgiving without her husband approaches, Gilbert remarks on how she and her family are "hyperconscious of what my grief books define as the danger of holidays for the bereaved" (*Wrongful Death* 237). Toward the end of the book, nearly two years after her husband's death, she and Susan Gubar bring flowers to his grave. Gilbert begins crossing herself and silently recites three Hail Marys. She then refers to the roots of the flowers trying to thrust themselves "toward the light and into the light, whatever light there is, wherever it is, the kindly light that my grief books talk about when they recount the 'near-death experience' as a way of comforting the bereaved" (326).

Therese A. Rando

Gilbert's major grief book is Therese A. Rando's *How to Go on Living When Someone You Love Dies*, originally published in 1988 as *Grieving*. Rando, a clinical psychologist who has written extensively on bereavement, offers many insights in her book that are of particular value to Gilbert. "Unless a couple dies together at the same time," Rando observes, "widowhood will be the inevitable conclusion of all intact marriages" (127). But not all spousal deaths result in the same type of grieving. Throughout her book, Rando shows how different forms of death produce different patterns of grieving. One of her most suggestive comments is that bereaved people "tend to grieve in much the same manner as they conduct the rest of their lives" (50), which recalls Roger Rosenblatt's statement that "People in grief become more like themselves." Both insights are true of spousal loss memoirists, including Gilbert.

Gilbert does not explicitly comment on *How to Go on Living When Someone You Love Dies*, but she chooses eight passages from Rando's book and uses them as epigraphs to different chapters of *Wrongful Death*. These passages illuminate the special problems for widows like Gilbert who are stunned by sudden spousal death. The first two passages explore the differences between sudden and anticipated death. "In both sudden and anticipated death, there is pain," Rando points out in the first passage Gilbert quotes. "However, while the grief is not greater in sudden death, the capacity to cope is diminished. Grievers are shocked and stunned by the sudden loss of their loved one. . . . If you are such a griever, you probably are suffering extreme feelings of bewilderment, anxiety, self-reproach, and depression, and you may be unable to continue normal life" (*Wrongful Death* 36, Rando 90). The second passage from Rando's book describes the incomprehensible events that take place on Elliot Gilbert's deathday "In unanticipated grief, you are unable to grasp the full implications of the loss. Your adaptive capabilities are seriously assaulted . . . and the death may continue to seem inexplicable" (*Wrongful Death* 43, Rando 83).

The third passage reveals one of Rando's most noteworthy insights: preventable deaths result in a more complicated grieving process than non-preventable ones. "If you perceive the death to have been preventable, and assume responsibility for having failed to prevent it, your grief will be greater and you will experience more guilt, which will further complicate your mourning process" (*Wrongful Death* 46, Rando 53). This is especially true of Gilbert's situation. The fourth passage emphasizes the need to understand the sequence of events leading to sudden death. "Because you were not prepared for the death and it had no understandable context, you will try to deal with your lack of anticipation by putting the loss into a series of events. You may find yourself looking back at the time leading up to the death and searching for clues that could have indicated what was to come" (*Wrongful Death* 57, Rando 91).

The fifth passage describes the widow's obsessive need for a retrospective reconstruction of her husband's death, a phenomenon that appears throughout *Wrongful Death*. "In an effort to gain some control and understanding over what often appears to be a meaningless, unmanageable event, you may repeatedly review the death, trying to make sense of it. Also, you may attempt to restructure the situation so that it seems that you had some inkling that it was going to happen. . . . This is especially important in circumstances of sudden death, when you must come to some cognitive understanding of what happened so suddenly to your loved one" (*Wrongful Death* 80, Rando 40–41). The sixth passage offers advice about the significance of funerals and other leave-taking rituals. "Participation in the funeral ritual—standing at a wake and repeatedly looking at your loved one in the casket, attending the funeral service, accepting the condolences of others, seeing the casket at the grave—graphically illustrates to you that the death has indeed occurred" (*Wrongful Death* 92, Rando 266–267).

The seventh passage is an extensive list of the physical symptoms of grief, most of which affect Gilbert, including "Loss of pleasure"; "Anorexia and other gastrointestinal disturbances"; "Apathy"; "Decreased energy"; "Decreased initiative"; "Decreased motivation"; "Decreased sexual desire or hypersensitivity"; "Physical exhaustion"; "Lack of strength"; "Lethargy"; "Sleep difficulties"; "Tearfulness and crying"; "Weight loss or weight gain"; "The tendency to sigh"; "Feelings of emptiness and heaviness"; "Feeling that something is stuck in your throat"; "Heart palpitations, trembling, shaking hot flashes, and other indications of anxiety"; "Nervousness, tension, agitation, irritability"; "Restlessness and searching for something to do"; "Shortness of breath"; "Smothering sensations"; "Dizziness, unsteady feelings"; and "Chest pain, pressure, or discomfort" (*Wrongful Death* 103, Rando 45–46). Gilbert suffers from nearly all these physical symptoms (as does Oates in *A Widow's Story*), including developing the flu during her deposition: "I guess the stress made me sick" (259).

Gilbert must have wondered, when she was involved with the details of her medical malpractice lawsuit, whether she had put grief "on hold," the term Rando uses in the eighth passage. "When a loved one dies from a physician's malpractice . . . grief is often put on hold until the legal proceedings are completed. For some, this contributes to a delayed grief reaction. For others, these proceedings themselves are therapeutic, since they afford a way to channel the rage and give it a focus" (*Wrongful Death* 221, Rando 109). Gilbert never directly answers this question, but the implication is that pursuing the lawsuit helps her channel and focus her rage. She does not quote the final two sentences in Rando's paragraph, but they suggest another way in which the lawsuit helps her work through her grief: "For still others, they provide a vehicle for achieving some meaning. If some good can come out of their loved one's death . . . then the death may seem less meaningless" (Rando 109).

Rando makes other observations about the widow's grief that apply to Gilbert's and Oates's situations. Some widows "are afraid to give up the pain, since it binds them closely to the deceased" (85), which recalls Gilbert's statement in *Wrongful Death* that her grief is "carved in stone," a "stone that journeys with me everywhere, a sometimes enigmatic, sometimes all too explicable burden I may never lose—and perhaps never want to lose" (2). Gilbert would agree with Rando's discussion of "illegitimate guilt," which is "out of proportion to the event." Such guilt is "normal in grief," Rando suggests reassuringly, "the natural consequence of a relationship that lacks perfection and contains ambivalence." The guilt comes from unrealistic expectations and standards—"for example, 'I should have been able to protect her from death' or 'I never should have felt any anger toward her during our relationship'" (Rando 34). Gilbert would agree with Rando's discussion of newborn death. "Like stillbirth, the death is socially negated. The loss is discounted, and therefore your grief is minimized." To work through this grief, Rando recommends "repeatedly going over the details of the pregnancy, the birth, and your child's short life" (187).

Gilbert would appreciate Rando's sensitivity to language, particularly the use of quotation marks when describing the need to "resolve" one's grief over the death of a loved one. "If the person you lost was truly significant to you, grief is not usually resolved in the sense of being finished and completely settled forever" (Rando 225). Gilbert would agree with Rando's recommendation to keep the dead alive in one's memory. "There are many healthy ways in which you can 'hold on' to your deceased loved one. It is not true that you have to sever all connection with that person who has been so much a part of your life" (235). Gilbert would endorse Rando's recommendation to find someone who can listen sympathetically to one's sorrow. And Gilbert would approve of Gilbert's apt reference to *Macbeth*: "Give sorrow words; the grief that does not speak whispers the o'er-fraught heart and bids it break" (249).

Shrink

Gilbert refers a half dozen times in *Wrongful Death* to her "shrink," though she never reveals her therapist's name or what she discusses in therapy. The first reference occurs in early March 1991, a time when she rarely leaves her house "except twice a week, when somebody drives me to Oakland to see my shrink" (116–117). Ten days later, she observes that both her daughter Susanna and her "shrink" worry that a positive outcome to her lawsuit might give her the false illusion that her husband will come back to life again. The UCDMC attorney asks her during her deposition whether she has incurred any medical bills as a result of her husband's death. She admits she has had "some counseling," and when he asks whether her treatment had anything to do with her marriage, she indignantly responds, "No," explaining to the reader: "He wants to show that I was seeing a shrink because my marriage was in trouble so . . . Elliot was of no use to me and therefore I'm not owed any damages and the case might as well be dismissed" (254–255). The final reference occurs on July 21, 1992, when she mentions that her "shrink" interprets her "weird dental abscess" as a symptom of the "tension and anxiety" surrounding her court deposition and the upcoming settlement conference (310–311). Gilbert never asserts, as Oates does repeatedly throughout *A Widow's Story*, that widowhood is the punishment for having been a good wife or that widows deserve to suffer, statements with which Gilbert's "shrink" presumably would have disagreed vehemently.

Self-Healing in Death's Door

Gilbert becomes her own shrink in *Death's Door*, which itself may be considered a landmark literary grief book. The chapter "Writing Wrong," only thirteen pages long, summarizes a paper she delivered at a conference on medical error held in Berkeley in May 2000. Asked to represent the viewpoint of patients and their families, she explores not only the details of her husband's wrongful death but also why she wrote her memoir. "Writing Wrong" offers one of the most compelling discussions of the risks and benefits of authoring books like *Wrongful Death*, an "activity that is as much a process of remembering, testifying, and reorganizing as it is of reiterating and striving to repair or readjust" (*Death's Door* 87). She knows from her own anguished experience that the "effort to write (record) and right (rectify) wrong involves both fear and ferocity" (87). She offers five linked propositions about writing wrong. She begins each proposition by conceding the difficulty, if not hopelessness, of writing wrong but then moves, albeit begrudgingly, toward a more positive conclusion. Her discussion is valuable not only to those who, like herself, are writing wrong, but also to anyone who writes about loss, which, in its broadest sense, may always feel wrong.

Gilbert's first proposition is her most draconian. Writing wrong is a "hopeless effort at a performative act that can never in fact be truly performed" (*Death's Door* 88). This proposition can be summarized as "weep and write," words from a poem by Elizabeth Barrett Browning that Gilbert uses near the end of *Wrongful Death*: "Weep and write. / A curse from the depths of womanhood / Is very salt, and bitter, and good" (341). Gilbert knows that writing will not bring back the dead. She quotes her husband's observation about the limits of converting knowledge into action in detective novels, and she then imagines him reminding her ruefully that writing about his death will not bring him back to life. Nor can writing undo catastrophe. Nevertheless, she points out, with undeniable if tautological logic, that writers write because they are compelled to write: there is nothing else to do. The second proposition is that writing wrong is *painful*. To "write wrong, whether in memoir or elegy, is to drive oneself into the heart of fear, pain, rage" (*Death's Door* 92). How can such writing *not* be fearful, painful, enraging? Without disagreeing with this proposition, Gilbert quotes the sentence she repeated to herself "like a mantra" while writing the story of her husband's death: "That which you fear the most, that you must do" (93).

The third proposition, closely related to the fourth and fifth, is that those who write wrong may themselves be wrong in their perceptions, facts, or motivations. Writing wrong may be "*un*cool or uncouth" (*Death's Door* 94). Gilbert acknowledges the possibility that the innocent may be unfairly accused. She never believes, however, that her husband's death was *not* wrongful. The fourth proposition suggests that writing wrong is wrong because, according to contemporary theory, "if you can write it, you've written it wrong" (95). She concedes there are parts of stories that writers must imagine and then quotes Picasso's observation that "Art is a lie one tells in order to tell the truth." She is aware of the epistemological challenges posed by poststructuralist criticism, which argues that history, reality, and biography are unknowable, but she never questions the possibility of knowing much or most of the truth in a situation like her husband's wrongful death. Her final proposition is that writing wrong is wrong because "it is *writing death*, writing *the* absence that can't be written" (97). She responds to this with a writerly credo: "the protest against death is what must be 'told,' as the beads of a rosary are 'told,' and what must be written, even if it's written wrong" (98). Gilbert might have added a sixth proposition about the problems implicit in writing wrong. The dead cannot speak for themselves, cannot talk about the moment of death, cannot explain the meaning of their dying statements. We'll never know the meaning of Elliot Gilbert's last words, "I feel lousy." Sandra Gilbert talks to her husband in *Wrongful Death* and hears him speak to her, but she knows this is an *imagined* dialogue. "Despite its brutal factuality as the close of life," Garrett Stewart suggests in *Death Sentences*, "dying is by nature the one inevitably fictional matter in prose fiction. Death for the self exists only as nonexistence, is not a topic so much as a voiding event, has no vocabulary native to it, would leave us mute before its impenetrable fact" (4). Nor can we know how the dead feel about the writer's effort to re-present them. Nevertheless, writing wrong is an attempt to bring the dead back to life, to honor and memorialize them, to explain how they have been wronged and why the living should attend to them.

The dedicatory grief that we saw in Oates's *A Widow's Story* is no less striking in Gilbert's *Wrongful Death*. Elliot Gilbert remains alive in Sandra Gilbert's scholarly books and poems, alive to his children, grandchildren, colleagues, students, friends—in short, alive to anyone who reads her writings. It matters little whether his death was wrongful or natural: he is gone, but his verbal portrait endures. It would be an exaggeration to claim that Elliot Gilbert has become "immortal." It is hard to imagine that even the greatest, most "immortal" art will last more than a few thousand years, which is not even a nanosecond in the history of the universe. Writing wrong creates, at its best, not immortal art but the illusion of immortality, an illusion that is nevertheless sustaining to the writer and reader.

Joyce Brothers

Gilbert turns to Dr. Joyce Brothers, the well-known clinical psychologist, television personality, advice columnist, and author of several best-selling self-help books, to understand the crushing feeling of emptiness that is part of sudden bereavement. Gilbert's favorite grief book is Brothers's auto-biographical *Widowed*, partly because she sees so many parallels between the psychologist's story and her own. "I like it because her husband was just about Elliot's age—well, maybe a few years older—and they had been married for more than thirty years, just like me and Elliot, and after Milt Brothers died, Dr. Joyce suffered from loneliness, confusion, and anxiety the same way I do. Of course, her husband died of a *disease*— he had terminal cancer of the liver I think—whereas Elliot was still pretty healthy" (*Wrongful Death* 170). Milton Brothers died of bladder cancer, not liver cancer, in 1989, two years before Elliot Gilbert's death. "In her book about her own experience with widowhood," Gilbert writes, "she says the loneliest time is coming home from a trip, when you're greeted by this kind of emptiness" (225). Gilbert even considers writing a letter to the psychologist asking how she dealt with depression.

One can understand why Gilbert identified so strongly with Brothers and what she learned about grief from reading *Widowed*. There are many similarities between the two women. Both were born near each other in downstate New York, Brothers in Long Island in 1927, Gilbert in Queens in 1936; both attended Cornell as undergraduates and received their doctoral degrees at Columbia; both had long and happy marriages to men who died in their early sixties; both became feminist pioneers in their respective fields; both write with intellectual and expressive power; and both have written extensively about widowhood, which they describe as the dark night of the soul. Joyce Diane Bauer married Milton Brothers, an internist specializing in the treatment of diabetes, in 1949, and shortly after he died she wrote *Widowed*, one of the earliest personal accounts of widowhood. "I cannot promise a widow that what I have to say in this book will blunt her raw sense of loss or banish her loneliness," Brothers admits at the beginning of her memoir. "What I can do is chart the course of the pain—horrendous, unceasing, and cruel—that we call grief and reassure her that this is normal and that all widows travel this same road. And I can offer hope" (Brothers 8).

Some of Joyce Brothers's observations apply mainly to those widows and widowers whose spouses die from protracted terminal illness, like her own husband, but other statements speak to those like Gilbert and

Oates whose spouses die suddenly and unexpectedly. Brothers quotes the British psychiatrist Colin Murray Parkes's comment that grief is the only "functional psychiatric disorder whose cause is known, whose features are distinctive and whose course is usually predictable" (Brothers 66). She remarks that the widow's first reaction to her husband's death is shock and then a "merciful numbness," usually followed by suffering, a "compound of emotions—longing, panic, helplessness, loneliness, anger, resentment, depression, self-pity, denial" (66). Using a simile that Gilbert must have appreciated, Brothers reveals that after her husband's death she felt "as if I were in a no-man's land between two lives—the familiar that was now forever lost to me and the unknown that I dreaded" (62).

Throughout her book Brothers speaks as both a psychologist and a widow, observing and theorizing her grief while caught up in it. She thus writes as a participant-observer. Gilbert may have felt at times that she could have penned *Widowed*: both write with the brutal honesty that allows them to reveal dark feelings they had not known existed before their husbands' deaths. It must have been especially difficult for a sensitive and empathic psychologist to acknowledge prejudices that went against her compassionate instincts and clinical training. For example, Brothers finds herself unexpectedly scorning other widows after her husband's death. "I shuddered at the idea of being a 'professional widow,'" by which I mean a woman whose chief identification was as a widow. I resented the social discrimination that relegated widows to second-class citizenhood" (Brothers 109). Brothers is not afraid to confess her "enormous self-pity," though she did not recognize it as self-pity at the time. She writes about how crying became "almost like breathing or blinking, an automatic, unthinking reaction" (68). The intensity of her anger shocks her. Her anger increases when she realizes that widows are "among our country's most oppressed minorities" and that, according to sociologist Helena Lopata, widowhood "means a plunge in social status in our society, which still bases a woman's worth on her relationships with men" (Brothers 81–82). Her anger imperceptibly changes over time into loneliness, which has nothing to do with being alone. "I was with people all day long," she admits, "yet I felt as if I were wandering in the wilderness" (Brothers 92).

There are many other insights in *Widowed* that must have resonated with Gilbert, as when Brothers cites research indicating it is more stressful to lose a spouse than a child. "If you lose your child, your husband shares your grief. The two of you comfort each other. You are not alone. If you lose your husband, your children may mourn as passionately as you do, but there is a different dimension to their grief. They lost a father; you lost a husband" (Brothers 106). She cites Thomas Holmes's study that the loss of a spouse is the most stressful event in life. Gilbert certainly must have agreed with Brothers's statement that the dead remain a part of their family, a belief that helped lessen Gilbert's own loneliness. The "hypotheticals" on which Gilbert muses in *On Burning Ground* resemble Brothers's advice to widows to ask the question "what if" when confronting their new selves: "I would advise every woman—single, divorced, or widowed—who is considering marriage to put herself through a series of similar 'what ifs.' I was surprised at what I learned about myself" (Brothers 139). And Gilbert would have been moved by the psychologist's "miracle dream" the second spring after her husband's death. Dreaming that they are holding hands and laughing on their beloved farm, she tells him, "How lovely it is to have a second chance to be with you," all the time knowing it is only a dream (156).

Perhaps the greatest similarity between Brothers and Gilbert is that they honored and memorialized their husbands by writing books about them, a process that helped both women—and Oates, too—through the agonizing months of early widowhood. Writing *Widowed* helped Brothers realize, to her astonishment, that her grief was subsiding. Citing Freud, she notes the paradox that remembering is the best way to forget the pain of loss and go on living. "It is as if each time you remember, a healing film grows over the memory until eventually it is no longer a raw wound. You are whole and healthy again. There may be a scar, but you are ready to forge ahead in life" (75). The paradox that remembering a painful memory is the best way to minimize its pain has been confirmed by recent neuroscience research on post-traumatic stress disorder, which suggests that we must revisit lacerating memories to overcome the trauma of memory.

Wrongful Death is not primarily a self-help book, as *Widowed* is. Nor is *Wrongful Death* a book that focuses mainly on the journey from grief to recovery. Nevertheless, Gilbert agrees with Brothers's observation that writing is a form of grief work. Near the end of *Wrongful Death*, Gilbert recalls that her husband was compelled to tell the story of his failed intubation again and again to friends and colleagues, "like some sort of medicalized Ancient Mariner, to repeat his tale again and again, each time with further details" (323). She, too, is an Ancient Mariner, repeating the story of his death to gain a degree of self-understanding and self-mastery. Repeating the story of her husband's death enables her to fulfill her promise to Toni Morrison to "do all the mourning things," thus honoring her husband's memory.

Ghost Volcano and Aftermath:
Elliot Gilbert's Continuing Presence

Gilbert's mourning rituals included two of her most distinctive volumes of poetry, *Ghost Volcano* (1995) and *Aftermath* (2011). Written at the same time that she was working on *Wrongful Death*, *Ghost Volcano* memorializes her husband and finds a way to keep his memory alive. She tells us in "A Note to the Reader" that the "Widow's Walk" poems "form a narrative of the stages of grief" with which she has struggled in the three years following his death. The poems don't chart a linear journey from denial to acceptance, certainly nothing like the "stage theory of grief" Elisabeth Kübler-Ross popularized in her many books on death and dying. Gilbert does not mention any of Kübler-Ross's books in *Wrongful Death*, though she cites three of them, including *On Death and Dying*, in *Death's Door*. Nevertheless, without implying that grief is predictable, *Ghost Volcano* suggests a gradual, tentative movement from despair to acceptance. Some of the poems relive the details of her husband's unexpected death while other poems focus on the desolation of loss. And yet the poems are not uniformly bleak: there are moments of unexpected happiness, even joy. Elliot Gilbert may be dead, but his ghostly presence is always palpable, like a volcano.

Several poems in *Aftermath* celebrate Elliot Gilbert as a continuing presence in his wife's life. Most of these poems appear in part 1, "Old Recipes," where she recalls the past, the "long-gone picnic-perfect days" (19) that remain a part of her present. Her references to her husband are sometimes bittersweet but always life affirming, evoking the medieval theme of *ubi sunt*, a meditation on mortality and transience. After describing Elliot's gastronomic talent, including cooking "snowy babies," she ends with a jarring rhymed couplet, "They didn't know they'd be chopped up and browned, / or end (like him) in an oven underground" (21). In "The Anniversary," written on February 11, 2005, she refers to the "two cycles of seven" that have passed since her husband's death, remarking discordantly that she, too, has "passed past too much memory" (45). "Anti-Sonnet" cleverly announces and repudiates her decision not to write anymore about her late husband. Even as she bids farewell to the content of the traditional sonnet, saying "goodbye to the seasons, to pastorals, to dopey / moping sheep, to brooding sky and sea," she hears Emily Brontë and the Australian poet Judith Wright urging her to "whistle a different tune"—one that doesn't "describe tough stuff in another sonnet!" (46).

Aftermath bespeaks Gilbert's auditory imagination, her sensitivity to the musicality of language, including perfect and imperfect rhymes, alliteration, and assonance. *Aftermath* also affirms her passion for life. Her poems reveal the sorrow that comes not from emptiness but from plenitude; she never surrenders to despair or sentimentality. She may be a literary historian of grief, but her poems demonstrate the courage and strength of survival.

Ruth Stone

The courage and strength of survival characterize not only Sandra Gilbert's poetry but also that of her friend and former colleague Ruth Stone, who was widowed in her fifties when her poet-husband committed suicide in 1959, leaving the mother of three daughters bereft and penniless. The suicide was the catalyst for Stone's most disquieting work, *Who Is the Widow's Muse?* Stone taught for a year at Indiana University in 1973 where she and Gilbert soon became friends. Gilbert was one of the earliest admirers of Stone's poetry, and in 1996 she and Wendy Barker edited a volume of essays on Stone's importance as a poet, *The House Is Made of Poetry*.

There is a world of difference between losing a husband to a wrongful death and losing him to suicide. Nevertheless, Gilbert identifies with Stone's journey through grief and rage, and her husband, no less than Stone's, has served as the widow's muse. Like Walter Stone, Elliot Gilbert is an absent presence who has become the poet's silent interlocutor. Again like Walter Stone, Elliot Gilbert evokes a wide spectrum of emotions in his wife, ranging from sorrow and grief, on the one hand, to playfulness and pathos, on the other. Gilbert's poem "For Ruth Stone on Her Ninetieth Birthday" pays homage to the poet's ability to conjure up the dead, as the final couplet suggests: "Walter left but he couldn't leave you alone: / your flesh and blood of stone" (*Aftermath* 148). Stone has that gift, and so does Gilbert.

Tellingly, many of Roger Gilbert's statements about Ruth Stone in *The House Is Made of Poetry* apply to his mother. "The desire to make the dead speak is of course a principal obsession in Stone's work" (Barker and Gilbert 142). It's also an obsession in Sandra Gilbert's work. Stone's "autobiographical poetry has for the last thirty years been dominated by the single fact of her widowhood, which inspires many of her most haunting poems" (142). Change thirty years to twenty years, and this statement describes Sandra Gilbert's widowhood. "If loss is a primary subject of poetry, then a combination of remembrance and grief is its work, and who has taken that task more seriously than Ruth Stone?" (153). Roger Gilbert no doubt intended his question to be rhetorical, yet he would probably agree that it also applies to his mother. "Stone's poetry of remembrance does not bog down under the excessive weight of self-importance or self-centeredness. Often buoyant, always powerful in its poignancy, her poetry on grief is an act of generosity, a study in resilient devotion, a tour through the underworld of loss that so many of us dare not enter" (154). This is also true of Sandra Gilbert's poetry.

Both Stone and Gilbert write about widowhood with unsurpassed insight and power. Both widows write poems that embrace love and loss, joy and sorrow. The two poets create an ongoing dialogue between the living and the dead that time does not silence. Both write about grief without despair. Both memorialize the dead not because they are fixated on the past but because they know that memory gives meaning and beauty to the present. Both write poems filled with "stone" images suggestive of elemental hardness and endurance. (*Aftermath* abounds in stone images.) And both write about widowhood elegiacally, ruefully, deftly, alert to the ambiguities and paradoxes of absence and presence.

The Widow's Search for New Love

Therese Rando and Joyce Brothers discuss the widow's search for new love after the death of a spouse, part of what the former calls "moving adaptively into the new life without forgetting the old." Rando lists four ways to achieve this new life: (1) "Developing a new relationship with the deceased"; (2) "Keeping your loved one 'alive' appropriately"; (3) "Forming a new identity based on your being without this person and encompassing the changes you have made to adjust to his death"; and (4) "Taking the freed-up emotional energy that used to be invested in your loved one and reinvesting it in other relationships, objects, activities, roles, and hopes that can offer emotional satisfaction back to you" (232).

Brothers, who writes more personally about widowhood than Rando, remembers how wrenching it was to begin dating after her husband's death, concluding that she probably will never remarry because "the odds are against me—against almost every widow. And one reason for this is that the average woman is fifty-six years old when her husband dies. And that really narrows the field" (Brothers 143). Apart from the far greater number of widows than widowers, nearly four to one in the early 1990s, along with the fact that widows have less money than widowers, there is the ubiquitous fear of rejection and failure that accompanies every new relationship.

Lynn Caine offers similar observations in her two books, *Widow* and *Being a Widow*, both of which Gilbert cites in the bibliography in *Wrongful Death*. Caine recounts in *Widow* her devastation when her husband died of cancer, leaving her with two young children. She quotes the same two psychiatrists, Colin Murray Parkes and Thomas Holmes, whom Brothers cites in *Widowed* more than fifteen years later. Caine admits in the chapter "The Trouble with Love Affairs" that she didn't want a "procession of affairs" after her husband's death but rather "a relationship" (*Widow* 185), something that does not happen by the time she completes the book. She concludes with an apt definition of "widow," a "harsh and hurtful word" that means "empty" in Sanskrit (221).

In her second book, *Being a Widow*, which is less of a narrative of her loss than a self-help guide, Caine advises other widows to keep a journal, which she calls her "paper psychiatrist," helping her to define her emotions and chart her progress. After enumerating the many problems besetting the widow, including disorientation and denial, sleeping and eating disorders, stress and anxiety attacks, and need for self-confidence rebuilding, she returns in the chapter "Dating and Sexuality" to the difficulty of finding another man to love. "Unless there is a definite outlet for sexuality, unless there is someone to whom a widow is attached for at least a period of time, it seems that for the majority of women, sexuality is put to rest" (182).

Caine mentions in the epilogue to *Being a Widow* that in 1983 she developed breast cancer and had a lumpectomy followed by chemotherapy. For a while she felt well, but then she had a recurrence that required another round of chemotherapy. Now, as she is completing her new book, she feels a worrisome lump in her throat and has difficulty swallowing. She has not yet seen a doctor. She ends the book by saying that "whatever time is left will be spent celebrating the life I have and trying to lighten the burden of those who will grieve for me" (244). A brief editorial note indicates that she died of cancer in 1987, one year before the publication of the book.

Falling in Love Again

In *Death's Door*, Gilbert cites Caine's observation that grieving widows, suffering from what one writer has called a "spoiled identity," feel compelled to hide because of embarrassment over spousal loss. Gilbert was fifty-five when her husband died, but she seems to have overcome quickly whatever embarrassment she may have felt over being a widow. She informs her readers in the second paragraph of the introduction to the paperback edition of *Wrongful Death* that she has a "new romantic companion—a kind, funny mathematician who loves to do a good many of the things I love to do, even though we inhabit such different professional spheres" (2). She refers to him by name near the end of the preface, where she thanks her "wise and loving companion, David Gale" (16). Gilbert dedicates *Aftermath* to the "memory of David Gale," and in the preface to *Rereading Women* she pays tribute to both deceased men as well as to a new man in her life. "In the beginning, and still, my beloved intellectual mentor was and has always been my late husband Elliot Gilbert, but in more recent years I was deeply enriched by the passionate energy of my late much-cherished partner David Gale. Today, I am intensely thankful for the loving companionship of Albert Magid" (xvii).

Gilbert never explicitly addresses one of Rando's most provocative statements: "Identify the gain that has come from your loss. In every loss there is a gain. This is not to dismiss the intensity of your grief, not to minimize its tragedy. However, whenever a loss takes place, there is a gain that comes about" (Rando 259–260). This is admittedly a daunting statement to confront in a book on wrongful death. Nevertheless, Gilbert has continued with her life, dedicating herself to the memory of her late husband while forming new romantic attachments. She never implies that she feels guilty for being in love again or that love for a new man dishonors the memory of a deceased man. Nor does she imply that widowhood is the end of life or the punishment for a good marriage, as Oates does throughout *A Widow's Story*.

Gilbert and Oates could not be more different in the ways in which they announced they have fallen in love again. There is never a "breach of narrative promise" in *Wrongful Death* as there is in *A Widow's Story*. We read *Wrongful Death* with the knowledge that Gilbert has fallen in love again, and though she may believe that her life is over, imagining herself as a "grieving widow who sits Shiva forever and a day, until even her children and best friends give up on her" (105), we know this scenario has not come true.

Gilbert never describes *falling* in love again after her husband's death. To my knowledge, we never see the *process* of falling in love again in any spousal loss memoir. But she does describe *being* in love again. No other spousal loss memoirist succeeds in doing this as convincingly as Gilbert does. She also dramatizes the disciplinary tensions that exist between the poet's and mathematician's worlds, tensions that enrich her art even if they complicate her life.

David Gale

A distinguished mathematician and economist, David Gale was born in Manhattan in 1921, earning a BA in mathematics at Swarthmore College in 1943 and a PhD in mathematics at Princeton in 1949. After teaching for a year at Princeton and then at Brown from 1950 to 1965, he was appointed a full professor in the mathematics department in 1966 at UC Berkeley (and, a year later, a full professor in the economics department), where he taught until his retirement. Gale shared the 1980 John von Neumann Theory prize for his work on game theory. Sylvia Nasar states in *A Beautiful Mind* that John Nash credited Gale for a clue that led to the concept of game theory, for which Nash shared the 1994 Nobel Prize in economics. Nasar describes Gale as coming from a "well-to-do-business family," "artistic," "a bit of a tinkerer," and an "aficionado" of mathematical games and puzzles. Gale met his future wife, Julie B. Skeby, while he was in Denmark in 1953; they had three daughters and were divorced in 1974. He died of a heart attack in 2008 at the age of eighty-six.

Gilbert dedicates *Death's Door* to "D.G., who brought new life." She acknowledges in the preface being "endlessly grateful to David Gale, my companion in daily life and *bien aimé*," adding wryly that he has "cheerfully joined me on more tours of cemeteries, memorials, and mortuary exhibitions than he may care to remember" (xxiv). In the chapter of *Death's Door* called "Yahrzeit," which marks the ninth anniversary of Elliot Gilbert's death, she explains that she and Gale have been together for nearly seven years. He's "always kind about the impulses to mourn that still master me from time to time. He understands quite well, I think, that one can love and grieve for the dead person who shaped the past even while loving and living with a new person who's central in the present." Some people in Gale's situation might feel threatened by Gilbert's devotion to her deceased husband, but there's no evidence he felt this way. Gilbert admits, however, that he has trouble understanding what he considers "my mystical tendency to brood on the chronological milestones that mark my personal narrative of loss" (41).

"When She Was Kissed by the Mathematician"

Gilbert wrote about David Gale first in her nonfiction and then in her poetry. Her most detailed description of their relationship appears in the nine love poems forming part 3 of *Kissing the Bread* (2000), "When She Was Kissed by the Mathematician." Throughout the sequence, she refers to her lover not by his name but by his professional identity. His passion for work continues even in his retirement. Gilbert captures the mathematician's otherness by developing a new poetic language based on formulas, vectors, matrices, axioms, algorithms, triangles, theorems, and equations. She writes about his world, including his inclination toward logic, order, and abstraction, with rapier insight and lively wit, and we are always aware of how vastly different his world is from her own.

The poems in "When She Was Kissed by the Mathematician" are alternately thoughtful, playful, witty, clever, and often startlingly erotic. The early poems in the sequence celebrate their physical relationship, as the opening of the title poem reveals: "The morning after the night she was / kissed by the mathematician, / she woke with a new intelligence" (*Kissing the Bread* 117). Gilbert's first scholarly book was a study of D. H. Lawrence's poetry, *Acts of Attention*, and the love poems in "When She Was Kissed by the Mathematician" have a Lawrentian vitality: "she embraced / a hypothesis she'd long forgotten: / *Energy*, she declared, / as she bounded out of bed" (118). The mathematician has helped her to reconnect with her vital, passionate self, and the entire world seems reborn, as the ending suggests: "Beyond her study door / the garden bloomed with glittering proofs" (118).

The playfulness, eroticism, and wit of the early poems give way to the koanlike questioning of the later ones. The mathematician's humor, warmth, and tenderness in the early poems morph into an almost mystical otherworldliness. The rebirth imagery in the first two poems, in which the mathematician and lover explore new pleasures, transforms into geometrical images and mathematical operations that have little to do with everyday reality. The mathematician never loses faith in his own world, but his faith proves to be cold comfort to his lover.

"AfterMath"

The center of *Aftermath*, part 3, is the title sequence of ten poems devoted to Gale's death. The longest poem, cleverly entitled "AfterMath," consists of ten sonatas focusing on the mathematician's dying and death and the poet's grief. "AfterMath" does not burn with the searing intensity of Ghost Volcano. Nor would we expect it to have the same furious power. Sandra Gilbert was shocked, horrified, and for a time incapacitated by Elliot Gilbert's sudden death, and she weeps in rage for much of *Ghost Volcano* and *Death's Door*. His death was nothing less than a geological eruption that violently transfigured every aspect of her life. He was much too young to die. It may be hard for her to determine whether he resembles an active or dormant volcano, but he is never extinct.

By contrast, David Gale's death is unexpected but natural; it is not a wrongful death. No one could have prevented it. Moreover, he was eighty-six, not sixty, when he died. Gale's death could not be more different from Elliot Gilbert's death. In addition, Gilbert knew that Gale, who was fifteen years older, would probably predecease her. Her grief is controlled and restrained. Nonetheless, both deaths produce grief that must be worked through publicly and privately. For Gilbert, there is no better way to honor the memory of her beloved companion, with whom she lived for fifteen years, than by transmuting him into poetry.

Gilbert never reveals any of the difficulties of a widow falling in love again that her "grief books" discuss. She never compares the two men to each other or implies that later love is inferior to earlier love. Elliot Gilbert and David Gale are separate but equal, each extraordinary in his personal and professional life. She is careful not to intrude on relatives' or friends' privacy. She never tells us, for example, how her children feel about their mother being in love again, nor does she explain her decision not to remarry. She expresses gratitude for the years she spent with both Elliot Gilbert and David Gale, idealizing neither relationship. Some of the poems in "When She Was Kissed by the Mathematician" reveal different relational problems, but their friendship endured. She lived with Elliot Gilbert, with whom she had three children, more than twice as long as she lived with Gale, and *Ghost Volcano* abounds in marital and parenting experiences that are absent from *Aftermath*. But her love for Gale appears no less genuine. She and her husband were both English professors, and they lived in the same disciplinary world; Gale's world was radically different, as the "Mathematician" poems show. And yet she did her best to understand that world and meld it with her own.

What is most remarkable about *Aftermath*, indeed, Gilbert's entire career, is its richness and fullness. Seize the day, her poems proclaim, regardless of sorrow. In a teaching and writing career that has spanned more than forty years, she is at the height of her poetic power. Her poems move from lamentation to luminous celebration. Neither age nor loss has weakened the septuagenarian's imagination. *Aftermath* sparkles with the golden afterglow of life, the poems bespeaking autumnal hues and shades that dazzle the eye.

Sandra Gilbert's writings reveal, no less than Oates's, how widows in grief become more like themselves. "Knowledge of life necessarily involves knowledge of death," Gilbert writes in *Acts of Attention*, "and to attend to life is to attend to death at the heart of life, to physical death as well as the spiritual death that is, as we shall see, a kind of precondition for heightened life" (59). She could not have imagined, when she wrote "as we shall see," that a catastrophic adverse event would indeed compel her to attend to a physical death that is a precondition for heightened life. Both Gilbert and Oates discover that widowhood has shattered their assumptive worlds, but they recreate their new identities in ways that are consistent with their old identities, revealing inner sameness and continuity.

Gilbert and Oates continue to write about widowhood while at the same time writing about mathematics and trepanation, the worlds of David Gale and Charles Gross, respectively. The two women see no contradiction or conflict between honoring past and present lovers. In calling attention to four men who were or are themselves authors, Gilbert and Oates create posterity selves. The two women demonstrate the truth of Robert Anderson's statement that death ends a life but not a relationship. They also show the possibility of growth and transformation through grief. Gilbert never addresses what Robert DiGiulio calls the "singular-love fantasy our society holds so dearly," the belief that "You can truly love only one in this life" (89), but it's apparent that she believes the opposite is true. Unlike Oates, who doesn't allow herself to write autobiographically about being in love again, Gilbert does. She lauds her romantic partner in both her scholarly bereavement writings and in her poems. Gilbert shares Oates's belief that those who have been magnanimous in life can be imagined as magnanimous in death.

In Rando's terms, Gilbert has moved adaptively into a new life without forgetting the old life by developing a new relationship with the deceased, keeping her loved one alive appropriately, forming a new identity based on love and loss, and developing new relationships. Gilbert's life and work demonstrate a continuing bond that affirms the resilience of relationships that survive even death. The poems near the end of *Aftermath* celebrate new life, including her grandchildren's lives: her "two-year-old princeling," Aaron David Gilbert-O'Neil, who in "Flocks" bleats like sheep; her young granddaughter, who in "Fourteen Fourteeners for Sophia at 14

Months" "sallied forth" high above the sea, her "tiny swaggering stagger along the cliffside path" (*Aftermath* 149); and her oldest grandchild, Val, to whom she expresses her love in the high-spirited "Anti-Valentine." The most joyful poem in the volume, "Hearing Aids," dedicated to her new companion, Albert Magid, is a tour de force that reveals the possibility of falling in love again during the twilight of life. "Sex Sounds" ends with the speaker's lover placing his head on her breast; the whistle of his hearing aid rises "delicate & sweet as mythic piping," and he says aloud in his sleep, "Oh boy," with a "certain satisfaction" (154).

—∼∼∼—

3

Gail Godwin

Evenings At Five

"Suffer, Joyce. Ray was worth it." Joyce Carol Oates quotes Gail Godwin's condolence four times in *A Widow's Story* (119, 198, 323, 407) as well as Godwin's prediction that Oates uses as an epigraph for the memoir: "Oh God—you are going to be so unhappy." Godwin's two statements become a haunting refrain in *A Widow's Story*, linking love with inevitable loss and grief. Midway through *A Widow's Story* Oates remarks on her thirty-year "epistolary, writerly" friendship with Godwin, in which they are like cousins or sisters of a bygone era—"the long-lost era of the Brontë sisters, perhaps."

Oates and her husband often visited Godwin and her longtime companion, the distinguished composer Robert Starer, in their Woodstock, New York, home. "Robert's unexpected death in the spring of 2001 had the sorrowful feel of the end of an era, though I had not dared to think that my husband would be next" (*A Widow's Story* 197). The men's sudden and unexpected deaths strike Oates as "uncanny" because they had been hospitalized "temporarily," implying they would soon recover. Early one morning, Oates writes, "as Gail was preparing to drive to the hospital in Kingston to see him, she received a call from a doctor whom she didn't know—who happened to be on duty at the time: 'I'm afraid Robert didn't make it' "—to which Oates then responds, "So we protest, in disbelief.

Clinging to what has seemingly been promised to us, like children" (197). Oates adds that Godwin, too, had driven to the hospital "in a trance" and that, like her, Godwin had difficulty believing her partner had died. Throughout *A Widow's Story* Oates hopes she will be able to follow Godwin's advice to be strong enough to suffer.

Gail Godwin was born in 1937 in Birmingham, Alabama, and raised in Asheville, North Carolina, by her divorced mother and grandmother. Godwin was brought up Episcopalian, and nondoctrinal religion remains a positive force in her life. She is among the most acclaimed novelists of our age. She has written thirteen novels, three of which have been nominated for the National Book Award and five of which have appeared on *The New York Times* Best Seller list. In addition, she has published two collections of short stories; one scholarly study, *Heart*; two volumes of her journal, *The Making of a Writer*; and libretti for ten musical works composed by Starer. Godwin won a Guggenheim Fellowship and the 1981 Award in Literature from the National Academy and Institute of Arts and Letters. In 1986 she was the chief fiction judge for the National Book Awards. Godwin's two marriages ended in quick divorces, but she lived with Robert Starer for nearly three decades until his death in 2001 at the age of seventy-seven. Godwin's *Evenings at Five: A Novel and Five New Stories*, with illustrations by Frances Halsband, first published in 2003, is a work of fiction, but it is closely based on her relationship with Starer, as she states in the introduction.

> I never considered the memoir form because I wanted to write a tale. The major experience was real—all too real—but I needed to reserve the right to add and subtract and embellish, to "make it up" when my instincts tugged me in that direction. After decades of writing fiction I have learned that in the middle of "inventing," the most amazing discoveries jump out at you: surprises of memory and feeling that shed new light on the literal happenings. So it was "Rudy" and "Christina" from the beginning; I even changed the name of the cat. (xvi–xvii)

Evenings at Five is only 116 pages long, but it is filled with illustrations that reduce the novel to the length of a novella, a quarter of the length of Oates's *A Widow's Story*. The two stories have much in common, but they are aesthetically different. *A Widow's Story* contains elements of gothic horror, while *Evenings at Five* evokes a different kind of ghost story, one in which the dead remain in communion with the living. The stories offer vastly different visions of mourning; Christina survives the ordeal of widowhood through her acceptance of death and religious faith.

The more one understands Godwin's and Starer's lives, both as individuals and as a couple, the more one appreciates the vision of bereavement in *Evenings at Five*. Each wrote a great deal about love and loss before meeting the other. There is no biography of Godwin, but *The Making of a Writer* allows us to see her struggle for fulfillment in both love and work.

The Making of a Writer

Like Oates, Godwin began her journal when she was an adolescent. She has published two volumes but has no plans for further publication. As editor Rob Neufeld observes, Godwin's journals "are at times expressions of *encouragement* from her 'cowriter,' her other self" (*The Making of a Writer*, I, 138, n. 22). Godwin invests her journals with the greatest significance: "As long as there is this outlet," she writes on November 26, 1962, "I can survive. There are worse things than being in a room by oneself. These journals, while seemingly over-personal & dead-end, are a panacea—and may, someday, serve as references when I find a route" (I, 191).

The "inner motive" for writing, Godwin suggests in a June 22, 1963, entry, is not only to discover and create meaning, but also to "go back and examine the past, remove the pain by changing it into form and thus free ourselves for the next battle" (I, 291). Occasionally she feels guilty about keeping a journal, as she reveals on July 3, 1963. "Nobody I know keeps one. I look over my shoulder and think: Who is that crazy girl sitting in her window and putting down versions of things that are happening to her?" (I, 298). Guilt notwithstanding, writing in her journal is a necessity. Two days later she speculates that "perhaps I am neurotic & have resolved my neuroses by using these notebooks" (I, 299). In volume 2 she continues reflecting on the value of journal writing, admitting that if she couldn't confide in her journals, she "risked losing track" of herself (II, 167).

"You Never Get Over It"

The Making of a Writer casts much light on the most traumatic event of Godwin's early life, the suicide of her father, Mose Winston Godwin, in 1958, twenty years after his wife divorced him and, according to Neufeld, "three years after he had reentered Gail's life in a supportive way following her high school graduation" (II, 13, n. 26). In volume 1 Godwin compares her father's suicide with that of Richard Cory, the doomed hero of Edwin Arlington Robinson's poem, who "one calm night / Went home and put a bullet through his head" (I, 25). Godwin returns several times in both volumes to her father's suicide, trying to understand its impact on her life and how she can transmute it into fiction. She begins writing about him in a story called "Mourning," developing the material that eventually appears in her 1978 novel *Violet Clay*. Ambrose, the heroine's uncle in *Violet Clay*, is based on Godwin's father.

Godwin also lost her half-brother, Tommy, to suicide. She writes about the event in her 1987 novel *A Southern Family* and expands on it in *Heart*. The official cause of his death was listed as a gunshot wound to the head, but Godwin maintains that he died of a broken heart. Following his death, she began having a "heartbreak dream" in which she finds herself trapped in a black box and feels "only stark, pure emotion. I wanted to die—or kill somebody—or both, because this person didn't, or couldn't, love me. The person didn't have a gender. I didn't have a gender. The whole thing was just the overwhelming agony of knowing myself not loved and wanting to kill/die to avenge myself and put an end to the pain" (*Heart* 153).

Godwin's heartbreak dream continues to haunt her, she admits, but in later versions "I am always at least myself—myself at an earlier age or myself now, trapped in a longing for someone I have outgrown in real life. The person doesn't, or cannot, love me, and I rage in anguish and wake flailing in a morass of hopelessness and shame" (*Heart* 153). One never gets over a loved one's suicide, she writes in a condolence letter to a father whose son recently took his own life, adding that she doesn't want to get over her brother's death. "Maybe that in itself is the hopeful part, and that is what I tried to convey in my letter. How you never get over it, and how as time goes on you realize you are *glad* you'll never get over it because the lost one remains alive in your heart as you continue to engage with the who and the why of him" (154). A frequent theme in Godwin's writings, as in Sandra Gilbert's, is that one must find a way to absorb the death of a beloved companion into one's life so that it doesn't become paralyzing.

What Godwin doesn't admit, except in *The Making of a Writer*, is her own ambivalence about committing suicide. "I am the type that will never commit suicide," she writes on March 26, 1963, a time when she is feeling depressed: "I hit bottom again. Anyway, the result was to feel that there was *nothing* at all to continue for—yet to be apathetic about doing anything about ending existence" (I, 251). From this passage and a scene in *Violet Clay*, when the eponymous heroine puts her Uncle Ambrose's unloaded gun to her head in an apparent reenactment, Neufeld concludes that Godwin is invulnerable to suicide. "Understanding suicide saves the heroine from feeling suicidal" (I, 251, n. 1). Yet on April 29, 1965 Godwin concedes disturbingly, "I have the seeds of destruction in me. Ambrose had them. I am attracted to people who have them" (II, 130). One month later she admits that her "big enemies are anger, proneness to depression, and laziness." Indeed, she is so despondent that she concludes her journals are a "waste of time. I have to produce more. No more anger" (II, 132). Nor is this the only reference to committing suicide. "Failing catastrophe," she writes on July 22, 1968, "I can hide in a university till sixty-five and maybe then have the courage to kill myself" (II, 197).

Growing up with a father who committed suicide left Godwin vulnerable to suicide and depression, as her journal entries indicate. On August 18, 1963, she can see how, in ten years' time, she might "come home from a Sunday afternoon walk, look in the mirror, add up my assets and liabilities, and then put a bullet through my head after the manner of MWG" (II, 13). She writes about suicide and depression in one of her most powerful novels, *Father Melancholy's Daughter*, where she appears as her father's melancholy daughter.

Godwin acknowledges in A Reader's Guide to her 2000 novel *Evensong* that she knows "a good deal about depression both from personal experience and from watching members of my family who have suffered from it" (n.p.). Many of the references to her father are implicit cautionary tales, as when she writes, "Dear God, don't let me be another MWG, babbling great nothings after a few drinks, running off to Florida (or its equivalent) every time responsibility raise its disagreeable head" (II, 141). She dedicates the novel "to my own Father Melancholy, the sorrowful but animating spirit who dwells within," suggesting a mysterious link between mood disorders and creativity.

Twice Married, Twice Divorced

Godwin's two failed marriages added to her depression. In December 1960 she married *Miami Herald* photographer Douglas Kennedy, with whom she worked for a year. They divorced five months later. In 1961 she boarded the SS *Oklahoma* and sailed to Europe, visiting Denmark and Spain and then England, where she began working at the US Travel Service at the

American Embassy in London. In a June 23, 1963, journal entry she refers to herself as a twenty-six-year-old-woman who has become "afraid that I will never marry again" (I, 292). In 1965 she met Ian Marshall, an English psychiatrist, at an evening fiction class at the City Literary Institute in London. Within a few months they married. The precipitous marriage introduced her to Scientology, in which she became interested briefly before concluding that it was authoritarian and fanatical, like her husband, whom she quickly divorced.

"I Do Not Believe I Can Do without a Man"

Godwin's journals offer us insight into the making of a writer and the kind of man with whom she wished *not* to spend the rest of her life. The journals document, sometimes with poignant sadness, other times with wry humor, her quest for the right man. She declares on July 22, 1968, that "I do not believe I can do without a man," explaining that she's not sure she wants to achieve the "dubious state of blissful independence" (II, 197). While a graduate student in the late 1960s, she has relationships with men whom she endows with romantic names, such as "Othello" and "Byron." She met a man who attracted her but realized after a week that he's "not husband material" (II, 205). She devotes many entries to a "new star on the horizon" at the university, a poet and printer whom she calls "Vulcan." "He propositions when drunk, wiggles out of an assignation when sober. He works like crazy, long hours alone at his job, then goes home and drinks himself to sleep" (II, 236).

"I Put Writing First Now"

Godwin did not allow problems with men to interfere with her deepening commitment to fiction. From the beginning, she sought to resolve personal conflicts through writing. "In my earlier books," she admits at the beginning of *The Making of a Writer*, "I was working out how independent women can be independent and still manage to love and be loved. *The Odd Woman, Glass People, The Perfectionists.* That was my initial concern. I've solved it to my satisfaction" (I, 24). Viewing art as a form of problem solving compels her to end her journals with a statement made by Lawrence Durrell: "Art is easy; it is life I find difficult" (II, 299).

Godwin's journals reveal not that she is an autobiographical writer, but that she saw life and art as interconnected. She uses her journal entries to develop ideas, such as her flirtation with Scientology, that would soon form the basis of her early novels. She ends a letter written to her mother on June 7, 1968, with the prophetic words, "I put writing first now" (II, 186). She committed herself entirely to fiction after her divorce from Marshall. In 1970 she published her first novel, *The Perfectionists*, in which she creates a cult-addicted husband-psychiatrist whose goal, based on that of the cult's founder, is to "clear the planet" by freeing patients of irrational impulses. During the next few years, Godwin put her own irrational impulses to good use, penning novels that were artistic and popular successes.

The Making of a Writer ends in 1969, three years before Godwin met Robert Starer at Yaddo, the prestigious artist's colony in Saratoga Springs, New York. Neufeld breaks chronology to quote some of Godwin's later observations about writing, as when he states near the end of volume 1 that journal writing became especially important to her after Starer's death. "There are times when I fill up a three-hundred-page journal in a month and a half—after Robert died—and times when a three-hundred-page journal lasts more than a year" (I, 285).

A Life in Music

We learn many details about Starer's life, both before and after he met Godwin, in his 1987 memoir *Continuo: A Life in Music*, dedicated to "Gail." There is much he tells us in this provocative and deftly written work and much that we can only infer. His early life could not have been more different from Godwin's, and yet they shared a long partnership that also turned out to be a remarkable artistic collaboration.

Born in Vienna to wealthy parents—his father owned a textile factory—Starer entered the State Academy for Music in 1937. A year later, he and the other Jewish students were expelled after the German annexation of Austria. Life would never be the same for him. We learn surprisingly little about his parents. As a youth, Starer wished to become a member of the Vienna Choir Boys, but his mother forbade it because she wanted him to have "what she considered a normal childhood." In the next sentence, however, he intimates that his childhood was not entirely normal. "In those days my mother was studying psychoanalysis with Alfred Adler, and I saw as little of her as I did of my father, who came home late in the evening, always was elegantly dressed and never carried a package" (*Continuo* 6). Was Starer's mother studying psychoanalysis because she wished to become an analyst or because she sought and needed therapeutic help? Why did her studies—or therapy—prevent her from being with her son? Starer does not raise these questions. Instead, he tells us that his long Sunday walks with his father helped shape his character. "Whatever I can trace of my moral and behavioral values seems to have been implanted then"—namely, politeness, courtesy, and consideration for others, all of which were considered "marks of civilization" (6–7).

Blessed with absolute pitch (the ability to name the exact pitch of any sound), Starer played the piano and delighted in *klimpern*, musical doodling, which foreshadowed his career as a composer. As Vienna came under Nazi rule, he was invited to study at the Jerusalem Conservatory of Music, and he left Austria when he was fourteen. He informs us, in one of the most understated moments in the memoir, about his unusual departure from the Vienna train station. Standing next to his "pale and speechless" mother was a fourteen-year old girl named Kitty whom he had once kissed shyly. "I had eyes only for Kitty, not for my mother, whom I was never to see again; she left for England with my father a few months later and died there during the war" (*Continuo* 19). Starer was among countless children who would never see their mothers again. Curiously, there is hardly a reference to his mother after this passage or her impact on his life.

Starer lived in Jerusalem for the next nine years, served in the British Royal Air Force for three years, then came to the United States in 1947 and studied at the Juilliard School in New York City, where he later taught. He was a precocious student, scoring so high on the entrance exams that he passed all of his courses before taking them. He became an American citizen in 1957. He returned to Vienna twice, the first time in 1957–1958 with a fellow student whom he married in 1942, a young German soprano with whom he had a son, Daniel, and the second time in 1978 with Gail Godwin.

Throughout *Continuo*, Stater emphasizes his life *in music*, but he reveals little about his life apart from music. He is far less self-disclosing than Godwin; one could not imagine him publishing his journals or writing about his romantic adventures and misadventures. He tells us nothing about his wife or the reasons for their divorce. He allows us only to guess at the significance of two unusual events that connect him with his son. In 1961, he was invited with his wife and young son to Shelter Island, near the Eastern tip of Long Island, to spend a weekend working with Martha Graham, for whom he wrote three ballets. He saw little of his family for the next two days, and as they were leaving, "little Dan went over to Martha and while we all thought he was going to hug her, he bit her right in the stomach, the height he could then reach. He must have been furious with the woman who had taken his father away from him so completely on the weekend. Martha laughed—I don't think Dan hurt her—but many years later, when I took him backstage after an evening of the Graham Company, she looked long and hard at him and then asked, 'Are you the young man who once bit me in the stomach?'" Everyone who heard her was mortified, including Daniel, but Starer sympathized with his son, "for when I was a boy I had evidently once punched Alfred Adler, with whom my mother was studying psychoanalysis in Vienna, in the stomach in a similar rage" (110–111).

Meeting Gail Godwin

Starer writes about Godwin in the chapter called "Composer and Librettist," but he reveals little about her or their relationship beyond their professional collaboration. There was no thought of musical collaboration at the beginning of their relationship. "About three years after our decision to live together, Gail and I were walking up one of the hills near our house in upstate New York while I complained bitterly about the insensitivity of a librettist who was sending me uninspired pages of dialogue and overly wordy, unmusical pages for a commission that I had accepted. As I ranted, it suddenly struck me that I lived with a highly musical writer, yet had never even thought of the possibility of collaborating with her" (*Continuo* 125). Godwin had just written a short story with a reference to Saint Pelagia, a fourteenth-century woman of pleasure who renounced her life and, disguising her gender, became a monk. Starer and Godwin decided to write a chamber opera together, *The Last Lover*, which had its premiere at the Caramoor Festival, a summer music series held in Westchester, New York. He quotes Godwin as saying that she felt uninhibited writing the words to the opera "because nobody ever remembers the librettist anyway" (129). The opera was not only a success but also the beginning of a long and fruitful collaboration.

After teaching at Juilliard until 1974, Starer was appointed distinguished professor of music at Brooklyn College and the Graduate Center of the City University of New York. He was a devoted teacher committed both to serious music, old and new, and to his students. He opens the chapter "Audiences" by noting that, during a performance of his third piano concerto with the American Symphony at Carnegie Hall in 1980, the man sitting next to him rose and walked out of the hall as soon as the first chord was struck. Many composers would instantly become angry or hurt and dismiss the man as ignorant, but Starer asserts counterintuitively that he admired Mr. X for leaving. "Too many people will sit through almost anything and tolerate it; at least he had convictions and acted according to them" (*Continuo* 146).

Evenings at Five

Godwin opens *Evenings at Five* with Rudolf Geber's demand for promptness. "Five o'clock sharp. '*Ponctualité est la politesse des roi*': Rudy quoting his late father, a factory owner (textiles) in Vienna before the Nazis came" (3). Starer makes the same observation in *Continuo*: "my father considered it proper to appear at an appointment exactly two minutes before the agreed-upon time. To be late was out of the question ("Punctuality is the politeness of princes'), and to be five minutes early showed too much anxiety" (7).

We learn other details about Rudy's life that are consistent with Starer's self-portrait in *Continuo*, including his service in the British Royal Air Force in Palestine during World War II; his attendance, despite being Jewish, at a Catholic *Gymnasium* in Vienna until he was fourteen; his sensitivity to anti-Semitism; his identification with five nationalities; his ability to speak fluent German, Hebrew, English, and Italian along with a knowledge of Russian and Arabic; and his love for Bach—Godwin quotes the same statement that Starer does in *Continuo*: "He has order, and stability, qualities one doesn't always have in one's life. Yet he's not predictable, sentimental, or personal" (*Evenings at Five* 115).

Rudy embodies the qualities he admires in Bach. He's not predictable, though he is consistent and dependable, and he doesn't come across as sentimental or personal. (Godwin never explains why Christina and Rudy disapprove of being personal—perhaps because they identify the word with narcissistic self-absorption.) We learn little about his personal life before meeting Godwin in 1972 at Yaddo—nothing about his failed marriage or his son, his childhood in Vienna and adolescence in Jerusalem, his immigration to United States, or his life spent teaching at Juilliard and then at Brooklyn College. We don't even learn that Rudy died of congestive heart failure—that detail appears in Starer's *New York Times* obituary.

Godwin doesn't mention the kind of contemporary music Rudy likes, but she doesn't hesitate to mention the kind he dislikes. She describes at Yaddo a "sneering nasal-voiced twelve-tone composer who told her melody was the enemy" (*Evenings at Five* 86). She hints at Rudy's efforts to "outsmart the Boulez crowd" (87), a reference to Pierre Boulez's well-known antipathy for tonal music. Starer conveys the same dislike for Boulez in his 1997 novel *The Music Teacher*, where his largely autobiographical protagonist Bernard Winter remarks that Boulez's piano composition "Structures" was the "last piece he wrote in strict serialism. After that, even he gave up" (119). Godwin doesn't try to soften Rudy's disdain for certain composers: "Sometimes Rudy exploded with a tirade against toneless composers or a particular enemy" (11). Rudy is more intimidating in *Evenings at Five* than Starer is in *Continuo* and *The Music Teacher*. Christina's friend Gilbert Mallows offers a telling characterization of the couple: "When Rudy was alive, you two barricaded yourselves, which was understandable with his health problems. You were both formidable, though you seemed the more accessible of the two" (47).

Rudy doesn't suffer fools gladly, as Godwin implies in *Evenings at Five*. He often speaks "brusquely" to her, and he has no patience for small talk at parties, erupting in anger when he hears Eve Mallows talking about an "outstanding cabbage," which he then repeats with sardonic mockery in his basso profundo voice. It is the only time in the story when Christina confesses to hating him, though later she finds herself "hooting with laughter" (57) over the incident. She never mentions the other women in Rudy's life, but there is one moment when she alludes to his wariness over a certain type of female. Describing Gilbert Mallow's sculptor-mother, the aristocratic Gertrude von Kohler Spezzi, who was married and divorced several times, Christina quotes Rudy as saying, "What a gorgon Gilbert's mother was. I've known women like that. There's only way to treat them: laugh at them and walk away" (69). Like Starer and Bernard, Rudy is overbearing at times, though Godwin qualifies this impression: "If arrogance is the refusal to squander yourself on the unpassionate and the unfascinating, then he is arrogant. But toward her there is a generosity of spirit she recognizes as rare, an attention that is larger than self-consciousness" (92). "My arrogance," Bernard observes in *The Music Teacher*, "is really only an absolute intolerance for ineptitude" (134).

Setting Fire to Their Respective Lives

Godwin implies in *Evenings at Five* that Christina and Rudy were immediately attracted to each other at Yaddo and that they "set fire to their respective lives in order to be together" (77). She doesn't elaborate on the nature of the fire or the opposition to their relationship, but she suggests that each made a major sacrifice to be with the other. "Rudy had left his ordered family life in Manhattan, and Christina had given up her tenure-track teaching job in Iowa" (16). They sacrificed everything except their work, to which they remained committed. A few pages later she refers to "having burned their bridges" at Yaddo by publicly announcing their intention to live together (87). The beginning of their relationship was tumultuous; she would jump into her blue 1970 Mustang, with her blue IBM Selectric, every time she and Rudy had a "big fight for the next ten years, until both machines were replaced and the fights got less dramatic" (85). She describes some of the reasons behind their arguments, such as his complaint that she didn't listen to her, along with her denial, and the different ways they responded to arguments: "Rudy blew up quickly, but he blew over almost as quickly. Christina marinated her resentments, then simmered them over a low flame for days" (10).

Nowhere in *Continuo* or *Evenings at Five* do we learn why Godwin and Starer never married. That information appears in an interview Godwin gave in 1989. "Robert and I have lived together for a blissful seventeen years, but we're not married. What—who—would we have been marrying for? (We would definitely have, if we decided to have a child). There was no one we wanted to impress or please except ourselves. Our whole tax situation would have been a mess. . . . It's not my time of life to be a bride. That time is over" (Westerlund 38–39, n. 27).

Rudy doesn't keep a journal, but Godwin quotes some of the entries from his appointment diary to indicate his visits to a long list of medical specialists who treated him for multiple myeloma, cancer of the plasma cells in bone marrow. The physicians include an oncologist, hematologist, nephrologist, and ophthalmologist. He receives chemotherapy for multiple myeloma along with blood transfusions. On five separate occasions Christina calls 911 for medical emergencies. Godwin doesn't give us a chronology of his illness, but she does refer to the "fifteen-year-long saga of Rudy's organs betraying one another and breaking down" (51). Six attendants transported him on a stretcher during his final trip to the ER. "You look like Pharaoh being carried forth on his litter," Christina mordantly tells him (43), eliciting his wan smile behind an oxygen mask.

Rudy reminds himself throughout his medical ordeal to remain "Positive but not exuberant, Resigned but not depressed" (37). He never loses his passion for work, his love for Christina, his will to live, or his sense of humor. Godwin quotes one of the remarks he always made to her when his music was being performed with that of the classic composers: "How I love being the only one on the program who still has a dash after his birth date" (34). Even as the end approaches, they both assume they will have more time together. Christina's last words to Rudy, "Don't you dare leave me," prompts his reply: "We still have some more time together" (20).

"I Wonder What My Last Words Will Be"

Toward the end of *Evenings at Five*, Godwin mentions how Christina walks into Rudy's study after his death and touches his baby grand piano, which he had bought on the same day he watched Laurence Olivier's deathbed scene in Evelyn Waugh's *Brideshead Revisited*. How would Godwin have depicted a deathbed scene in *Evenings at Five* if Christina had been with Rudy during his dying moments? What were his final thoughts? In an example of art eerily imitating life, these questions, only hinted at in *Evenings at Five*, become the central event in Godwin's 1994 novel *The Good Husband*, her most powerful fiction to date.

Magda Danvers is a fifty-eight-year-old English professor who displays her daunting intellect, vast erudition, and acerbic wit to friends and foes alike. One of her most memorable observations, part of which Godwin uses as the epigraph to *The Good Husband*, is "Mates are not always matches, and matches are not always mates. Many people in this world are mated to people who are not their match, just as, conversely, people who may be matches for each other should never have gotten together as mates" (*The Good Husband* 24). Magna is married to Francis Lake, twelve years her junior, who is almost slavishly devoted to her and self-effacing to a fault. The other marriage in the novel is between Hugo Henry, a novelist whose ego demands constant praise and validation, and his wife, Alice, who lost her parents and brother in a car accident when she was seventeen and, more recently, has given birth to a stillborn child.

As the novel opens, Magda is dying from ovarian cancer. Far from engaging in denial, she holds court for the many people who visit her in her bedroom crammed with scholarly books. "I wonder what my last words will be" (*The Good Husband* 66), she states matter-of-factly to Francis, indifferent to the anguish the question evokes in him. An omnivorous reader, she then quotes the last words of literary masters, beginning with what is commonly assumed to be Henry James's last words: "Here it is at last, the distinguished thing." She knows from reading Leon Edel's biography, however, that it is more likely James's final words were "Stay with me," addressed to his sister-in-law, who was sitting at his bedside. Magda also quotes Goethe's dying words, a plea for "More light," and Beethoven's,

"I shall hear in heaven" (66). Ever the professor, she regards dying as her "Final Examination," and she orders Francis to bring her the "blue books" on which college students write their tests. "Her Final Examination was how she thought of the time she had left to lie here and account for her life" (205).

Throughout the story Magda tests her husband's goodness, hurling obscenities at him and treating him like a simpleton. She has a dream in which she imagines teaching a class of high-school students about to graduate, and though she is in intense pain, she wants the class to be memorable. To capture her students' attention, she begins talking about a dying woman—herself. "She was done for and they all knew it. She lay there rotting away, because that was her destined mode of expiration. Some of us will be snuffed out quickly and painlessly, but with no time to reconnoiter the mysterious route by which we have arrived at where we are. Others of us are charted for a slower, more agonizing exit, but with the consolation prize of being allowed to take stock of our lives as we lie there and disintegrate" (*The Good Husband* 299).

Magda's agonizing exit allows her to take stock of her life. She reaches few Tolstoyean epiphanies during her Final Examination; darkness does not yield suddenly to light at the end of her life, as it does at the end of *The Death of Ivan Ilych*. And yet Magda, despite her self-centeredness, develops a remarkable insight into other people's lives and hearts. As she tells the students in her dream, "The reason she could see was because *she didn't want anything from any of them anymore*. Once you get yourself out of the way, you can see everything the way it is. Your self isn't blocking the world from you, once you have sidestepped its shadow" (299–300).

Magda's deathbed scene is fraught with irony. Alice has come to visit her and help Francis with his many caregiving responsibilities. Godwin allows us to enter Magda's consciousness; she is confused, disoriented, and petulant, but she intuits that Francis and Alice would be good mates for each other. With Francis momentarily out of the room, Magda has an inspired idea. " 'I know what I'll do,' I tell kind Alice, whoever she may be. 'I'll leave him to you in my will. Go get me a . . .' " (303). Shocked, Alice cannot believe Magda is in her right mind. The dying woman makes the same bequest to her husband when he returns to their bedroom. " 'Have Alice,' I croak my instructions against the warm whorl of his ear, 'she'll suit you. I'd like you to have her after I'm gone.' " Like Alice, Francis cannot believe what he hears, and yet Magda has a greater insight into their lives than they do themselves. Magda's dying words remain with the reader long after completing the novel.

"You're not making sense, Magda," he says, resistant as a stone wall. Unlike her, he hasn't entertained a single thought of any attachment, not even unconsciously. I can feel it through his skin: his pure unreceptivity. Yes, boys and girls, the husband of the dying woman, a good husband, as husbands go, was completely faithful right to the end. Amazing, isn't it, in these wanton times! Are the obtuse more easily virtuous? A possible exam question, though I may think up more beguiling ones.

"You're on your own," I say, pushing him away. I feel the counterthrust of his sweet release. Go, good-bye, go. (303–304)

Recall Garrett Stewart's observation that "dying is by nature the one inevitably fictional matter in prose fiction." Any novelist who can create a deathbed scene as memorable as the one in *The Good Husband* could have imagined what her dying partner's final thoughts might have been, particularly because Godwin realized that through the imagination the "most amazing discoveries jump out at you." Did Rudy have time to reconnoiter the mysterious route by which his life led him to Christina? Was he allowed to take stock of his life before he disintegrated? Why does Godwin refuse to imagine Rudy's final thoughts in *Evenings at Five*, a story that is not a memoir but a work of fiction? The answer to the last question, we suspect, is that Godwin did not wish to stray too far from autobiographical truth. Her literary instinct was to use her dedicatory grief to memorialize Robert Starer, to bring him back to life verbally, as only a writer can do. To pretend to know his dying thoughts in a story that is largely autobiographical, however, would be to claim too much.

"Four Stimulating but Often Puzzling Parts of My Own Character"

Godwin's observation in the dedication to *The Good Husband* that Magda, Francis, Alice, and Hugo are "four stimulating but often puzzling parts of my own character" offers several clues to her character and to those of Christina and Rudy in *Evenings at Five*. Godwin's description of Magda as "wickedly irreverent," wanting to "shine light on things even if it's unflattering," applies to her own inclination to write truthfully about Christina's relationship with Rudy, shining light on their occasional conflicts and arguments. So do Oates and Gilbert write truthfully about their own absent loved ones, shining light on their occasional conflicts and arguments. Magda tells Francis that she thinks about his life as a widower because "imagining it with you now is a way of keeping company with you after I'm gone" (*The Good Husband* 105). Similarly, Godwin remains close to Starer's spirit by writing about him. Magda speaks about "haunting" Francis after her death, a haunting he welcomes. Godwin calls *Evenings at Five* a ghost story: "an encounter with a real absence can lead to a sounding through of certain values and energies of the absent person, qualities that transcend death" (xvii). The ghost manifests itself, she explains in A Reader's Guide to *Evenings at Five*, as a "leftover life that refuses to die," a life that "can inhabit the person and use the living person as an instrument" (277).

Godwin gives Magda a husband who serves her needs, but in doing so, he inadvertently thwarts her creativity. The critically and popularly acclaimed monograph Magda writes as a doctoral student, *The Book of Hell: An Introduction to the Visionary Mode*, remains her only book. Godwin confesses ruefully that although she loves Francis for the satisfaction he receives from serving other people, "there's very little of that in me!" Unlike Magda, Godwin has remained a steady and prolific novelist, as was Starer a consistently productive composer. Each was the other's lover and muse. Creativity was the hallmark of their relationship. They were far better matched in their talents and interests than were Magda and Francis.

Godwin sees Alice as a person who has been "damaged by what's happened to her," evoking the tragedies in the novelist's own life. Reflecting on her many losses, including her baby's death, Alice ponders a question that remains implicit in most of Godwin's novels, especially *Evenings at Five*. "Were losses supposed to teach you something? Did they eventually link up to meaning and growth? Or were they simply random occurrences in the planet's diurnal spin: so many infants don't make it through the birth journey, a certain number of families (minus the one who stayed at home) are extinguished in holiday traffic" (*The Good Husband* 81). Alice suffers a breakdown after her family members' deaths and visits many physicians who reach vastly different interpretations of and treatments for her depression. Dr. Anita Starling offers the most perceptive prognosis. " 'You'll always be fragile, Alice,' Dr. Starling told her at the end of their intensive therapy, 'but it's not the brittle kind of fragility that shatters like glass and can't be mended; it's more like . . . well, you've seen long-stemmed flowers after a heavy rain, how they bow all the way down to the earth. But unless their stems got broken, they rise again when the sun dries them out. Yours is that resilient kind. It goes *with* nature, not against it" (193).

Dr. Starling expresses these insights in moving figurative language and natural imagery, suggesting that she represents the authorial point of view. She advises Alice to educate her feelings as well as her mind, telling her at the end of therapy that there is always something more to learn in life. " 'You never graduate, Alice, you keep taking the courses. But what I hope we've done together is lay the groundwork for your continuing education" (194). Godwin does not rely on "grief books" in *The Good Husband* or *Evenings at Five*, as Gilbert does in *Wrongful Death*, but she affirms, through Alice and her "shrink," the power of resilience and emotional intelligence, qualities that we see throughout *Evenings at Five*. It remains unclear whether Alice and Francis will enter into a union at the end of *The Good Husband*, but she is strong enough to survive on her own, as Godwin does after Starer's death.

The novelist Hugo Henry is the least sympathetic of the four characters in *The Good Husband*. Despite his disintegrating marriage with Alice, which produces a "state of shared isolation" for both of them, the idea of a new book energizes him. He lives through his writings, and it is for this reason that Godwin identifies the most with him, as she admits self-mockingly. "Yes, he's the most me. Any scene that you see him in, I've been there: ruining a vacation in Switzerland because my books weren't in the English bookstore, and always worrying about my literary status. But, thank goodness, having written Hugo and made fun of him a little helped me distance myself from that aspect" (A Reader's Guide n.p.). Writing humorously about one's narcissism can be a de-narcissizing experience, allowing one to escape from self-importance.

Godwin's gifts as a novelist allowed her imagination free play in *The Good Husband*, but life's unpredictability, to which she remained committed, dictated the events in *Evenings at Five*. "I know I can't be with her every single moment," Francis says to Alice, "but I'd like to be with her when she dies" (296). Godwin grants Francis his wish, but she was not granted her own wish to be with Starer at the end of his life. Magda is "satisfied with the results" of her Final Examination (300); no one can say how Starer felt during the last moments of his life. Magda has insights into the lives of those around her. Did Starer? Francis, unable or unwilling to be as self-analytical as Magda wanted him to be, experiences a jolting epiphany as he strokes his wife's forehead and feels the warmth leave her body. "If only he could tell Magda this. It was exactly the sort of thing that she was always trying to pull out of him: the way he'd stood over his mother's casket and felt the terrible but exhilarating abyss of freedom

122 / Writing Widowhood

opening around him" (310). Insights like this are expressed more easily in a novel than in a fictional memoir.

"We Still Have Some More Time Together"

Irony surrounds Rudy's statement to Christina when she leaves the hospital, "We still have some more time together" (20, 109), for they turn out to be his last words to her. Nor do they realize they have run out of time together. Rudy knows he is seriously ill but not that he is dying. Neither of the two types of deaths Magda mentions—being snuffed out quickly and painlessly, with no time to prepare for one's Final Examination; and dying slowly, agonizingly, taking stock of one's life—applies to Rudy. He has been ill for more than a decade, on a slow, downward trajectory, battling both blood cancer and a weakening heart, but he and Christina assume that the end is not yet in sight.

From the opening pages of *Evenings at Five*, however, Godwin has carefully prepared readers for Rudy's death. Sometimes he brusquely shouts to her at five o'clock, their prearranged time to conclude work and begin their cocktail hour, "I won't be here forever, you know" (4). Two pages later Christina muses, returning home from the hospital where she has left him in a stable condition, *"What did I think that we had forever?"* (6). During an argument, she tries to change the subject by asking him whether he will be traveling to Boston to attend the performance of one of his compositions. "Yes. Maybe we'll go if I'm still here," he responds (10), an ominous allusion she tries to ignore. Godwin touches lightly on these intimations of mortality. Do Rudy's statements indicate anger or self-pity over his medical condition? Has he been able to follow his own advice to remain resigned but not depressed? It's not clear. "Don't you dare leave me," she warns him as she leaves the hospital for the last time, suggesting that death is never far from her mind. Their many references to the end of life suggest an apotropaic motive, as if by talking about mortality they can keep death at bay.

"Death Had Always Fascinated Rudy"

Rudy's 2001 appointment diary indicates that he and Christina continued to engage in professional activities, he composing and rehearsing, she writing novels and lecturing. There is no discussion of retirement or slowing down. Nor are there conversations about an afterlife. "Death had always fascinated Rudy far more than eternal life," Christina acknowledges, wondering whether this was a "Jewish thing" (21). Rudy remains a secular Jew, like Elliot Gilbert, and he never observes any Jewish practices or rituals. Starer spends little time in *Continuo* or *The Music Teacher* brooding over God or an afterlife.

Religion and spirituality are a vital part of Christina's life, however, far more so than with Joyce Carol Oates or Sandra Gilbert. After Rudy's funeral she sits shiva for the required weeklong mourning period, as Gilbert does after her husband's death, lighting a yahrzeit candle each night, then taking the empty glass container with the Star of David to a candle store to be refilled. These rituals comfort her and maintain her social relationship with the community. A "cradle Episcopalian" who attended a Catholic school in North Carolina, Christina, like Godwin, who attended Peace Junior College, a women's college founded by Presbyterians, thinks often about God but remains unsure about the existence of an afterlife. When a priest and parishioner visit and ask her whether she would like to pray, she replies, "I'm not sure I can."

In the emotional climax of *Evenings at Five*, the priest reads from *The Book of Common Prayer* and gently reminds Christina of the necessity for hope. " 'Hope that is seen is not hope,' Father Paul read from Romans. 'Why hope for what is already seen? But if we hope for what we do not see, we wait for it with eagerness and patience' " (108). Her body convulsing in paroxysms of crying and gasping, Christina begins to pray and immediately feels better. Godwin never mentions C. S. Lewis, but, like him, she observes her own grief, declaring that amid Christina's uncontrollable shaking her mind "coolly" registers not only her own thoughts but also those of the two people with her. Like Gilbert, Godwin would agree with Lewis's observation that "the more joy there can be in the marriage between the dead and the living, the better" (54).

In her conversation with Rob Neufeld, Godwin repeats the priest's statement and admits that her feelings about the "spirit world" are stronger than ever. After Rudy's death, Christina maintains her "sense of the quest" (*Evening at Five* 276). Agreeing with the priest's statement that "We might as well learn to accept our inseparability from God" (280), Godwin stresses the value of engaging with death. "Death is not an enemy at all; it's a room I haven't been allowed into yet. The barriers may open into unexpected landscapes" (287).

"Two Old Hearts, Still Entwined"

In *Dream Children*, Godwin cites Jung's observation that "Neurotics may be simply people who cannot tolerate the loss of myth" (48). After Starer's death, she must have thought about her discussion in *Heart* of Ovid's story of Baucis and Philemon, whom she calls "two old hearts, still entwined." She describes how in the Roman poet's story two devoted lovers, Baucis and Philemon, befriend the gods Jupiter and Mercury, who pose as poor wayfarers, and, as a reward, the lovers are granted one wish. After briefly conferring, they ask to die at the same time so one will never have to bury the other. Their wish is granted. "One day they were reminiscing about former times in their cozy little hut with the cheerful fire, when suddenly each saw the other putting forth leaves. They had only time to cry, 'Good-bye, dear heart,' and then the bark grew all around them until they became the linden and the oak entwined in each other's branches" (*Heart* 253). Godwin calls Ovid's story a "worthy example of the marriage of true minds as well as hearts" (250), an example of love that finds a way to survive human death.

Like Ovid's couple, Christina seeks a way to remain united with Rudy. After saying farewell to his body in the hospital, she hears a voice sounding like a mantra, "Absent in his presence, present in his absence." She then realizes that "somewhere in the gulf between those opposites, 'absence and presence' or 'presence and absence,' might lie the secret of eternal life." Or maybe, she wonders, "it's all one and the same, only the order of opposites is reversed: absence in presence, or presence in absence. Depending on where you are in your journey" (21). This is Christina's major discovery. Paradoxically, she listens to Rudy more closely now that he is a present absence and pays more consistent attention to him than when he was alive, something he might have pointed out to her sarcastically. The most valuable consolation notes and letters she receives are those that "opened up new possibilities for her connection with Rudy after death or because they provided models for future condolence letters she would be writing to others." She awards "first prize" to a widowed friend who told her recently that, "in his experience, love operates at a higher frequency after the death of the partner, and so it's easier to get through" (76). If this is true, then perhaps the best part of her life is not necessarily over, as she thought earlier.

"Stop All Alcohol"

Christina's religious faith does not solve all her problems, however, including a growing dependency on alcohol. Her favorite ritual with Rudy was cocktail hour at five o'clock sharp, but she drinks by herself after his death. The first hint of a problem occurs on the seventh day after his burial, when she "stumbled tipsily" to bed. Seven months later, she has changed from a "faithful" to an "increasingly immoderate observer of the ghostly cocktail hour" (*Evenings at Five* 28). Dr. Gray, the primary care physician she visits because of a frightening episode of blurred vision, gives her a prescription slip in which he prints in large block letters, "STOP ALL ALCOHOL" (50). She goes home and takes down a *New Yorker* cartoon that had "enjoyed pride of place" on the kitchen bulletin board, about a couple sitting on a sofa, drinks in hand, with the caption, "I love these great evenings at home battling alcoholism" (50).

The cartoon has been on the bulletin board long enough to have gone "brown and curly at the edges," suggesting that drinking may have been a problem for Christina, and perhaps for Rudy, *before* his death. The discreet Dr. Gray uses the expression "blotto" to describe her problem, which "left less room to wriggle out of than the euphemisms she had grown up with" (52). Recommending that it would be better for her to take a pill than to "get blotto every evening," he gives her a prescription for sleep medication. Later Christina eavesdrops on an Alcoholics Anonymous meeting. She objects to what she perceives as the exhibitionism of those who disclose at AA meetings their drinking problems. She also resents being told that she cannot have another drop of alcohol. She appears to gain control over her addiction by the end of the story, though it remains ironic that her favorite ritual with her lover now has a dark side.

Differences between *Evenings at Five* and *A Widow's Story*

Godwin never doubts the love and devotion Christina and Rudy feel for each other, and she has little interest in describing the composer's life before their meeting in 1972. She never hints at the existence of *Continuo* or *The Music Teacher*, both of which reveal much about Starer's earlier professional and personal lives. Unlike *A Widow's Story*, *Evenings at Five* does not regard a partner's or husband's past as a clue to his present life. Rudy's life before meeting Christina is not a dark mystery to be solved, as Raymond Smith's life is to Oates. The first decade of Christina's long relationship with Rudy was tempestuous, each confronting the painful scars of failed marriages, but she never writes about a crisis of doubt after her partner dies.

We don't see the intense yearning for death in *Evenings at Five* that pervades *A Widow's Story*, or the regressive desire to remain in bed, though we do see a problem with alcohol that threatens to become an addiction. The preoccupation with magical thinking that informs *A Widow's Story* and appears in *Wrongful Death* is largely absent from *Evenings at Five*. Like Oates, Godwin blames herself for not being with her partner when he dies, but she is far less guilt ridden, and she does not hold herself responsible for Starer's death. Godwin never implies, as does Oates, that widowhood is the punishment for having been a wife. Lost love leads inevitably to suffering, but that is different from self-punishment. Godwin takes to heart the consolation she offers to Oates seven years later: love is worth the suffering that accompanies loss. Godwin is stricken by loss, but she does not experience the mind-numbing depersonalization and derealization in *A Widow's Story*. Godwin finds a lifeline in writing, but unlike Oates, she finds another lifeline in religious faith.

Evenings at Five may be read as a ghost story about the ways in which a leftover life inhabits the bereft living person, but it is not a gothic horror tale. Unlike *A Widow's Story*, which is based largely on Oates's journal, *Evenings at Five* does not appear diaristic, despite Godwin's observation that she filled a 300-page journal in a month and a half after Starer's death. *Evenings at Five* combines, in Goethe's words, poetic inspiration and truth. Oates's prose in *A Widow's Story* is dense and hypercharged; Godwin's prose in *Evenings at Five* is economical and understated. Oates's story is dramatic; Godwin's lyrical. *Evenings at Five* contains a quiet dignity befitting its emotional and spiritual profundity. In *Evensong*, Godwin distinguishes between two types of grieving and quotes lines by Emily Dickinson: "Safe despair it is that raves—Agony is frugal" (119). In *Evenings at Five*, we see frugal agony.

The biggest difference between *Evenings at Five* and *A Widow's Story* is that Godwin has not fallen in love again while writing her spousal loss story. The reader thus does not feel astonished by a sudden, unexpected development, as occurs at the end of *A Widow's Story*, a "breach of narrative promise," as Julian Barnes suggests. Godwin remains closer to Rudy's spirit at the end of her story than Oates is to her deceased husband's; Rudy's presence is palpable despite his absence. Starer remains, aesthetically, a more evocative absence than either Raymond Smith or Elliot Gilbert in *A Widow's Story* or *Wrongful Death*, respectively. Christina's bond with Rudy is as strong in death as it was in life. Rudy remains alive in Christina's heart as she continues to "engage with the who and the why of him," as Godwin wrote about her deceased half-brother in *Heart*. To quote Goethe, Christina and Rudy live in and with each other; his spirit remains with her after his death. And she is comforted when she recalls his confidence in her ability to survive his death and invent new rituals without him.

Roger Rosenblatt's observation that people in grief become more like themselves applies to Godwin, who is quietly grief stricken but spiritually comforted. She remains connected with her beloved companion despite his absence, alert to the possibility that the barrier between life and death may open into unexpected landscapes. Her earlier novels, abounding in love and loss, are rehearsals for Starer's death. She writes with unflinching insight, restraint, and control. Christina and Rudy are two unique voices that are independent in rhythm yet harmonically interdependent. Godwin intuitively understands what Bernard's lover and piano accompanist fails to grasp in *The Music Teacher*: the parts of music written for two pianos are equal, like a marriage or a longtime partnership. Companionship in grief soon yields to companionship in joy.

Completing the Story

Godwin is not with Starer when he dies, but she uses the testimony of a nurse, Edward, who was there to complete the story. Edward becomes a reliable, almost omniscient narrator who tells Christina everything she wants and needs to hear about Rudy's ending. Rudy shares with Edward the happy events of the preceding years, when he and Christina traveled abroad and wrote operas and musical plays together. The composer's brief narration to Edward does not conjure the image of Magda's "Final Examination" in *The Good Husband*, though it suggests how illness compromised his life at the end. " 'But then,' you told him, 'my life slowly changed and I could do less and less' " (*Evenings at Five* 110).

Edward informs Christina about Rudy's chest pains around ten o'clock in the evening, for which he is given a nitro drip with morphine. A few hours later, his blood pressure drops precipitously, and he is soon gone, despite the best efforts of the staff. Edward's description of the nurses' response to Rudy's death is strikingly different from the coldness and impersonality surrounding Raymond Smith's death at the Princeton Medical Center or Elliot Gilbert's wrongful death at the UC Davis Medical Center. "We were devastated," Edward recounts. "We stood around the bed holding hands. We were in a daze. This man was affecting all of us. His energy was still there." Christina responds to this description by gently apostrophizing her absent lover, "You were conscious enough to bring your life story to completion, with Edward as the listener" (111).

Edward helps Rudy achieve a good ending to his life. *Evenings at Five* concludes with what Hugo Henry calls in *The Good Husband* a "closed ending," the kind of satisfying ending found in the great nineteenth-century

English novels, in which two characters stay together by overcoming early difficulties. "We get what we hoped for, or some version of what we hoped for, for the characters in the story—or for ourselves if we're talking about real life. Our lovers stay married and grow to love each other in larger ways, but they're the same lovers who started together in the beginning" (415). Disappointed in their early marriages, Christina and Rudy begin a relationship in the middle of their lives that sustains them until the latter's death—and even then the relationship continues, albeit in altered form.

By contrast, Godwin uses an "open ending" in *The Good Husband*, where Francis and Alice do not get married, as we want and expect them to do; they love each other but go their separate ways. Open endings are characteristic of most twentieth- and twenty-first-century novels, which usually conclude ambiguously, but closed endings are usually more appropriate in widowhood memoirs or, in the case of *Evenings at Five*, a fictional autobiography. A closed ending does not imply the resolution of mystery, for when Christina sees Rudy shortly after his death, she cannot describe the expression on his face. "Superiority? Bemusement beyond caring? A distanced, tranquil amusement? Satisfaction at a task completed?" (113). Christina cannot figure out how to interpret Rudy's final expression, but she knows he has led a good life and that he is at peace.

Pointers toward Wholeness

Godwin ends *Evenings at Five* with a short coda—an appropriate ending to a story about a composer, because many classical-era compositions conclude with a coda (Italian for "tail") that brings the work to a convincing resolution. " 'I used to try to be original,' you said about your work not long before you died. 'Now I try to be clear and essential' " (115). Starer comes across in *Continuo* and *The Music Teacher* as clear, essential, *and* original, as does Godwin in her writings. If Godwin remains surprisingly silent about Starer's career as a memoirist and novelist, she seizes the opportunity to promote his career as a composer, for which he will be remembered in the future. She creates, in fact, posterity selves for both of them, a gift for which her readers will be grateful.

Throughout *Evenings at Five*, Rudy appears as a present absence who remains a part of Christina. In the end, the fear expressed by Godwin in her journals that she would never love or be loved gave way to the knowledge that she loved and was loved by Starer. She has been an independent woman happy in love and work. And Starer found a woman with whom he achieved an equality that eludes Bernard Winter's grasp in *The Music Teacher*. Christina's statement to the absent Rudy, "You are with me always" (22), implies their inseparability and continuing bond. In death, he continues to protect her, as he had done in life.

Reflecting on her Final Examination, Magda thinks about what she has done for her readers in *The Book of Hell* and distinguishes between *arousers* and *fulfillers*. "I have shown them some pointers toward the wholeness, led them on day-trips toward it, but I haven't provided the wholeness myself. That is art's purpose. It may be the only way we can get what we strive for in this life. The human condition is notorious for its lack of wholeness" (*The Good Husband* 168). Magda characterizes herself as an arouser. Godwin and Starer are fulfillers, and *Evenings at Five* remains an eloquent testimony of a fulfilling union of true minds and hearts.

~~~

4

Joan Didion

The Year of Magical Thinking and *Blue Nights*

"Thank you for the Joan Didion memoir, which I'd already read—but will happily reread," Joyce Carol Oates writes to Arthur Vanderbilt on February 27, 2008, two weeks after her husband's death, adding, "I know that there is much melancholy wisdom here" (*A Widow's Story* 154). Oates refers to Didion's best-selling 2005 memoir *The Year of Magical Thinking*. The only other explicit reference to Didion is a few pages earlier when Oates reveals she is "astonished" that "writers married to each other—for instance Joan Didion and John Gregory Dunne—should share virtually every page they write" (123).

These are the only two explicit references to Didion in *A Widow's Story*, but there is a third allusion that almost certainly refers to her. Oates recalls receiving a letter from another widow who writes, *"it took me a long time to get beyond being stunned by [my husband's] death, which was in fact quite predictable. (I see now.)"* (332). Oates tells us that the "author of these words is in fact a very well-known writer whose memoir of her husband's death and her own survival a few years ago was a highly acclaimed best seller. Rereading her letter now, I wonder if it was the fact of being 'stunned' that propelled my widow-friend into writing the memoir, that so combines the clinical and the poetic—if she had understood at the time of her husband's death that his death was 'in fact quite predictable' would she have written the memoir? *Could* she?" (333). There is nothing here that is offensive, so why not name Didion? Because of what comes next. "Now I am being made to think: is there a perspective from which the widow's grief is sheer vanity; narcissism, the pretense that one's loss is so special, so very special, that there has never been a loss quite like it?" (333).

It is a distinctly curious and unempathic question to raise, particularly because the reader who feels this way about *The Year of Magical Thinking* is likely to feel the same way about *A Widow's Story*. Most readers, however, will be moved deeply by these two memoirs and recognize that there is nothing vain or narcissistic about the widow's grief. Every loss is special and devastating, as these two memoirs demonstrate.

There are many striking similarities between Joyce Carol Oates's *A Widow's Story* and Joan Didion's *The Year of Magical Thinking*. Both widowhood memoirs combine the clinical and the poetic. Both widows, married for forty years or longer, are stunned by their husbands' unexpected deaths. Both are filled with guilt, self blame, and self-loathing, replaying every "mistake" they make after their husbands' deaths. Both want to believe that knowledge is power but conclude that self-awareness does little to diminish the pain of bereavement. Both describe the acute somatic distress caused by bereavement, including tightness in the throat, insomnia, and weight loss. Both are filled with massive rage followed by acute depression. Both reread their husbands' writings for clues to their deaths and realize how little they knew their spouses. Both feel compelled to bear witness to their husbands' deaths and honor their memories. Both describe the attempts to undo loss through what Oates calls "primitive thinking" and what Didion calls "magical thinking." Both write about the derangement of grief, with Oates's basilisk resembling Didion's "vortex." Both use refrains for ironic effect—Didion repeats Gawain's statement from the *Chanson de Roland*, "I tell you that I shall not live two days." Both have no use for psychotherapy and "grief books." Both pen memoirs that record the shock, trauma, and grief of the first year of widowhood. And both turn to writing as a lifeline, a means for survival.

Like Oates, part of Didion's assumptive world is the core belief in her ability to control events, a belief that is shattered forever by the events she describes in *The Year of Magical Thinking*. Like Oates, she recognizes that grief is disabling. "Grief has no distance. Grief comes in waves, paroxysms, sudden apprehensions that weaken the knees and blind the eyes and obliterate the dailiness of life" (27). Both writers are honest enough to admit feeling self-pity and expand their sympathy for other grief-stricken widows. "I remember despising the book Dylan Thomas's widow Caitlin wrote after her husband's death, *Leftover Life to Kill*," Didion recalls. "I remember being dismissive of, even censorious about, her 'self-pity,' her 'whining,' her 'dwelling on it.' *Leftover Life to Kill* was published in 1957. I was twenty-two years old. Time is the school in which we learn" (198).

Tellingly, Didion discovers that the experience of sudden widowhood shatters forever the perspective that grief is vanity or narcissism. Like Oates, she understands "for the first time the meaning in the practice of suttee" (75) and experiences the loneliness, sorrow, and stigmatization of widowhood. Like Oates, she cannot trust herself "to present a coherent face to the world" (168). And like Oates, she feels compelled to create a written account of her husband's death, partly to make sense of sudden loss, partly to help her through the dangerous first year of bereavement, and partly to conjure up the dead to remain connected with them.

Like Sandra Gilbert, Didion recalls several arguments she had with her husband shortly before his death. Like Gilbert, she tells her husband angrily that he should not have married her. "You want a different kind of wife" (*208*). Like Gilbert, she fears she has allowed her husband to be buried alive. And like Gilbert, she uses her research skills to understand the reasons for her husband's death.

Like Gail Godwin, Didion tries to bring her husband's life to completion by writing about him and the importance of his work, in the process creating a posterity self. Like Godwin, she has written about her struggle with depression and suicidal thinking. She is Episcopalian, like Gilbert, though Didion derives little comfort from spiritual faith. Didion's fictional world is bleaker than Godwin's, and her female characters are less able to take charge of their lives and recover from tragedy. And like Godwin, Didion reveals remarkable strength and resilience in a long career devoted to writing.

The differences between *A Widow's Story* and *The Year of Magical Thinking* are worth noting. Didion's story is much shorter than Oates's, and *The Year of Magical Thinking* is not based on journal entries. Unlike Raymond Smith, who had no serious health problems before developing pneumonia and then a secondary infection in the hospital, John Gregory Dunne had a long family and personal history of cardiac problems, which he wrote about in his fictional and nonfictional books. Didion acknowledges in *The Year of Magical Thinking* that only when she reread her husband's 1989 autobiographical *Harp*, in which he reports telling her about his serious heart condition, does she realize she "had *not sufficiently appreciated*" this fear (155). John Gregory Dunne's death at the age of seventy-one was sudden—he suffered a fatal heart attack while having dinner with his wife in their Manhattan apartment on December 30, 2003—but, in view of his long cardiac history, his swift death was not surprising.

The greatest difference between *A Widow's Story* and *The Year of Magical Thinking* is that Didion experiences a second devastating loss. On the night of her husband's death, their only child, Quintana Roo Dunne Michael, had been unconscious for the previous five days in the intensive care unit of Beth Israel Medical Center in New York City, where what seemed to be a severe case of the flu developed into life-threatening pneumonia and septic shock. She made a slow recovery, but shortly after her father's funeral, when she and her new husband were in Los Angeles, she developed a massive hematoma in March 2004 and underwent a six-hour brain surgery at the UCLA Medical Center. Later she was flown to the Rusk Institute of Rehabilitation Medicine at New York University Medical Center in New York, where she spent fifteen weeks as an outpatient. Didion began writing *The Year of Magical Thinking* on October 4, 2004, completing it in eighty-eight days; by the end of the memoir Quintana had made a shaky recovery. By the time the book was published, however, Quintana had died of acute pancreatitis, on August 26, 2005, at the age of thirty-nine. Didion writes about the death in her 2011 book *Blue Nights*. And so *The Year of Magical Thinking* and *Blue Nights* describe a widow's worst nightmare, losing not only her spouse but also her only child.

One can reread John Gregory Dunne's stories to see how he was often imagining and rehearsing his own death through heart disease. The event that terrified him in life provided rich material for his art. By contrast, nothing in Quintana's life could have predicted her untimely death. And yet Didion's novels reveal that the loss of a child was, indeed, her greatest fear, one that may be seen in nearly all her stories.

Slouching towards Bethlehem

Didion's earliest reference to Quintana appears in *Slouching towards Bethlehem*, her first nonfictional book, where she writes about returning to her parents' home in the Central Valley of California with her husband and one-year-old daughter. "On Going Home" is mainly about Didion's ambivalent feelings toward her parents and the institution of marriage, which she describes as the "classic betrayal" (165). Her apprehensiveness over being a mother is tangible. She characterizes her unnamed daughter as an "open and trusting child, unprepared for and unaccustomed to the ambushes of family life" (167). She would like to promise her daughter that she will grow up "with a sense of her cousins and of rivers and of her great grandmother's teacups," but she can make no such promise because "we live differently now" (167–168). The mood of "On Going Home" is somber, even bleak, largely because Didion evokes the "nameless anxiety" that she feels about the home in which she grew up, the feeling of "neurotic lassitude" associated with the past (165–166). She feels no excitement when she shows her baby to her relatives, from whom she feels disconnected. "Questions trail off, answers are abandoned, the baby plays with the dust motes in a shaft of afternoon sun" (167). Didion knows the kind of life that is now lost to her but not the one that lies ahead.

Play It as It Lays

The feeling of loss that pervades *Slouching towards Bethlehem* dominates *Play It as It Lays*, published in 1970, when Quintana was three. One can see from the beginning of Didion's novelistic career how her worst fear is a mother's loss of her only child, a fear that predates her own daughter's death by more than three decades. The mother-child relationship has always evoked the specter of catastrophic loss in Didion's fiction. In *The Year of Magical Thinking*, she quotes a long passage from *Play It as It Lays* in which her protagonist, a thirty-one-year-old former model and actress, Maria Wyeth, learns about a friend who had an illegal abortion—an event that foreshadows Maria's own harrowing abortion near the end of the story. Didion might have quoted an even more significant detail about *Play It as It Lays*, Maria's relationship with her four-year-old daughter, Kate, who is born with a fatal birth defect. Kate screams when Maria unexpectedly visits her, a scream that reverberates throughout the mother's life. Maria's fear that Kate will soon die seems to be related to a wish for her own death.

Didion observes in *The Year of Magical Thinking* that "Things happened in life that mothers could not prevent or fix" (97), a conclusion that Maria also realizes in *Play It as It Lays*. Maria knows that it is useless to look for reasons in life to explain suffering or to believe, as her father did, that life will improve. She endures one traumatic experience after another, including having a suicidal friend, BZ (an abbreviation for benzodiazepines, on which he overdoses), die in her arms, but nothing is as horrifying as not being able to help her daughter.

Motherless, Maria comforts herself by thinking about Kate. Lying on her daughter's empty bed, she "cradled Kate's blanket, clutched Kate's baby pillow to her stomach and fought off a wave of the dread" (*Play It as It Lays* 21). Maria's frequent visits distress her child, as the authorities inform Maria's husband, Carter. "They called me to point out that unscheduled parental appearances tend to disturb the child's adjustment," to which she rightly asks, "Adjustment to what" (41). When Maria tells Carter that she is pregnant again, he demands that she have an abortion, and when she refuses, he blackmails her by threatening to take Kate. The termination of Maria's fetus, associated with the future, recalls the loss of her mother, associated with her past. With both the future and the past destroyed and her daughter Kate helpless and unavailable, Maria's present becomes unbearable. She can only dream of having the baby and being with Kate, but this dream is even more remote and unrealistic than the films that her husband-director shoots in the desert. Maria's illegal abortion turns out to be one more disaster in her life, and she almost bleeds to death. She remains obsessed with death, as can be inferred from her wish to travel to New York City, where she imagines "fetuses in the East River, translucent as jellyfish, floating past the big sewage outfalls with the orange peels" (117).

A Book of Common Prayer

Rereading *Play It as It Lays* after Quintana's death, we see not only how Didion projects her darkest fears onto the mother-daughter relationship but also how she views both motherhood and childhood as a time of heightened vulnerability. The same theme appears in her next novel, *A Book of Common Prayer*, set in the imaginary Central American country of Boca Grande. Charlotte Douglas cannot stop obsessing over her two daughters: Marin, who disappears when she is eighteen years old (we later discover that she has run off with a band of Marxist radicals), and Carlotta, who is born prematurely, hydrocephalic, with a defective liver. Charlotte's husband urges her to let the baby die in the New Orleans hospital where she was born, but she refuses and takes Carlotta to Mérida, Mexico, where she cares for her. The baby dies of convulsions in the parking lot of a Coca-Cola bottling plant. The doctor doesn't speak English but marks the death certificate in English: *death by complications*. When Charlotte asks, "Complications of what," she is told, "Complications of dying" (151).

The White Album

The most revealing self-disclosure found *anywhere* in Didion's writings appears in *The White Album*, in which she includes a psychiatrist's report written in 1968, when she entered the outpatient psychiatric clinic at Saint John's Hospital in Santa Monica for an attack of vertigo and nausea. The report is based on the results of four diagnostic tests she takes: the Rorschach, the Thematic Apperception Test, the Sentence Completion Test, and the Minnesota Multiphasic Personality Index. The tests characterize her as a "personality in process of deterioration with abundant signs of failing defenses and increasing inability of the ego to mediate the world of reality and to cope with normal stress" (14). The report details her emotional alienation; her fantasy life, "virtually completely preempted by primitive, regressive libidinal preoccupations many of which are distorted and bizarre"; and her defense mechanisms, including "intellectualization, obsessive-compulsive devices, projection, reaction-formation, and somatization, all of which now seem inadequate to their task of controlling or containing an underlying psychotic process and are therefore in process of failure" (14). The patient has a "high average or superior intelligence" but is now "functioning intellectually in impaired fashion at barely average level."

Emphasizing Didion's "fundamentally pessimistic, fatalistic, and depressive view of the world around her," the report concludes with a statement that in retrospect sounds like it could have been written *after* her husband's and daughter's deaths. "It is as though she feels deeply that all human effort is foredoomed to failure, a conviction which seems to push her further into a dependent, passive withdrawal. In her view she lives in a world of people moved by strange, conflicted, poorly comprehended, and, above all, devious motivations which commit them inevitably to conflict and failure" (*The White Album* 14–15).

Anti-Psychiatry

It is never clear why Didion includes her psychiatric diagnosis in *The White Album* or how much credibility she attaches to it. Nowhere in Didion's writings do we see her in the process of self-deterioration, not even in *The Year of Magical Thinking*, where she *tells* us that she is incapable of thinking "rationally" (35) but *shows* us her remarkable self-control. For authors like Didion, it is not living well that is the best revenge but doing well, *writing* well; publishing a book about the writer's "failing defenses" represents, in her view, a rejection of the accuracy of the diagnosis. Didion's observation that she was selected by the *Los Angeles Times* as a "Woman of the Year" in 1968 further calls into question the diagnosis of being intellectually impaired. Including her psychiatric diagnosis in *The White Album* is admittedly a risky strategy, but it allows Didion to suggest how repressive and out of touch psychiatry was in the 1960s, a decade that saw the publication of such antipsychiatric novels as Ken Kesey's *One Flew Over the Cuckoo's Nest* and Doris Lessing's *The Golden Notebook*.

Like Oates, Didion has familiarized herself with clinical theory and consistently derides psychology, psychiatry, psychoanalysis, and psychopharmacology in her fictional and nonfictional writings. In *The Year of Magical Thinking*, she attacks Vamik D. Volkan, a professor of psychiatry at the University of Virginia and the creator of "re-grief therapy," in which patients are encouraged to keep lost loved ones alive. Admitting that her anger toward Volkan is "irrational," she nevertheless disparages all mental health professionals. As in Oates's fictional world, no psychotherapist in any of Didion's fictional or nonfictional writings offers real insight, help, or compassion.

Didion's hostility toward psychiatry appears at the beginning of *Blue Nights*, when she discusses Karl Menninger's classic 1938 study of suicide, *Man Against Himself.* Menninger, who along with his father founded the Menninger Clinic in Topeka, Kansas, which became the largest psychiatric center in the world, cites, in Didion's words, "the young woman who becomes depressed and kills herself after cutting her hair. He mentions the man who kills himself because he has been advised to stop playing golf, the child who commits suicide because his canary died, the woman who kills herself after missing two trains." She agrees with part of Menninger's discussion, particularly his statement that these instances of suicide are examples of "severed emotional bonds" to which she adds, "Yes, clearly, no argument." She then takes issue with Menninger's question, "But why should such extravagantly exaggerated over-estimations and incorrect evaluations exist?" She answers the question with two rhetorical questions. "Did he imagine that he had answered the question simply by raising it? Did he think that all he had to do was formulate the question and then retreat into a cloud of theoretical psychoanalytic references?" (10–11).

Man Against Himself is not simply a cloud of psychoanalytic references, however. Many of the psychiatrist's statements are illuminating, such as his belief that suicide must be regarded as a "peculiar kind of death which entails three internal elements: the element of dying, the element of killing, and the element of being killed" (24). Menninger recognizes that "persons prone to suicide prove upon examination to be highly *ambivalent in their object attachments, that is, masking with their conscious positive* attachments large and scarcely mastered quantities of unconscious hostility" (29), an observation that is consistent with contemporary attachment theory. He understands that what is "characteristic of a very large number of suicides is the apparent inadequacy of the precipitating event" (35), a statement that applies to the suicides in Didion's and Dunne's novels. It is true, as Didion notes, that Menninger raises the question of why "such extravagantly exaggerated over-estimations and incorrect evaluations exist," but he follows it up with a statement that indicates his refusal to be content with rhetorical questions. "We cannot dismiss the matter by saying they were foolish people; we must know why their folly expressed itself in this particular way, if we are to understand why aggressive tendencies can become self-directed" (*Man Against Himself* 36). And almost certainly Didion would agree with Menninger's assertion that suicide is not only symbolic murder of another person (or persons) but also the turning inward of aggression against the self, resulting in self-punishment for the guilt arising from murderous violence.

In short, Didion's rejection of psychiatry does not invalidate the insights arising from psychiatric theory and practice. Nor must we accept at face value her rejection of her own psychiatric diagnosis. We do not see in *The Year of Magical Thinking* the writer in the "process of self-deterioration," the observation made in her psychiatric diagnosis that she includes in *The White Album*, but there is at least one way in which the psychiatric report is true. Throughout Didion's writings, her vision has remained "fundamentally pessimistic, fatalistic, and depressive." Many of her novels and essays are undeniably dark, stark, and bleak. For this reason, it is startling to hear Didion state in *The Year of Magical Thinking* that her impression of herself "had been of someone who could look for, and find, the upside in any situation. I had believed in the logic of popular songs. I had looked for the silver lining" (171). We see a silver lining in none of Didion's books, including those written decades before her husband's and daughter's deaths.

Self-Help Books

To understand Didion's—and Oates's—mistrust of psychiatry, we may raise the larger question of their disapproval of self-help books. As Sandra K. Dolby points out in a nuanced study, self-help books tend to arouse suspicion and mistrust from intellectual readers, even when the self-help books are written by academics themselves. This is particularly true of popular psychology books written by trained mental health professionals. Authors of self-help books propose simplistic solutions or "cures" to "wounded," "addicted," "needy," or "dysfunctional" readers, which explains why this genre is so often dismissed and parodied.

And yet Dolby suggests that despite their limitations, self-help books have value. "People use contemporary self-help books in their own learning projects, much as people have used classical philosophy and the Bible in the past" (xi). As we have seen, highly intellectual readers like Sandra Gilbert have learned much from "grief books." Readers of self-help books enhance their understanding of physical and mental health, relationships, and the universe. One function of self-help books is that they provide their authors "with an opportunity to bear witness to their own transformation or conversion" (48). Another function is that they demonstrate the importance of seeking help. The popularity of the genre reflects a cultural paradox. "Americans think they are simple selves—broad-shouldered, active, natural, and unreflective—but the popularity of the self-help book demonstrates that they are not" (66). A folklorist, Dolby acknowledges that many academics are ambivalent about self-help books. Scholars often consult self-help books in their private lives even as they believe it is their duty to stamp them out in their professional careers.

Didion is certainly one of those writers, along with Oates, who has studied psychiatric textbooks and self-help books in order to eradicate them. All of Didion's books reveal more than a casual knowledge of the burgeoning number of psychiatric and psychological self-help books on depression, mourning, and bereavement. Didion has put her depression to good use, as Doug Underwood suggests in *Chronicling Trauma*, by showing the "capacity to turn compulsive ruminations into creative products" (175). She remains, nonetheless, dismissive of psychiatric self-help books, suspicious of any clinical or popular text that offers relief from suffering. The psychiatric diagnosis in *The White Album* appears to be one of the counternarratives that Didion must resist in order to keep living and writing.

Dutch Shea, Jr.

Didion's two fictional daughters, Kate in *Play It as It Lays* and Carlotta in *A Book of Common Prayer*, reveal the novelist's generalized fear of losing a child to the "complications of dying." Didion's husband, John Gregory Dunne, imagines an even worse fate for his major fictional daughter. In *Dutch Shea, Jr.*, the eponymous protagonist, a disillusioned criminal lawyer who plays life on the dark keys, and his bitter ex-wife, Lee, lose their only child, eighteen-year-old Catherine, "Cat," when she is blown up in a French restaurant by IRA terrorists. Cat is the sole victim: Lee has gone to the ladies' room when the explosion occurs. Dutch Shea Jr. cannot exorcise the image of his daughter's horrific death. The death haunts him throughout the novel, especially because he had made the reservation at the restaurant in which she was blown up. Guilt ridden, he fears he will forget his lost daughter. He tries to immerse himself in work, "chemotherapy for a metastasizing memory," but nothing diminishes his despair, and at the end of the story the bereft father commits suicide, invoking Cat's name and God's in his last breath.

Dunne establishes two biographical connections between his daughter, Quintana, and Cat. The first connection is that they are both haunted by the same nightmarish figure. Dutch Shea Jr. sees, in a secret drawer of his maple desk on the third floor of their home on Asylum Street in West Hartford, Connecticut, a note he had written when Cat was a young child about "the Broken Man," her personification of fear, death, and the unknown. "I had a bad dream about the Broken Man, she would say. Don't let the Broken Man catch me. If the Broken Man comes, I'll hang onto the fence and won't let him take me" (*Dutch Shea, Jr.* 25). He wonders whether the Broken Man had time to frighten her before she died. That's all we learn about the Broken Man in *Dutch Shea, Jr.*, but Dunne reveals in *Harp* that this was also Quintana's fear. "When my daughter was a child, she would often have nightmares about death. In these terrifying dreams, death was not an abstraction, but a person she called 'the Broken Man.' If the Broken Man comes, she would sob, I'll hold on to the fence so that he cannot get me." Dunne adds that he thought about the Broken Man often as one of his aunts drifted toward death. "Life seemed to be the fence to which she clung in terror, trying to stave off the grasping fingers of the Broken Man" (*Harp* 222). Dunne never reveals that he used his daughter's fear of the Broken Man in *Dutch Shea, Jr.*

In *The Year of Magical Thinking*, Didion quotes the passage about Cat and the Broken Man from *Dutch Shea, Jr.* She returns to the Broken Man in *Blue Nights*, quoting some of her daughter's actual notes about the monster and then adding that Quintana's descriptions were so frequent and vivid that Didion herself began to believe in his presence. There's a double irony associated with the Broken Man. "After I became five," Quintana discloses, "I never ever dreamed about him" (51), a statement that Didion finds so startling that she repeats it several times in the book. The other irony, more unsettling, is that Didion's fear of the Broken Man has darkened her entire life, a fear that comes true.

Adopted Daughters

The second biographical connection between Quintana and Cat is that both are adopted daughters. "It was a private adoption," Dutch Shea Jr. muses to himself. "He had never had the slightest interest in Cat's natural parents until her death. One day he wanted to tell them what sort of child she had been, what sort of daughter. But then Cat never had been their daughter. He wondered if Cat were even of interest to them. Cat. This angel boarder. *That* angel boarder" (*Dutch Shea, Jr.* 96). Dunne's convoluted plot leads to his protagonist's discovery near the end of the story that a priest is Catherine's biological father, a discovery he then imagines revealing to her in a mordant apostrophe: "Father. Pater. Père. Poppa. Pop. Pa. Daddy. Dad. *Your dad is your dad*" (388).

Dunne could imagine using a daughter's adoption as one of several details in a terror attack in a novel, but he took great pains to avoid sensationalism when he discussed his own daughter's adoption in *Quintana & Friends*. The title essay, "Quintana," less than seven pages long, is one of Dunne's best: insightful, warmhearted, elegantly written. The opening sentences—"Quintana will be eleven this week. She approaches adolescence with what I can only describe as panache, but then watching her journey from infancy has always been like watching Sandy Koufax pitch or Bill Russell play basketball" (3)—capture a father's fierce pride in his daughter. These sentences have special pathos for Didion, for we learn near the end of *Blue Nights* that they were read aloud at Quintana's memorial service. Dunne, who is spared this poignant irony, recalls how he and his wife visited the newborn in the hospital nursery seventeen hours after her birth, looking at the letters "NI" on her name tag, "No Information," and then ends the paragraph with three words: "Quintana is adopted."

Dunne's essay gives us a good deal of information about raising an adopted daughter, beginning with his awareness of the complexity of adoption for the biological mother, the adopted child, and the adoptive parents. The essay charts Quintana's journey from childhood to the beginning of adolescence. Changing cultural attitudes and laws only heighten the confusion and uncertainty surrounding adoption. Many young unwed mothers gave up their babies for adoption in 1966, when Quintana was born, an era when abortion was still illegal in the United States and when children were seldom told they were adopted or given the details of their biological parents. "Today we are more enlightened," Dunne observes, "aware of the psychological evidence that such barbaric secrecy can only inflict hurt" (*Quintana & Friends* 4). He also conveys the frustration of adoptive parents when they hear the well-meaning but thoughtless comment "You couldn't love her more if she were your own," to which he replies, "At moments like that, my wife and I say nothing and smile through gritted teeth" (3). The only official information Dunne and Didion were given at the time of adoption was the biological mother's age when she gave birth, where she was from, and a certified record of her health. Through one bureaucratic slipup, the adoptive parents learned of the name of Quintana's birth mother, and through another, the birth mother learned of their names and Quintana's.

Quintana's parents "tried never to equivocate" that she was adopted, and because they always had "Spanish-speaking help," one of the first words she learned, before she knew its meaning, was *adoptada*. "I tried to explain that adoption offered to a parent the possibility of escaping the prison of genes, that no matter how perfect the natural child, the parent could not help acknowledging in black moments that some of his or her bad blood was bubbling around in the offspring; with an *adoptada*, we were innocent of any knowledge of bad blood" (*Quintana & Friends* 5). It's impossible to tell from this passage whether there was indeed bad blood bubbling around in Dunne or Didion, which might explain why they decided not to have their own children, a fear that may be seen in the two infants born with fatal birth defects in *Play It as It Lays* and *A Book of Common Prayer*, or whether Dunne was understandably telling Quintana what he thought she wanted to hear.

Dunne's delight in storytelling is evident in "Quintana" when he recounts to his daughter the details of her adoption. Realism soon gives way to mythology. "As she grew older, she never tired of asking us how we happened to adopt her. We told her that we went to the hospital and were given our choice of any baby in the nursery. 'No, not that baby,' we had said, 'not that baby, not that baby . . .' All this with full gestures of inspection, until finally: 'That baby!' Her face would always light up and she would say: 'Quintana'" (5). In *Blue Nights*, Didion calls this, with bittersweet irony, the "recommended choice narrative," a story that does not lead in Quintana's case to a happy ending. Quintana asked her parents, when she was young, how old her "other mommy" was when she was born, and she was told "eighteen," the age, we recall, at which Cat is blown up in *Dutch Shea, Jr.* We discover late in the novel that Cat meets her mother at the ill-fated restaurant mainly to tell her she is pregnant. In *Quintana & Friends*, Dunne refers to the "twin traumas of birth and the giving up of a child" experienced by his daughter's birth mother, but he projects onto Dutch Shea Jr. the traumas of losing both his beloved daughter and future grandchild in a horrific explosion. Dunne can imagine as a novelist a father losing his daughter, but he is not willing to imagine this grim possibility in real life. And yet he is certainly aware of some of the similarities between Quintana and Cat, apart from their common fear of the Broken Man, which he does not include in "Quintana." Using the same angelic term that his fictional father uses in *Dutch Shea, Jr.*, Dunne concludes "Quintana" by remarking that "All parents realize, or should realize, that children are not possessions, but are only lent to us, angel boarders, as it were" (10).

Dunne's love for his daughter is palpable throughout "Quintana," and she appears "remarkably well adjusted," to use his brother's words. Indeed, she is so proud of being adopted that the twenty girls who attended her eighth birthday party were jealous that they were *not* adopted, one classmate even claiming, "Well, I was almost adopted" (6).

Dunne concedes that difficulties may arise when adopted children grow up and seek to discover their biological mothers, who may or may not wish to meet their offspring. He recognizes the potential problems of disclosing too much personal information about his daughter. "I of course discussed this piece with her before I began working on it. I told her what it was about and said I would drop it if she would be embarrassed or if she thought the subject was too private" (*Quintana & Friends* 7). Quintana thought about the questions and then said she wanted him to write about her. He knows that in a few years she may wish to seek out her birth mother; if so, he and his wife will support Quintana in whatever ways they can. He also knows that because writers are "at least semipublic figures," the publication of the essay may prove upsetting to his daughter's birth mother. His hope, what he calls a "romantic fantasy," is that the birth mother will welcome Quintana's efforts to locate her. What's not fantasy, Dunne continues, is that Quintana asked her parents when she was ten for her birth mother's name, and, taking a "deep breath," they told her. Later he asks what she would do if she met her birth mother. "I'd put one arm around Mom,' she said, 'and one arm around my other mommy, and I'd say, 'Hello, Mommies.'" If it turns out this way, Dunne adds, "that is what she will do" (10).

Nothing diminishes Dunne's joy over Quintana or his belief in her bright future. He acknowledges on the final page of "Quintana" that he does not know the end of the story. How can he if his daughter is only eleven? He imagines only the best for her, and we are left with a father's unwavering confidence that his daughter's passage into adulthood will continue to be joyful.

We see a continuation of the story in Jill Krementz's edited volume *How It Feels to Be Adopted*, in which Quintana offers her own perspective at age sixteen. The essay, even shorter than Dunne's "Quintana," never names her parents, though there is a photo of them with their daughter. There's also a photo of Quintana sitting at her desk, next to a typewriter, looking like a young writer. Many of Quintana's observations repeat, sometimes word for word, those appearing in her father's essay, including her parents inspecting every baby in the nursery until they found the right one; her bracelet with the letters NI; her nickname, *L'adoptada*; her birth mother being eighteen when Quintana was born; her adoptive parents' willingness to tell her everything they know about her adoption; and her response if she found her real mother: "I would put one arm around Mom and one arm around my other Mommy, and I'd say, 'Hello, Mommies'" (Krementz 61).

A comparison of the two brief essays reveals that Quintana views her early life, including her adoption, in the same way that her father does. Writing enables father and daughter to convey their stories intergenerationally. One new detail in Quintana's essay is that her biological father was twenty-one when she was born. (Dunne remarks parenthetically in his essay that the birth mother had never named the birthfather and that, "even more interesting, Quintana has never asked about him"). Another new detail is that when Quintana gets into arguments with her parents, "I think maybe my *real* parents would be more understanding. It's a terrible thing for me to do, and I've never said anything about it" (Krementz 58).

Quintana takes pride in her ability to see life clearly and deeply. "My parents always tell me that I have a great ability to sense things that are going on, like observing other people the way a writer does; and if that's true, then that's a quality that probably emerged from the way I was brought up, because my parents are both writers" (Krementz 58). She attributes her interest in writing, then, not to genes but to upbringing. Ironically, most of the material in Quintana's essay comes from her father's own essay about her, raising the question who "owns" the story of Quintana's young life, the daughter or the father?

The Year of Magical Thinking

Flash forward twenty-seven years from Dunne's *Quintana & Friends* to *The Year of Magical Thinking*. Quintana, now in her late thirties, newly married, lies gravely ill in a New York City hospital as her father dies suddenly from a heart attack. The mother, devastated by her husband's death, visits her daughter every day, hoping she will soon be able to leave the hospital. In March, Quintana and her husband fly to Los Angeles, beginning their new life, when suddenly she is struck down once again, this time by a cerebral hemorrhage that requires emergency brain surgery. Didion flies to Los Angeles to accompany her daughter back to New York City, where she will begin rehabilitation. Apart from revealing in *The Year of Magical Thinking* Quintana's two medical crises and tentative recoveries, along with the ways in which Dunne included her fear of the Broken Man in *Dutch Shea, Jr.*, Didion offers us little insight into her daughter's personal life. Didion's focus is mainly on her husband, where it should be in a spousal loss memoir. Moreover, she doesn't wish to invade her daughter's privacy.

John Gregory Dunne's death shatters Didion's lifelong hope that intelligence and control can keep the Broken Man at bay. Though she is struck by the irony of a social worker's characterization of her as a "pretty cool customer," Didion has always operated under the assumption that knowledge is power. *"Information is control"* has been her mantra *(The Year of Magical Thinking* 94), a guiding assumption she has put to good use in her journalistic and political writings. She shared the "core belief" in her "ability to control events" (98). And yet in the same paragraph she admits that because she was "born fearful," she knew that some events would remain beyond her control. Fear produces in her, as in many people who value intelligence and control, strong counterphobic motivation that compels her to learn everything she can about her daughter's two medical crises.

Researching Quintana's cerebral hemorrhage, Didion reads everything she can on the subject. She doesn't believe her daughter is the victim of medical malpractice, but she uses her research skills to make recommendations to Quintana's physicians, as Gilbert does in *Wrongful Death*. Didion reads a paperback copy of John F. Murray's *Intensive Care: A Doctor's Journal*, paying close attention to his discussion of the difficulty of deciding when it is the right time for extubation, the removal of a patient's endotracheal tube. She notices a "stiffening" among Quintana's physicians when she uses the word "edema," suggesting their anger over her implicit criticism of their expertise. In recording with scientific precision the details of her daughter's illness and treatment, she casts an ironic eye on her own involvement in the story. She tells us, for example, that upon landing in Los Angeles, she bought several sets of cotton scrubs to wear while she visited her daughter. "So profound was the isolation in which I was then operating that it did not immediately occur to me that for the mother of a patient to show up at the hospital wearing blue cotton scrubs could only be viewed as a suspicious violation of boundaries" (*The Year of Magical Thinking* 106).

Didion is also willing to reveal when her memory fails her, especially her knowledge of her husband's writings about Quintana. Dunne recalls in *Harp* the family tragedies that struck in the 1980s, including the suicide of his brother Stephen and the murder of a young niece, Dominique:

> "Most of my friends have never been to a funeral," my daughter Quintana said after Dominique was killed. "I've had a murder and a suicide in my family." Quintana was sixteen.
>
> I told her that eventually things would even out. This is the kind of placebo parents give children to help explain tragedy.
>
> I am not altogether sure that things do even out. (*Harp* 106)

Didion elaborates on this passage in *The Year of Magical Thinking*, recalling her husband telling Quintana, "It all evens out in the end," an answer that seemed to satisfy her daughter at the time but not Didion herself. Several years later, Didion's friend Susan Traylor, whose parents had recently died, repeated Dunne's statement:

> "He was right," Susan said. "It did."
>
> I recall being shocked. It had never occurred to me that John meant that bad news will come to each of us. Either Susan or Quintana had surely misunderstood. I explained to Susan that John had meant something entirely different: he had meant that people who get bad news will eventually get their share of good news.
>
> "That's not what I meant at all," John said.
>
> "I knew what he meant," Susan said.
>
> Had I understood nothing? (173).

Didion never mentions that this incident appears in *Harp*. One who has not read Dunne's book is likely to accept her conclusion that she understood "nothing." The passage in *Harp*, however, is more ambiguous, and one can certainly conclude, as Didion initially did, "mistakenly," that there might be a degree of truth in the "placebo" a father offers to his teenage daughter.

Didion's willingness in *The Year of Magical Thinking* to accept blame for events beyond her control and for memory lapses that only those with a photographic memory can recall reminds us of the similar self-blame in *A Widow's Story* and *Wrongful Death*. Didion's self-blame is entirely in character in the sense that most of her fictional female characters are also self-blaming. But on some level Didion must know, as we suspect Oates and Gilbert must know, that readers will hold them blameless for events beyond their control.

Toward the end of *The Year of Magical Thinking*, Didion reveals that she does not want to complete her memoir—or the first year of mourning. "The craziness is receding but no clarity is taking its place," she admits, adding, "I look for resolution and find none" (225). Had her husband heard her, he might have repeated what he wrote in *Harp*: "Clarity only comes when pen is in hand, or at the typewriter or the word processor, clarity about what we feel and what we think, how we love and how we mourn; the words on the page constitute the benediction, the declaration, the confession of the emotionally inarticulate" (15–16). Dunne knew that writing is a way to achieve control and clarity: that's why he created so many autobiographical characters who brood over their cardiac problems. Writing enabled him to keep his demons at bay, though he eventually succumbed to what he feared most. Writing about grief allowed Dunne and Didion to master their demons or at least to live with them, all the while transmuting potentially paralyzing fears into lively stories.

The Year of Magical Thinking: The Play

And so it is in character that Didion, always the writer, returned to *The Year of Magical Thinking* after Quintana's death and transformed it into a one-woman play. Directed by David Hare and starring Vanessa Redgrave, *The Year of Magical Thinking: The Play* did not achieve the literary success of the memoir, which won the 2005 National Book Award for Nonfiction and was a finalist for the National Book Critics Circle Award and the Pulitzer Prize for Biography/Autobiography. Nevertheless, the play received generally positive reviews, and acclaimed productions have taken place in London, Australia, and Canada.

Writing the play enables Didion to hold onto her memories of her husband and daughter while acknowledging her double loss. She observes, at the beginning of the memoir, that "the way I write is who I am, or have become" (7). Writing the play compels her to create a new prose style and a new identity. She has always been a master stylist. In his introduction to *We Tell Ourselves Stories in Order to Live*, a collection of Didion's nonfiction published in 2006, John Leonard points out her inimitable prose. "I have been trying to figure out why her sentences are better than mine or yours . . . something about cadence. They come at you, if not from ambush, then in gnomic haikus, icepick laser beams, or waves. Even the space on the page around these sentences is more interesting than it ought to be, as if to square a sandbox for a Sphinx" (x).

One of the major differences between the memoir and the play is that Didion directly addresses the audience in the latter, something she does not do in the former. The viewers, whom she addresses repeatedly as "you," become a part of the drama. This heightens the urgency of her cautionary tale by reminding viewers that they too will find themselves in her situation. "This happened on December 30, 2003," the play begins. "That may seem a while ago, but it won't when it happens to you. And it will happen to you. The details will be different, but it will happen to you. That's what I'm here to tell you" (1).

Didion has long cultivated a tough, staccato prose style—austere, detached, spare, cool, ironic—but she takes this to an extreme in the play, which consists of more single-sentence paragraphs than does the memoir, along with more "white space." The single sentences read like lines in a poem, contributing to the poetic nature of her prose. Perhaps because of the spectacular success of the memoir, which popularized the idea of magical thinking and the deranging nature of grief, she knew that most viewers of the play would be familiar with her double loss. She knows she cannot surprise or shock her audience. Instead, she chooses a narrative strategy of reminding viewers that sooner or later they will find themselves in her situation. Near the end of the play, she quotes a paragraph from her memoir beginning with the sentence "Grief turns out to be a place none of us know until we reach it" (*Play* 58), but she now insists that her "lesson for survival" should be heeded.

The play contains a didactic tone that is absent from the memoir. Didion shares her experiences, praiseworthy and blameworthy, telling viewers what they can expect when they accompany a severely ill relative or friend to the hospital in an ambulance. She offers a chronology of her daughter's medical events to assure viewers that she can "still do dates" (27). She also anticipates viewers' efforts to call into question her sanity to distance themselves from her story. "If I'm sane, what happened to me could happen to you" (44). She remains "sane" even when she claims that occasionally she was deranged by grief. She cannot save her husband or daughter from death—no one could—but she never doubts that she can write an account of their deaths.

Blue Nights

Blue Nights is a memoir, not a play, but Didion continues to use the second-person pronoun, partly to achieve greater closeness and directness with her readers. She sometimes sounds like a college lecturer reminding her audience about past statements made in good faith that are now cruelly ironic, as when she recalls toasting Quintana and her husband, Gerry, on their wedding day, July 26, 2003: "we could see no reason to think that such ordinary blessings would not come their way. Do notice: We still counted happiness and health and love and luck and beautiful children as 'ordinary blessings' " (29–30). She uses the imperative form of verbs to remind readers to pay attention: "notice," "think that over," "do note," "you notice."

Sometimes Didion becomes impatient with her readers, annoyed that they may not grasp what is obvious. She and her husband authorize their lawyer to give Quintana whatever help she requests to locate her biological parents, but Didion begins to feel that "there comes a point, I told myself, at which a family is, for better or worse, finished." She immediately anticipates a reader's objection that Quintana may not believe her family is finished. "Yes. I just told you. *Of course* I had considered this possibility. Accepting it would be something else" (124). As in the play, the dialogical "I-you" relationship in *Blue Nights* creates a conversational, confessional quality that implicates the reader in the story.

In *Blue Nights*, Didion aims for maximum directness in her prose. She contrasts the ease with which she penned her 1996 novel *The Last Thing He Wanted*, which she implies was written spontaneously, almost formulaically, with the difficulty of crafting *The Year of Magical Thinking* and *Blue Nights*. "For a while I laid this to a certain weariness with my own style, an impatience, a wish to be more direct. I encouraged the very difficulty I was having laying words on the page. I saw it as evidence of a new directness. I see it now differently. I see it now as frailty" (105). After elaborating on this frailty, including her growing fear of falling, Didion wonders whether the "absence of style" that she encouraged has now "taken on a pernicious life of its own" (110). But it would be misleading to characterize the directness she achieves in *Blue Nights* as an "absence of style." Rather, it is a direct, intimate, colloquial style, one whose surface simplicity conceals highly wrought prose.

Didion never fears that her frailty will prevent her from telling a "true story" (109). She doesn't define true story, but she would probably insist that everything in the story has taken place as she describes it and that nothing has been withheld that would significantly change the story. Part of the challenge of writing a true *personal* story is knowing what to include and exclude, a challenge that is daunting in *The Year of Magical Thinking*, when Quintana is still alive, and even more daunting in *Blue Nights*, when she is dead.

Didion mentions in the play that she asked her daughter to read *The Year of Magical Thinking* before submitting it for publication. "Because the book was about events that touched the heart of Quintana's life and of which she had no firsthand memory, I asked her to read the manuscript. She said it was 'very good.' 'Really interesting'" (*Play* 53). Another reason for showing her daughter the manuscript was to be certain that Quintana did not believe her privacy was being invaded. John Gregory Dunne had given his daughter a copy of "Quintana" for the same reason: to make sure she did not feel her privacy was being violated.

Borderline Personality Disorder

One can only guess how Quintana would have responded to her mother's disclosures about her life in *Blue Nights*, where Didion refers to her daughter's "startling depths and shallows" of expressions, the "quicksilver changes of mood" (36). This is not surprising or problematic in itself, for many people experience sudden mood changes; but what *is* surprising and problematic is Didion's decision to reveal her daughter's extensive psychiatric problems. "Of course they were eventually assigned names, a 'diagnosis.' The names kept changing. Manic depression for example became OCD and OCD was short for obsessive-compulsive disorder and obsessive-compulsive disorder became something else, I could never remember just what but in any case it made no difference because by the time I did remember there would be a new name, a new 'diagnosis.' I put the word 'diagnosis' in quotes because I have not yet seen that case in which a 'diagnosis' led to a 'cure,' or in fact to any outcome other than a confirmed, and therefore an enforced, debility'" (47).

Didion's pessimism over her daughter's diagnosis may have been influenced by her own history of mood disorders. Ruth Davis Konigsberg suggests plausibly that Didion's depression before her husband's death "would make her more likely to experience a recurrence after a cascade of tragic events such as the death of her husband and fatal illness of her only child" (49–50). Didion's discouraging experience with psychiatry would thus prevent her from being hopeful about her daughter's own treatment.

Didion implies in *Blue Nights* that her daughter was depressed for a long time and that she medicated with alcohol. The clinical diagnosis that seemed the most accurate to her "least programmatic doctor" was "borderline personality disorder," which Didion then defines. " 'Patients with this diagnosis are a complex mixture of strengths and weaknesses that confuse the diagnostician and frustrate the psychotherapist.' So notes a 2001 *New England Journal of Medi ,ne* review of John G. Gunderson's *Borderline Personality Disorder: A Clinical Guide.* 'Such patients may seem charming, composed, and psychologically intact one day and collapse into suicidal despair the next.' The review continues: 'Impulsivity, affective lability, frantic efforts to avoid abandonment, and identity diffusion are all hallmarks.' " To which Didion adds, dejectedly, "I had seen most of these hallmarks" (48).

Reading Didion's comments about this review, written by Glen O. Gabbard, one would conclude that borderline personality disorder is untreatable. Reading both the review and Gunderson's book, however, one would reach the opposite conclusion. Gabbard states that although borderline patients were once seen as having an "untreatable and irrevocably chronic disease," new psychotherapeutic approaches have resulted in a sea change: "Guided by a growing body of empirical research, psychiatrists can now feel guardedly optimistic about the outcome when a carefully thought out treatment plan has been implemented" (Gabbard 1003).

Gunderson lays out the treatment plan in his 2001 book *Borderline Personality Disorder: A Clinical Guide,* a sequel to an earlier edition published in 1984. Gunderson's 2001 book illuminates what is generally a misunderstood psychiatric diagnosis. The book also deepens our understanding of Quintana's complex character. Widely recognized as one of the world's experts on the subject, Gunderson notes that borderline personality disorder is a relatively recent clinical diagnosis, entering the American Psychiatric Association's *DSM-III* in 1980. "It is easily the most widely and commonly used diagnosis for personality disorders in modern clinical practice" (1). Those with borderline personality disorder constitute about 2 to 3 percent of the general population, 25 percent of all inpatients, and about 15 percent of all outpatients. For reasons that Gunderson never explains, about 75 percent of borderline personality disorder patients are female, while roughly the same percentage of antisocial personality disorder patients are male.

Some clinicians have dismissed borderline personality disorder as a "wastebasket" diagnosis, implying it has no real clinical meaning. Patients who receive this diagnosis may mistakenly believe there is little possibility for therapeutic improvement. The label "borderline" captures an unhappy truth, Gunderson admits: "most clinicians don't like borderline patients. More to the point, most clinicians don't like patients who are angry, critical, rejecting, mocking, or even contemptuous toward them" (21). Nevertheless, Gunderson remains optimistic about diagnosing and treating what was first considered a personality *organization*, then a *syndrome*, and now a *disorder*.

One of the main symptoms of BPD, and the one that Didion spends the most time discussing in *Blue Nights*, is the fear of abandonment. "Although borderline patients are quite aware of abandonment fears," Gunderson observes, "some are so accustomed to acting out in response to such fears that they do not recognize the fears" (14). The fear of abandonment, he points out, is now viewed as a symptom of early insecure attachment. Along with abandonment fear are related symptoms: unstable relationships that alternate between idealization and devaluation, impulsivity, affective instability (including anxiety, depression, and irritability), intense anger or lack of control of anger, suicidal threats or self-mutilating behavior, identity disturbance and unstable self-image, chronic feelings of emptiness or boredom, and stress-related paranoia or dissociation.

As with nearly all psychiatric diagnoses, there are many genetic, developmental, and familial risk factors associated with the development of BPD. Families rarely wish to be told that they have contributed to the formation of a borderline patient. The few clinical books published during the 1980s and 1990s "combined to paint a very bleak and very critical picture of the health, function, and motivation of borderline patients' families" (Gunderson 191). Families of mentally ill patients are often defensive, fearing they may have contributed to their child's psychiatric problem; their defensiveness is "exaggerated when the offspring has borderline personality disorder and thus is particularly angry and devaluative" (198). The portrait of the borderline patient's parents has changed recently, however, along with treatment options, and Gunderson describes how he speaks to a patient's family, avoiding both clinical jargon and a judgmental tone:

> People with a borderline personality disorder have grown up feeling that they were unfairly treated, that they didn't get the attention or care they needed. They are angry about that, and as young adults, they set out in search of someone who can make up to them for what they feel is missing. Hence, they set in motion intense, exclusive relationships, which then fail because they place unrealistic expectations on the other person. Upon

failing, they feel rejected or abandoned, and they can either become enraged again about its unfairness (as they did when growing up), or they can feel they are bad and unlovable, in which case they become suicidal or self-destructive.

Either their anger at being mistreated or their feeling bad and being self-destructive can cause others—especially parents—to feel guilty and try to make it up to them; it naturally evokes wishes to protect or rescue. Such responses from others, especially parents, unfortunately validate borderline persons' unrealistically high expectations of having their needs met, and the cycle is apt to repeat itself. (197)

Gunderson cites evidence from other researchers that borderline patients have three major assumptions: "1) The world is dangerous and malevolent. 2) I am powerless and vulnerable. 3) I am inherently unacceptable" (180). Marsha M. Linehan, the creator of a new therapeutic approach, dialectical behavior therapy, proposes that there is a marked discrepancy between borderline patients' perceptions of themselves and their parents' perceptions. For this reason, Gunderson suggests, communication between borderline patients and their families is essential, along with the therapists' validation of patients and their families.

Family interventions for borderline patients are important, Gunderson suggests, mainly because traditional psychoanalytic approaches end quickly—and badly. "Borderline offspring can batter the parents into alienated flight, or the borderline individuals themselves can leave feeling betrayed and ganged up on" (189). He lists the "principles of psychoeducation" for families of borderline patients: mental illness is a problem within the patient, not a symptom of a family problem; family support is helpful to the patient; the family should be informed about the therapy, prognosis, and course of treatment; the family should recognize the psychological cost of illness, including alienation and isolation for both patient and family; "bad" parents are not evil but uninformed or ill themselves; and the family's burden can be eased by new therapeutic strategies (192).

Gunderson remains an advocate for patients, families, and therapists, urging empathy, tolerance, patience, and good faith. He is especially sensitive to the challenges posed to therapists. He is hopeful without being pollyannaish, and his portrait of a vexing diagnosis relies solidly on clinical theory and empirical evidence. His goodwill and humor are evident, as when he admits in the preface that, unlike many therapists, he enjoys working with borderline patients. "I think my growth in tolerance and understanding of life's terrors and cruelties has been expedited by the companionship of these patients. Like Dr. Seuss's Grinch, my heart has grown a little bigger" (xvi). Gunderson refers to a number of novelists and memoirists who have written about borderline personality disorder, though he makes one factual mistake, stating that psychiatrist Martin Orne tape-recorded his sessions with Sylvia Plath, when, in fact, Orne treated Anne Sexton (281).

How would Didion respond to Gunderson's *Borderline Personality Disorder*? Warily, at best, one senses; angrily and defensively, at worst. The best she can say about the psychiatrist who diagnosed Quintana with borderline personality disorder is that he or she was the "least programmatic doctor"—hardly a ringing endorsement.

Fragments of a Novel

Didion saw nearly all of Quintana's "hallmarks" except her "frantic efforts to avoid abandonment." She learns about the depth and duration of this fear when she comes across a story Quintana wrote when she was an adolescent. "I recently read for the first time several fragments of what she had referred to at the time she wrote them as 'the novel I'm writing just to show you.' She must have been thirteen or fourteen when this project occurred to her. 'Some of the events are based on the truth and the others are fictitious,' she advises the reader at the onset. 'The names have not yet been definitively changed" (*Blue Nights* 49). The protagonist in the novel, "Quintana," is pregnant, heeds her pediatrician's advice to tell her parents, and hears them say they will pay for her abortion but that they have given up on her. She can continue to live in their Brentwood, California, home, but it doesn't matter to them anymore what she does. "That was fine in her book," Quintana writes. "Her father had a bad temper, but it showed that they cared very much about their only child. Now, they didn't even care any more. Quintana would lead her life any way she wanted" (50).

But Quintana doesn't continue leading her life in her story. "At this point the fragment skids to an abrupt close," Didion informs us. " 'On the next pages you will find out why and how Quintana died and her friends became complete burnouts at the age of eighteen.' " Didion then adds, "So ended the novel she was writing just to show us" (*Blue Nights* 50). She can only wonder plaintively what her daughter wished to show her, why and how she imagined dying in the story, how Quintana wished her parents to react to the story of her death, and why she felt the parents in the story wouldn't care for her anymore. "She had no idea how much we needed her," Didion writes. "How could we have so misunderstood one another?" (51).

What does Quintana's story mean? She doesn't mention she is adopted, but the story nevertheless hints at the multiple losses present for everyone in the adoption scenario. On one level, she appears to be writing about herself as an unwanted child, rebelling against parental authority by becoming pregnant. On another level, she is the unborn fetus, coming into the world unappreciated and unloved. And on another level, she is the biological mother, imagining what it is like to give birth to a baby whom no one wants.

Reading the fragments of Quintana's unpublished story is as distressing to Didion as reading Raymond Smith's unpublished novel, *Black Mass*, is to Oates. Both Didion and Oates are stunned by what they read; both realize how little they knew about their daughter and husband, respectively. They are stunned, however, for different reasons. Oates suddenly realizes that her husband never disclosed to her his romantic interest in another undergraduate student or the fact of his breakdown. Didion suddenly realizes that her daughter's fear of abandonment by her parents was so intense that she imagined herself dead. Both writers discover after the deaths of loved ones a dark, haunting secret that complicates bereavement. Didion concludes pessimistically that "our investments in each other remain too freighted ever to see the other clear" (*Blue Nights* 53), an observation with which Oates would sadly agree.

Writing is for Quintana an act of revenge, a way to "show" her parents how angry and hurt she was over their treatment of her. Dying, perhaps by suicide, is another form of revenge, a strategy to punish others and then to expiate one's guilt. Recall Menninger's observation that suicide is both symbolic murder of another and the internalization of aggression, resulting in self-punishment. Didion may have been able to see the destabilizing ironies of her daughter's life, but Quintana was probably too young to understand the situation. Writing a story about suicide may have been a way for the child of two novelists to show that she could succeed at their chosen profession. By imagining her own death, and perhaps by acting out the fantasy, the young writer would merge with the many suicides who appear in her parents' novels. And perhaps Quintana imagined that one day her parents would write about her death, as her father had written about Cat's death in *Dutch Shea, Jr.*

Suicidal ideation is one of the symptoms and hallmarks of borderline personality disorder, which has a frighteningly high suicide rate. Kay

Redfield Jamison reports in *Night Falls Fast* that nearly three-quarters of those with this diagnosis attempt suicide, with 5 to 10 percent succeeding (123). This is one of Didion's worst fears. "I had seen her wishing for death as she lay on the floor of her sitting room in Brentwood Park, the sitting room from which she had been able to look into the pink magnolia. *Let me just be in the ground,* she had kept sobbing. *Let me just be in the ground and go to sleep*" (*Blue Nights* 49). Didion repeats the last two sentences two more times in the story, each time suggesting the depth of her daughter's and her own despair.

One of the effects of Quintana's slow recovery from her brain hematoma was that she tried not to brood over the details of her illness. "She wanted to believe that if she did not 'dwell' on them she would wake one morning and find them corrected." Didion offers an example: " 'Like when someone dies,' she once said by way of explaining her approach, 'don't dwell on it' " (155). Quintana's approach, however, was not her mother's approach. Quintana strongly opposed her mother's desire to read W. H. Auden's sixteen-line poem "Funeral Blues" (which is quoted in its entirety in *Blue Nights*) at John Gregory Dunne's memorial service. "She implored me not to do so. She said she liked nothing about the poem. She said it was 'wrong.' She was vehement on this point" (157). Didion thought at the time that her daughter objected to the poem's anger, but now she feels that Quintana objected to her mother's "dwelling" on dark emotions. She implies that Quintana's determination not to dwell on dark emotions was the result of her recovery from the two illnesses preceding her death, but it may have also been part of Quintana's strategy for psychological health. The expression "don't dwell on it" appears *five* times in *Blue Nights*, each time suggesting the mother's refusal to follow her daughter's advice.

Some people may succeed in "not dwelling" on dark emotions by compartmentalizing their thinking or focusing on positive emotions. Others cannot avoid rumination. Like Oates, Didion has always possessed a catastrophic imagination; dwelling on dark emotions is part of her identity as a person and as a writer. She has spent a lifetime dwelling on dark emotions; all of her writings arise from such dwelling.

The Ethics of Self-Disclosure

We never learn whether Didion agreed to Quintana's request not to recite "Funeral Blues" at her father's memorial service. Nor do we know whether she worried over disclosing her daughter's psychiatric history in *Blue*

Nights. If Quintana objected vehemently to reading Auden's poem because it unnecessarily dwelled on dark emotions, it's likely that she would have been opposed to her mother exposing her psychiatric history to readers of *Blue Nights.* How did Quintana's husband feel about the publication of his wife's psychiatric diagnosis? Quintana was not only a daughter but also a wife, and one would expect a mother to seek and receive her son-in-law's permission for such a personal disclosure. There's no social stigma in revealing Quintana's physical illnesses near the end of her life: pneumonia, septic shock, cerebral bleeding, and pancreatitis. There *is* stigma in revealing Quintana's psychiatric problems: her history of depression, obsessive-compulsive disorder, and borderline personality disorder.

Didion never mentions whether she consulted Quintana's husband before writing *Blue Nights.* She remarks that there is no uniformity in the way she refers to him, calling him "Gerry" at times and Quintana's "husband" at other times (160), but she doesn't raise the larger questions of whether she showed him the manuscript before publication and, if so, whether she solicited his advice about what to include and exclude about his wife. Gunderson suggests that "when the borderline patient is married, a clinician should inform the spouse about the borderline illness, in the hope that supportive allowance will be made for the spouse's handicaps" (196). Writers are not bound by clinicians' respect for patient confidentiality, but a memoirist's decision to make public her deceased daughter's diagnosis of borderline personality disorder will undoubtedly prove problematic to many spouses.

What are the ethics of memoirists revealing information about deceased biographical subjects? Does a writer's ethical obligations change—or end—when a biographical subject is no longer alive? G. Thomas Couser raises these questions in his book *Vulnerable Subjects: Ethics and Life Writing.* The "representation of vulnerable subjects in life writing is fraught with questions that bioethics, perhaps the most highly developed form of contemporary ethics, has considered because they often arise in biomedical scenarios" (x). Principlism governs biomedical ethics: respect for autonomy, beneficence, and justice. Couser admits that whereas physicians and mental health professionals must protect the confidentiality of their patients and clients, no such obligation exists in life writing. Couser does not believe that life writers should be bound by codified rules and regulations, but he raises ethical questions about life writing worth pondering by writers and readers.

One of these questions is whether a biographical subject's death releases a writer from ethical responsibilities. On the one hand, one cannot libel a dead person, and the right of privacy is held to terminate with death; on the other hand, although death would seem to suggest complete invulnerability to harm, it entails "maximum vulnerability to posthumous misrepresentation because it precludes self-defense" (Couser 16). Dead biographical subjects cannot talk back, cannot explain their actions, cannot offer their own points of view. Couser's conclusion is that life writing requires weighing competing values: "the desire to tell one's story and the need to protect others, the obligation to truth and the obligations of trust" (198). The interest of life writers has historically been favored over their biographical subjects, but perhaps we should consider those who, deceased, are represented by others, usually without permission.

These ethical questions have particular relevance to *Blue Nights* not only because of the private nature of Quintana's psychiatric history that is now made public for the first time but also because of Didion's past statements about the writer's relationship to biographical subjects. In *Slouching towards Bethlehem*, she observes that *"writers are always selling somebody out"* (xvi). In a *Paris Review* interview with Linda Kuehl, Didion characterizes writing as "hostile in that you're trying to make somebody see something the way you see it, trying to impose your idea, your picture. It's hostile to try to wrench around someone else's mind that way" (342). In "Why I Write," she asserts that the act of setting words on paper "is the tactic of a secret bully, an invasion, an imposition of the writer's sensibility on the reader's most private space" (5). Didion may believe that the only reader to whom she listens, and who may be hurt by her writings, is herself— "very possibly I'm committing an aggressive and hostile act toward myself" (Kuehl 342). Surely she knew, however, that her words as a journalist and memoirist have consequences for the people about whom she writes.

Didion may have included her daughter's psychiatric history to be as truthful as possible, believing that the only way to describe the intensity and duration of Quintana's fear was to show that it was an essential symptom of borderline personality disorder. By discussing her daughter's psychiatric problems, Didion involved her readers in what Gunderson calls "psychoeducation," public awareness and advocacy. The value of Didion's discussion remains limited, however, by her refusal to acknowledge the progress that has been made in the understanding and treatment of mental illness, in general, and borderline personality disorder, in particular.

Marsha M. Linehan, who has made a career developing a treatment for borderline personality disorder, disclosed in 2011, at the age of sixty-seven, that she herself was diagnosed with the disorder when she was seventeen. "So many people have begged me to come forward, and I just thought—well, I have to do this. I owe it to them. I cannot die a coward" (*New York Times*, June 23, 2011). In the same article, Elyn R. Saks, a professor at the University of Southern California School of Law, talks about the value of disclosing her experience with schizophrenia. "There's a tremendous need to implode the myths of mental illness, to put a face on it, to show people that a diagnosis does not have to lead to a painful and oblique life. . . . We who struggle with these disorders can lead full, happy, productive lives, if we have the right resources."

Fear of Abandonment

Quintana told her mother that she never dreamed about the Broken Man after the age of five, but the real Broken Man was the terror of abandonment that haunted her entire life. Quintana often worried about what would have happened to her if she had not been adopted. *"What if you hadn't answered the phone when Dr. Watson called,* she would suddenly say. *What if you hadn't been home, what if you couldn't meet him at the hospital, what if there'd been an accident on the freeway, what would happen to me then?"* (*Blue Nights* 63).

Quintana's fear of abandonment, Didion comes to believe, originated from adoption. Perhaps Didion also believes that Quintana's borderline personality disorder originated from the same event, though Gunderson never implies that adoption heightens the risk of developing borderline personality disorder. Didion nevertheless remains convinced that there is something intrinsic to the process of adoption that generates the fear of abandonment. "All adopted children, I am told, fear that they will be abandoned by their adoptive parents as they believe themselves to have been abandoned by their natural. They are programmed, by the unique circumstances of their introduction into the family structure, to see abandonment as their role, their fate, the destiny that will overtake them unless they outrun it"—to which she adds starkly, "Quintana" (*Blue Nights* 118). Didion then states what she thinks is the corollary to this belief: "All adoptive parents, I do not need to be told, fear that they do not deserve the child they were given, that the child will be taken from them" (119).

What's troubling about these two statements is Didion's belief that there is no way for adopted children or their adoptive parents to avoid the fear of abandonment. Didion's generalization allows no exceptions, no possibility of avoiding abandonment fear, no hope of human agency, no value in intervention, clinical or otherwise, no possibility for change. Nor does she cite any experts on adoption, clinical statistics, or experiences of other adopted children and their adoptive parents. There are major differences between infants adopted at birth, like Quintana, and those adopted months or years later, but Didion ignores these differences. So, too, are there differences between adopted children who are told the details of their adoption and those who are not told.

The "Delicate Life Dance" of Adopted Children

The research on adoption is extensive, and while there are many controversies among clinicians, none of the many books I consulted suggests that adopted children or their adoptive parents are "programmed" to see abandonment as their role. In *The Adoption Life Cycle*, Elinor B. Rosenberg suggests that the "issue of abandonment" experienced by school-aged children "tends to compromise their feelings of adequacy and call into question their basic human status," but she also remarks that struggling with these issues is a "normal and necessary process" for adopted children, part of a "delicate life dance" (103–104). Like other researchers, Rosenberg acknowledges that adopted children are overrepresented in inpatient, outpatient, and residential treatment settings. "Such children made up from 4% to 15% of the clinical population, although they constituted only 2% of the population at large." She offers several reasons for this phenomenon:

> It is possible that the facts speak for themselves and that adopted children (for whatever reasons) have more emotional and behavioral problems and thus are aptly overrepresented in mental health facilities. But other explanations are also possible. One is that adoptive parents tend to be representative of a more educated, higher socioeconomic class whose members would be more likely to turn to mental health professionals and therefore their children are no more overrepresented than are the biological children of demographically similar parents. Another possibility is that adoptive parents, having successfully turned to agencies to receive their child, feel more trusting and more ready to seek further help than their nonadoptive counterparts. Some clinicians have suggested other psychological motivations for adoptive parents, for instance, a secret wish to return the child to an agency or to have the agency "fix" what they feel are damaged goods. (118–119)

The history of adoption reveals a changing story of love, loss, identity, and belonging, as Ellen Herman documents in her 2006 book *Kinship by Design*. In the final chapter, "Damaged Children, Therapeutic Lives," she traces an idea that gained currency in the early 1960s: "adoption per se placed children at risk for emotional disturbance and psychopathology" (253). Far from denying these risks, Herman demonstrates that neither adoption nor modernity has been a "straightforward story" of improvement. "The knowable is haunted by the specter of the inexplicable." Her conclusion is that "if we can find the grace to accept what we do not know, perhaps it will be possible to reckon with risk differently" (299). The risks of adoption, while real, are generally manageable for most adopted children and their families. According to Jeffrey Seinfeld, the "vast majority of adoptees are reportedly well-enough adjusted in adult life" (182).

Didion implies throughout *Blue Nights* that the mother-daughter relationship was fraught with anxiety, tension, and misunderstanding. Quintana must have been acutely sensitive to her mother's fears, which became her own. "Once she was born I was never not afraid," Didion admits and then lists her fears: "I was afraid of swimming pools, high-tension wires, lye under the sink, aspirin in the medicine cabinet, The Broken Man himself. I was afraid of rattlesnakes, riptides, landslides, strangers who appeared at the door, unexplained fevers, elevators without operators and empty hotel corridors. The source of the fear was obvious: it was the harm that could come to her" (54). Some of these fears predated Quintana's birth; others were associated with the uncertainties over adoption, including Didion's fear that she might fail to take care of her baby along with the fear that the baby might fail to love her. The worst fear, however, is one that Didion can hardly express and then does so, with blunt honesty: "And worse yet, worse by far, so much worse as to be unthinkable, except I did think it, everyone who has ever waited to bring a baby home thinks it: *what if I fail to love this baby?*" (58).

Quintana's fantasy of meeting and greeting her two "Mommies" never came true. The hope that one day her adopted daughter would meet her biological family proved to be a stinging disappointment, not because the meeting never occurred, but because it turned out so badly for everyone involved. Didion recalls how in 1998 Quintana received a FedEx letter from a young woman who convincingly identified herself as Quintana's sister. A few months later the two sisters were united, and then Quintana traveled to Dallas to meet her birth mother and biological family. Quintana welcomed the reunion in the beginning, but she soon found herself unexpectedly burdened when her birth mother called her repeatedly in the morning just as Quintana was leaving for work. Finally, after discussions with her psychiatrist, Quintana told her birth mother and sister that she needed to "step back" from them. "In reply she received a letter from her mother saying that she did not want to be a burden and so had disconnected the telephone" (128). Unlike her husband's and daughter's "recommended choice narratives" of adoption, Didion leaves us with a heartbreaking abandonment narrative.

Without talking specifically about her own parenting difficulties, Didion generalizes: "I do not know many people who think they have succeeded as parents" (93). Her pessimism, here and elsewhere, is undeniable. It's unlikely she would be cheered by the idea of the "good enough parent," an expression that releases parents from the onus of failing to achieve perfection. Skeptical of parents who live vicariously through their children, and who regard them as narcissistic extensions of themselves, Didion goes to the other extreme, reciting, though without being specific, the "rosaries of our failures, our neglects, our derelictions and delinquencies" (93). There is much truth in Gunderson's observation that "because issues of causality are usually so heavily loaded with feelings of anger and guilt, these issues are rarely constructive for dealing with the present situation and recurrent crises" (199).

Self-Blame

Didion's fears here are part of a larger pattern of self-blame that pervades *Blue Nights*. She blames herself for failures large and small. The self-blame begins with the hauntingly evocative title of her book. She tells us in chapter 1 that "Blue Nights" refers to a physical and atmospheric blueness as the sky darkens and fades, but it also refers to a state of mind, the "end of promise, the dwindling of the day, the inevitability of the fading, the dying of brightness" (4). She blames herself for believing that life will never end, that she will never lose her family, that time will never pass. She ends chapter 2 with the refrain *Time passes*, which she knows is a "banality," but she cannot avoid raising the question: "Did I believe the blue nights could last forever?" (16–17).

Part of Didion's spiritual or existential self-blame lies in her perceived failure not only to appreciate the moment but also to construct a meaning to life that will not be destroyed by the inevitability of death. She doesn't cite E. M. Forster's observation in *Howard's End* that "Death destroys a man: the idea of Death saves him" (239), but it's doubtful that she would find it liberating. She holds onto her Episcopalian beliefs, though they provide her with little comfort. A memorial service for her daughter takes place at the Dominican Church of St. Vincent Ferrer in Manhattan, and the ashes are placed in a marble wall in St. Ansgar's Chapel at St. John the Divine along with those of Didion's mother and husband. She doesn't seem to fear her own death. Ironically, when an MRI reveals an aneurism deep in one of her arteries, she is now afraid *not* to die, afraid, that is, that she might suffer a devastating stroke that will leave her paralyzed.

This fear may explain her dislike of *The Diving Bell and the Butterfly*, Jean-Dominique Bauby's riveting account of "locked-in syndrome," the result of a catastrophic cerebrovascular stroke. Unable to move except for blinking an eye, Bauby "writes"—or blinks—a miraculously lyrical and affirmative story about the ability to survive in the most frightful existence possible. "*The Diving Bell and the Butterfly* had been when it was published extremely meaningful to Quintana," Didion writes, "so markedly so that I never told her that I did not like it much, or for that matter even entirely believe it" (*Blue Nights* 152). Only after Quintana found herself in her own locked-in condition, confined to a wheelchair, did Didion see the point of Bauby's story.

Didion also blames herself for the promise she made to Quintana to protect her from harm. It is a promise that every parent has made to a child, a promise made out of love and in good faith, and a promise that cannot possibly be kept. Surely Didion must know that no reader can blame her for breaking such a promise. A parent's promise to protect a child implies hopefulness for the future that creates secure attachments along with what Erik H. Erikson calls "basic trust," an "essential trustfulness of others as well as a fundamental sense of one's own trustworthiness" (96). Didion implies that there were many times when Quintana lost hope, partly because she sensed that her mother was not hopeful. Quintana feared that if something happened to her father, she would not be able to take care of her mother. "How could she have even imagined that I would not take care of her?" Didion laments. "I used to ask her that. Now I ask the reverse: How could she have even imagined that I *could* take care of her? She saw me as needing care myself. She saw me as frail. Was that her anxiety or mine?" (*Blue Nights* 101)

Indeed, we are never sure whether Didion's questions here and elsewhere are real or rhetorical, whether she accepts too much or too little blame for the problematic mother-daughter relationship. "Didion's writing has managed to be both candid and performative, unusually direct and totally evasive," Nathan Heller suggests in an article published on

November 4, 2011, in the *New York Times Magazine*. "These paradoxes are the dark center that every interpretation of her work orbits. They're also what gives her prose its strange allure."

Didion notes several times in *Blue Nights* that a parent's greatest grief is to lose a child. Losing a spouse is losing the past and present; losing a child is losing the future. She quotes statements by Napoleon and Euripedes about the grief of losing a child, then observes, *"When we talk about mortality we are talking about our children"* (13). The death of a spouse is a natural event; the death of a child in not. What makes Didion's loss of her daughter even worse is that Quintana may not have realized how much her parents loved and needed her. After disclosing her daughter's "frantic efforts to avoid abandonment," Didion asks sorrowfully, "How could she have ever imagined that we could abandon her? Had she no idea how much we needed her?" (49).

Losing a Child

Is the ubiquitous self-blame in *Blue Nights* characteristic of other books about the death of a child? Didion doesn't mention John Gunther's *Death Be Not Proud*, which describes the death of his seventeen-year-old son, Johnny, in 1947 from brain cancer, but the book offers an instructive contrast to her own. *Death Be Not Proud*, the title of which comes from a John Donne poem, became a best seller when it was published in 1947, and it has never been out of print. Gunther married Frances Fineman in 1927, and they had a daughter who died four months after her birth in 1929. The Gunthers divorced in 1944, three years before their son died after battling cancer for fifteen months. One finds not a trace of self-blame in John Gunther's account of his son's dying and death, though, tellingly, Frances Gunther confesses near the end of the book that she is "haunted" by her shortcomings, which include existential and marital regrets. "I think every parent must have a sense of failure, even of sin, merely in remaining alive after the death of a child. One feels that it is not right to live when one's child has died, that one should somehow have found the way to give one's life to save his life" (193).

No trace of self-blame appears in Roger Rosenblatt's memoirs *Making Toast* (2010) and *Kayak Morning* (2012) about the death of his thirty-eight-year-old physician-daughter, Amy, from an asymptomatic heart condition. But Rosenblatt makes no attempt to conceal his dark emotions. "My anger at God remains unabated," he admits in *Making Toast*, "and it may

166 / Writing Widowhood

be that I do not wish to concede to Him anything as good or as kind as providing the superintending presence of my daughter" (133). Like Didion, he refuses to be comforted over the death of a child, and he struggles, like her, to find a way to cope with loss. "All I have to keep me afloat," he remarks in *Kayak Morning*, which might also be called *Kayak Mourning*, "all I have ever had, is writing" (14). *Death Be Not Proud, Making Toast*, and *Kayak Morning* are filled with grief, but they generally avoid the self-blame, self-doubt, guilt, and pessimism that characterize *Blue Nights*.

"Memories are what you no longer want to remember," Didion declares midway through *Blue Nights* (64), adding a few pages later that some of her memories of Quintana fill her with pleasure while others break her heart. *Blue Nights* abounds in a mother's recollections of her daughter. Nowhere in the memoir does she fear losing her memory of her daughter. Didion needs these memories to survive. "I find myself thinking exclusively about Quintana," she observes five years after her daughter's death. "I need her with me" (150). She uses Quintana's words *all mudgy* (102) to describe her trouble remembering the five weeks she spent in the ICU at UCLA, but Didion's memories are sharp and unforgettable.

Didion's memories are so sharp and unforgettable that she ends *Blue Nights* with a startling sentence. In fourteen single lines that read almost like a sonnet, she describes her daughter's cremated ashes lying in a church wall behind locked doors, then addresses the reader in the penultimate sentence, "You may see nothing still to be lost," to which she responds: "Yet there is no day in her life on which I do not see her" (188). One must reread this sentence several times to realize that Didion is not saying what we may think she is saying, namely, that not a single day goes by without her seeing Quintana. Rather, the sentence implies that Didion can see, and thus remember, every day of her *daughter's* life. If this is not a typographical error, or wishful thinking, the memoir ends with the image of a mother who has not only been with her daughter every day of the latter's life but who also seems merged with her, dissolving the boundary between self and other.

"An Inadequate Adjustment to Aging"

Didion reveals near the end of *Blue Nights* that she turned seventy-five on her last birthday, December 5, 2009, and then notes sarcastically that a doctor to whom she "occasionally talks" suggests she has made "an inadequate adjustment to aging." Wrong, she wants to tell him: "I have made no adjustment whatsoever to aging" (137). Didion's mother lived to be nearly ninety-one, but Didion herself doesn't appear to be optimistic she will live as long. Her medical problems intensify after her husband's and daughter's deaths. She goes from one neurologist to another to find out why she feels unsteady and unbalanced, and she is told that she has a neurological inflammation, caused by "not weighing enough," a sensitive issue to her because her earliest memories involve being urged by her mother to gain weight, "as if my failure to do so were willful, an act of rebellion" (113). She begins falling in her apartment, losing consciousness, lacking the strength to summon help. Hospitalized, she feels immediately demoralized, infantilized, and even though several MRI and full-body PET scans show no abnormalities, she feels frail for the first time in her life. She finds it increasingly difficult to fulfill the promise she has made to herself to "maintain momentum" (165). She recalls the exact day when ill health overtakes her: August 2, 2007, when she is diagnosed with shingles, inflammation of the nervous system—the same illness Oates develops after her husband's death.

Didion never fails to acknowledge her increasing frailty in *The Year of Magical Thinking* and *Blue Nights*. The frailty is palpable, but, as she admits in the *Paris Review* interview, she has long cultivated the myth of her fragility. For whatever reason—modesty, superstition, or habit—she never writes about her legendary resilience. It takes resilience to survive the death of one's husband and daughter, to give interviews and lectures, and to write about frailty. She has always written with power and conviction, and her creativity shows no sign of failing her.

Nevertheless, Didion maintains an elegiac tone throughout *Blue Nights*, but the end of the story feels like she is bidding farewell to her readers, like the sorcerer Prospero breaking his staff in Shakespeare's *Tempest*. She is, almost certainly, working on another book-length project, as she has throughout her life, but *Blue Nights* reads like an end-of-life memoir. Just as we will always associate Fitzgerald's Gatsby with the green light, symbolizing the hope and promise of the elusive future that each year recedes before us, so will we identify Didion with the blue light, the dying of the brightness implicit in the memoir's title. *The Year of Magical Thinking* and *Blue Nights* are bookends, presenting us with the deaths of her husband, daughter, and soon, she implies, her own, three posterity selves. Both *The Year of Magical Thinking* and *Blue Nights* are grief memoirs, focusing on loss and bereavement. Both are survival memoirs as well. Dutch Shea Jr. wonders who will be the "custodian" of his daughter's memory after his death. Didion leaves no doubt that she has become the custodian of her husband's and daughter's memories after their deaths. The two stories contrast the golden days of Didion's past and the blue days of her posthumous present.

Amid the darkening of Didion's vision, a perspective that has been dark from the beginning of her career, there is only one activity that seems to diminish her sorrow: watching performances of *The Year of Magical Thinking: The Play*. In perhaps the most noteworthy passage in *Blue Nights*, she explains what she likes best about watching the play. "I liked it all, but most of all I liked the fact that although the play was entirely focused on Quintana there were, five evenings and two afternoons a week, these ninety full minutes, the run time of the play, during which she did not need to be dead" (167). Watching each performance allows Didion to experience the power of magical thinking, not the "omnipotence of thought" Freud discusses in *Totem and Taboo*, the "overvaluation of mental processes as compared with reality" (87), but the ability of art to conjure up the dead. Watching the play enables the playwright to remain connected with her daughter, a continuing bond. "We tell ourselves stories in order to live," Didion observes famously in *The White Album* (11). We also tell ourselves stories in order to die, that is, to understand the deaths of our loved ones and to prepare for our own deaths as well. In writing *The Year of Magical Thinking*, *The Play*, and *Blue Nights*, Didion honors the memory of her husband and daughter, preventing them from passing into nothingness. At the same time, she pens an extended survival story, filled with melancholy wisdom, taking us on a harrowing journey to a place, grief, that we can never know until we find ourselves confronting expected and unexpected losses.

5

Kay Redfield Jamison

Nothing Was the Same

The landscape of widowhood for Joyce Carol Oates, Sandra Gilbert, Gail Godwin, and Joan Didion is a bleak and lonely terrain associated with depression, grief, and guilt. Losing their companions was the most devastating experiences in their lives, a tragedy compounded for Didion when she lost her daughter. Kay Redfield Jamison's 2009 memoir *Nothing Was the Same* reveals that her heart was also shattered when her husband died from cancer, but, unlike the other memoirists, losing her heart was different from losing her mind, an event she recounted in her earlier memoir, *An Unquiet Mind*.

Jamison is a professor of psychiatry at the Johns Hopkins School of Medicine and an honorary professor of English at the University of St Andrews in Scotland, joint appointments that demonstrate the interdisciplinary nature of her teaching and scholarship. The recipient of a 2001 MacArthur "Genius" grant, she has expanded our understanding of moods and madness. She has received several other prestigious awards: *Time* chose her as a "Hero of Medicine," and the National Mental Health Association selected her for the William Styron Award in 1995. She has also earned the American Foundation for Suicide Prevention Research Award.

Jamison began her career as a clinical psychologist, receiving her PhD at UCLA in 1975, where she founded and directed the Affective

Disorders Clinic. Her first book, *Manic-Depressive Illness*, coauthored with Frederick K. Goodwin, remains the definitive textbook on the subject. "By any standard," writes Lewis L. Judd, director of the National Institute of Mental Health, *"Manic-Depressive Illness* is a monumental work. It is monumental in its size, its breadth of vision, its insight into the nature of affective disorders, and its mastery of the scientific basis for understanding and treating them" (ix).

Mood Disorders and Creativity

Jamison's next book, *Touched with Fire*, remains the most authoritative study of the complicated and controversial relationship between mood disorders and creativity. She presents compelling biographical, literary, and genetic evidence that scores of eighteenth- and nineteenth-century British writers, including Samuel Johnson, William Blake, William Wordsworth, Samuel Taylor Coleridge, Lord Byron, Percy Bysshe Shelley, and John Keats, suffered from recurrent depression or manic-depressive illness. She cites hundreds of scientific articles to support her findings, including a 1987 study of participants at the famed University of Iowa Writer's Workshop, which concluded that fully 80 percent of the study sample experienced symptoms associated with mood disorders. "Of particular interest, almost one half the creative writers met the diagnostic criteria for full-blown manic-depressive illness" (74)—an incidence that is much higher than the 1 percent of the general population who suffers from this disorder. An insatiable reader of poetry, Jamison cites many twentieth-century poets afflicted with mood disorders, including Robert Lowell, whom she quotes asking in a late poem, "Is getting well ever an art, / or art a way to get well?" (124).

In *Touched with Fire*, Jamison supplies abundant evidence for the genetic basis for mood disorders, showing how depression or manic-depressive illness appears in certain writers' families, including those of Virginia Woolf and Ernest Hemingway. Hemingway's family is unusual, she points out, for the "unnerving number of suicides—four, in just two generations of the family: Hemingway's father, brother, sister, and Hemingway himself" (228). Since the publication of *Touched with Fire*, that number has jumped to five in four generations of the family: Margaux Hemingway died at the age of forty-one from an overdose of phenobarbital, which a coroner ruled was a suicide. Her death occurred on July 1, 1996, one day before the thirty-fifth anniversary of her grandfather's own suicide.

In *Night Falls Fast*, one of the most far-reaching studies of suicide, Jamison remarks that most nonpsychiatric illnesses, such as Huntington's disease and multiple sclerosis—diseases that produce intense suffering, disfigurement, loss of dignity, and death—do not lead to an increased risk of suicide. By contrast, psychiatric illnesses dramatically increase the vulnerability to suicide. "Mood disorders, or mood disorders in combination with alcohol and drug abuse, are by far the most common psychiatric conditions associated with suicide. In fact, some type of depression is almost ubiquitous in those who kill themselves. An estimated 30 to 70 percent of people who kill themselves are victims of mood disorders; the rate is even higher when depression coexists with alcohol or drug abuse" (103–104).

Mood disorders confer certain advantages to creative writers, allowing them to explore states of mind that may be less accessible to ordinary consciousness. The link between mood disorders and creativity is best seen in hypomania (mild mania), which is often associated with ebullience, self-confidence, and boundless energy. Writers may find their creativity heightened during hypomania, but they are soon thrown into despair by full-blown mania or deep depression.

The best treatment for mood disorders, Jamison suggests in *Touched with Fire*, consists of both medication and psychotherapy. "Lithium has radically altered the course and consequences of manic-depressive illness, allowing most patients to live reasonably normal lives" (17). She elaborates on the value of lithium in *Night Falls Fast*, stating that it is "the most effective, most extensively studied, and best documented antisuicide medication now available" (239). She cites evidence from twenty-eight published studies involving seventeen thousand patients with major depressive or manic-depressive illness indicating that "those who had not been treated with lithium were nearly nine times more likely to commit or attempt suicide than those who had been treated with it" (240). Newer drugs, both anticonvulsant medications and antidepressants, have also proven effective.

Every drug has unwelcome side effects, and lithium is no exception: it can result in mental slowing and loss of concentration. Jamison understands why some people, including writers and artists, are reluctant to remain on medication for mood disorders, fearing the loss of creativity, but she is blunt about the sometimes fatal consequences of going off medication. "No one is creative when paralytically depressed, psychotic, institutionalized, in restraints, or dead because of suicide" (*Touched with Fire* 249). One of the values of psychotherapy with manic-depressive patients, she remarks in *Touched with Fire*, is that it can result in lower doses of lithium, thus minimizing its side effects.

Coming Out of the Closet

Manic-Depressive Illness and *Touched with Fire* reveal Jamison's professional interest in the relationship between mood disorders and creativity, but it was not until the publication of her third book, *An Unquiet Mind*, that she disclosed her personal interest. *An Unquiet Mind* is a searingly confessional book, filled with pain and shame about living what she considers to be a life based on a lie. "Clinicians have been, for obvious reasons of licensing and hospital privileges, reluctant to make their psychiatric problems known to others," she states in the prologue. "These concerns are often well warranted. I have no idea what the long-term effects of discussing such issues so openly will be on my personal and professional life, but, whatever the consequences, they are bound to be better than continuing to be silent. I am tired of hiding, tired of misspent and knotted energies, tired of the hypocrisy, and tired of acting as though I have something to hide" (7). Many authors have written about their personal struggle with mental illness: William Styron's *Darkness Visible* is perhaps the best-known example. It is risky, however, for mental health professionals to do so for fear of being shunned by members of their own profession and by their patients, who may worry that therapists who cannot help themselves will not be able to help others.

Jamison makes no effort to minimize both the seductive highs of hypomania or the crushing lows of severe depression. Nor does she conceal her early ambivalence toward the drug that ultimately saved her life. Appointed an assistant professor of psychiatry at UCLA in 1974, at the age of twenty-eight, she soon found herself "manic beyond recognition" (*An Unquiet Mind* 4). She knew about the genetic basis of the disease. Her father, a meteorologist and former pilot in the United States Air Force, suffered from manic-depressive illness and, like so many who resist treatment, self-medicated with alcohol. In graduate school she learned about mood disorders but remained in denial that her violent mood swings and mercurial temperament were characteristics of manic-depressive disorder. Intense highs were soon followed by abysmal lows, when Jamison felt withdrawn from the world and unable to get out of bed.

The result was a ruined first marriage, impulsive shopping that resulted in a thirty-thousand-dollar debt, and the loss of her self-confidence and will to live. Jamison finally summoned the courage to seek medical help. She found a sympathetic psychiatrist who diagnosed her illness and prescribed lithium, which had recently been approved for manic-depressive illness. She discovered that her form of the mood disorder "is a textbook case of the clinical features related to good lithium response" (93), but for the first ten years that she was on the drug, the side effects, exacerbated by the high dose, were difficult for her to accept. She began to miss the seductive highs of hypomania and made the disastrous decision to stop taking her medication.

Jamison's refusal to continue lithium produced first a floridly psychotic mania and then an eighteen-month black depression culminating in a suicide attempt, when she took a massive overdose of lithium. In *Night Falls Fast* she describes how she "unambivalently wanted to die and nearly did" (6). In *An Unquiet Mind* she explores the details of her suicide attempt, the coma she drifted into and out of for several days, and her slow recovery. She pays tribute to the psychiatrist who saved her life, a person who knew what to say and *not* say. "The debt I owe my psychiatrist is beyond description," she observes, and then gives us a moving description:

> I remember sitting in his office a hundred times during those grim months and each time thinking, What on earth can he say that will make me feel better or keep me alive? Well, there never was anything he could say, that's the funny thing. It was all the stupid, desperately optimistic, condescending things he *didn't* say that kept me alive; all the compassion and warmth I felt from him that could not have been said; all the intelligence, competence, and time he put into it; and his granite belief that mine was a life worth living. He was terribly direct, which was terribly important, and he was willing to admit the limits of his understanding and treatments and when he was wrong. (118)

Jamison's writing, here and elsewhere, is insightful, honest, and engaging. She writes from the heart as well as the head, and she avoids jargon of any type: all her books are mercifully free of psychobabble. She has an empathic understanding that allows her to imagine what her psychiatrist is thinking and feeling, and she is attuned to both sounds and silences. Although the above passage is not particularly metaphorical, as many of her others passages are, she is gifted with the ability to use figurative language effectively, often poetically. She establishes a close relationship with the reader, to whom she speaks as a trusted friend. There is nothing condescending, aloof, or clinical about her prose style, nothing that is off-putting. She writes from hard-earned experience, and she never gives easy solutions to vexing problems. She is, in Arthur W. Frank's words, a wounded storyteller, "trying to survive and help others survive in a world that does not immediately make sense ' (xiii). Jamison is always a reliable and trustworthy narrator, sharing her painful wisdom with others. She is generous to the many people who have helped her. Her vulnerability is a sign of strength, not weakness. Early failures lead to later successes. She embodies none of Oates's or Didion's negative stereotypes of mental health professionals. She is, above all, a skillful storyteller, bearing witness to the events leading to her illness and healing.

One of Jamison's most surprising admissions in *An Unquiet Mind* is that she was unable to pursue a lifelong passion during the years she was mentally ill. "Reading, which had been at the heart of my intellectual and emotional existence, was suddenly beyond my grasp. I was used to reading three or four books a week; now it was impossible. I did not read a serious work of literature or nonfiction, cover to cover, for more than ten years. The frustration and pain of this were immeasurable." She would throw books and medical journals against the wall in a black rage. She could read professional articles but had to take copious notes to comprehend and retain their meaning. "Even so, what I read often disappeared from my mind like snow on a hot pavement" (95).

From her experience, Jamison learned that life with lithium is worth living despite the loss of the intense highs associated with hypomania. She also learned to cope with sudden loss when the Englishman with whom she had fallen in love died unexpectedly. "I drew into myself and, for all intents and purposes, shuttered my heart from any unnecessary exposure to the world" (*An Unquiet Mind* 153). She traveled to England to research the study of mood disorders in British writers that forms the basis of *Touched with Fire*. She reveals, tellingly, that some of her clinical examples of hypomania and mania in her coauthored textbook came from her own experience. She never wavers in her pursuit of knowledge, but she knows the limitations of understanding, particularly with respect to intractable medical and psychiatric illnesses.

Richard Wyatt

Near the end of *An Unquiet Mind*, Jamison mentions meeting in the mid-1980s Richard Wyatt, a schizophrenia expert and chief of neuropsychiatry at the National Institute of Mental Health. Like her, he was a prolific writer, authoring more than eight hundred scientific papers and six books.

She and Wyatt were a "complete mismatch," she remarks wryly. Their differences were striking. He detested poetry, disliked visiting museums and art galleries, and couldn't understand her delight in walking her dog. A "man of moderation" (172), he found it difficult to adjust to her volatile moods. Unlike Jamison, who has spent a lifetime studying mood disorders to understand her own illness, Wyatt had not become a psychiatrist because of counterphobic motivation. He was, however, severely dyslexic, and he had to add four or five extra hours of work each day in college and medical school. "He accepted this as a fact of life, grateful to be able to pursue his ambitions" (*Nothing Was the Same* 14). He insisted that every prescription he wrote had to be read back to him to catch any errors.

Jamison's disclosure of her psychiatric history stunned Wyatt. She is under no illusions that people can truly imagine what it is like to suffer from a mood disorder unless they have experienced it. Love cannot cure madness, she argues, though madness can most assuredly kill love. In 1986 she resigned her tenured professorship at UCLA and moved to Washington, DC, to live with Wyatt, whom she married in 1994. The biggest disappointment in her life, she confesses, is that she always wanted to have children, but because her husband had three children from his previous marriage, she accepts being childless.

Jamison ends *An Unquiet Mind* by revealing the difficulty of writing her life story. She knows that some people may view her illness and suicide attempt as symptomatic of weakness. She dreads the responses of colleagues like the one she bitterly calls "Mouseheart," who responded judgmentally to her disclosure during lunch that she had tried to kill herself. Her honesty and openness throughout *An Unquiet Mind* are striking. At UCLA she put into place "safeguards" in the event her clinical judgment became impaired. She then observes that most physician suicides are due to untreated mood disorders. She also records her department chair's response when she told him she was in treatment. "I watched his face for some indication of how he felt. Suddenly, he reached across the table, put his hand on mine, and smiled. 'Kay, dear,' he said, 'I *know* you have manic-depressive illness.' He paused, and then laughed. 'If we got rid of all the manic-depressives on the medical school faculty, not only would we have a much smaller faculty, it would also be a far more boring one'" (209).

Exuberance

Jamison's marriage to Wyatt lasted until his death in 2002, at age sixty-three. The book she wrote after *An Unquiet Mind* helped her to deal with his loss. *Exuberance*, published in 2004, is itself an exuberant book, astonishingly so in that she wrote it while her husband was dying and in the years immediately following his death. Insights abound in this ebullient book that has the power to lift the reader's spirit. Noting that until recently, psychology textbooks have been far more preoccupied with "negative" emotions like sadness and fear than 'positive" ones like joy and happiness, Jamison calls for a renewed effort to study passion, optimism, and strength. It has long been assumed that creativity produces elation, but she suggests that expansive moods *precede* creativity. She quotes AIDS researcher Robert Gallo's statement that exuberance is in part the " 'capacity to reemerge, not seeing all the reasons why one should not'; it helps to buffer one against hurt and setback" (203).

Exuberance and the next book, *Nothing Was the Same*, allowed Jamison to cope with her husband's death. *Nothing Was the Same* is not an exuberant book—how can it be?—but it is a hopeful one, filled with insights about love, loss, and recovery. The two books illustrate her thesis that a "close familiarity with both exuberance and despair may lead to a profound understanding of human nature as well as an ability to more complexly express it in the arts and sciences" (*Exuberance* 275). She ends *Exuberance* with a tribute to her late husband. "He was delighted by the idea of writing about exuberance, and he encouraged me in every conceivable way. He supported my ideas with enthusiasm, made many imaginative suggestions, and never let a day go by without expressing his love and encouragement. I admired him enormously: he was an excellent scientist and physician, as well as a gentle, immensely curious, and quietly exuberant man. I miss him more than I can say" (381).

Nothing Was the Same

Nothing Was the Same has much in common with *A Widow's Story*, *Wrongful Death*, *Evenings at Five*, and *The Year of Magical Thinking*. The five widowhood memoirs are written by women of extraordinary achievement, all leaders in their fields, whether they be psychiatric research, fiction writing, literary criticism, journalism, or creative nonfiction. Each honors a man who gained distinction in his own field. Each woman was fortunate enough to find fulfillment in love and work. Each writes about a man who was her best friend and confidant, the person with whom she lived for many years until his death. In honoring her companion, each writer celebrates the most important relationship in her life. Each writer tries not only to bring her beloved partner back to life but also to show the importance of his life, in the process creating a posterity self. Like Oates, Gilbert, and Didion, Jamison rereads her husband's books to gain insight into his life and work. Like Oates, Gilbert, and, for many years, Godwin, Jamison is an academic, spending her entire adult life as a university professor, researcher, and writer. Like Oates, Gilbert, Godwin, and Didion, Jamison is devastated by loss, realizing, in words that come from a poem by the Scottish writer Stuart Macgregor, that nothing is the same after her companion's death. Each writer is willing to expose her private life to make public her story of bereavement. Each turns to writing as a lifeline, a way to remain connected with her lost loved one while at the same time moving on with her life. And each writer re-creates herself through writing.

There are also conspicuous differences between Jamison and her contemporary writers. She is, to begin with, a clinical psychologist, not a novelist. She was in love with a man of great accomplishments not in literature or music but medical science. We don't see the glaring antipsychiatric bias in *Nothing Was the Same* that we do in *A Widow's Story, The Year of Magical Thinking,* and *Blue Nights.* Instead, there is a close marriage between the arts and sciences, both linked to humanistic expression and the expansion of knowledge. Nor do we see the predominantly dark emotions that appear in *A Widow's Story, The Year of Magical Thinking,* and *Blue Nights.* Unlike Oates, Gilbert, and Didion, Jamison experiences relatively little guilt or self-blame over her husband's death. Medical science did everything possible to prolong Wyatt's life, and she doesn't second-guess any of their medical decisions. Unlike Raymond Smith, Elliot Gilbert, and John Gregory Dunne, Richard Wyatt was seriously ill for a long period of time; his suffering was intense and protracted. Unlike the other men, who died suddenly and unexpectedly, Wyatt became a mentor on dying and death, sharing his insights with readers. Jamison experiences fewer moments of magical thinking than does Oates or Didion. She remains close to her deceased husband, who guides her in death as he did in life.

Oates, Gilbert, Godwin, and Didion write about their experience with depression, but none of them has experienced Jamison's long history of manic-depressive illness, including a nearly successful suicide attempt. Unlike the other writers, Jamison distinguishes between two different forms of grief: one arising from mental illness, the other from spousal loss. She writes with quiet authority when she observes in the prologue that she disagrees with those who maintain that grief is a kind of madness. "There is a sanity to grief, in its just proportion of emotion to cause, that madness does not have. Grief, given to all, is a generative and human thing" (*Nothing Was the Same* 5).

It was harder for Jamison to write *An Unquiet Mind* than *Nothing Was the Same*. The publication of *An Unquiet Mind* elicited disapproval and sometimes censure by colleagues, acquaintances, and strangers. Mental illness remains a stigmatized subject and represents a form of disenfranchised grief. Grief is disenfranchised, according to Kenneth J. Doka, if a person "experiences a sense of loss but does not have a socially recognized right, role, or capacity to grieve" (1). Suicide involves disenfranchised grief because it evokes anger and condemnation in many people. By contrast, writing about a broken heart involves the kind of grief many people can begin to imagine even if they can't fully appreciate or understand it. "Depression, less comprehensible than grief, does not elicit the same ritual kindness from others," Jamison writes in *Nothing Was the Same*. "Human nature keeps us at a greater distance from those who are depressed than from those who grieve. Grief does not alienate in the same way that depression does" (178).

This is not to say, however, that it is easy to write a memoir like *Nothing Was the Same*, especially if one is as honest and forthright as Jamison is. She never glosses over the tensions that sometimes arose with her husband when he could not understand her moods, or her terror of being alone and bereft after his death. He was not only her husband, colleague, soul mate, and friend but also her anchor, the stabilizing figure in her life. He reminded her every day to take her medications, get enough sleep, and avoid overextending herself. He was not a substitute for her personal psychiatrist, but he was there for her in a medical emergency. Losing him was losing the most essential part of her life support system.

"Imperfect"

Both Jamison and Wyatt know that medicine is "imperfect" (*Nothing Was the Same* 23), but they use the word differently than does Didion, who twice in *Blue Nights* characterizes medicine as an "imperfect art" (15, 47). Referring to the many different psychiatric diagnoses Quintana received, none of which leads to an outcome other than a "confirmed, and therefore an enforced, debility," Didion concludes dismissively that psychiatry is yet "another demonstration of medicine as an imperfect art" (47). Wyatt uses the word more affirmatively. In a revealing passage in which she describes how her husband found her illness immensely challenging at times, Jamison recalls how one evening he asked her to describe the symptoms of neuroleptic malignant syndrome, a rare but potentially deadly reaction to antipsychotic medications. Disturbed by something in his tone and word choice, she nervously glances around his office at home and sees his black doctor's bag, which she hadn't noticed before. She asks him if she can look inside, and when he reluctantly opens it, she spies a syringe and a vial of antipsychotic medication. "I didn't have to ask. It was for me, in case I became manic." Feeling "trapped and, more fundamentally betrayed," she confronts him:

> After a long silence, he spoke with an unnerving calm. "Kay," he said. "I don't know what to do." He was silent for a long while. "Medicine is imperfect." He paused again. "I am imperfect," he said. "You are imperfect." He looked tired and sad as he sat down at his desk. Neither of us said anything for a long time, caught in the cold realities of the choices we had. Then he added very quietly, "Love is imperfect." It was the most true, most chilling thing I had heard about dealing with the uncertainties of an illness such as mine. Richard was doing the best he could; we both were. Love was imperfect, but it was what we had. (23)

This passage remains one of the epiphanic moments in *Nothing Was the Same*. Wyatt and Jamison both know that antipsychotic medication has its own risks and that psychopharmacology is imperfect. Lithium and psychotherapy have kept Jamison alive and generally well since her near-fatal suicide attempt, but she and her husband understand that there are no guarantees. Wyatt errs on the side of caution, even if it results in his wife feeling trapped and betrayed.

Experience teaches Jamison that many psychiatrists are imperfect in their bias against those who suffer from mental illness. She gives several examples of how her self-disclosure evoked insensitive statements from psychiatrists in private practice and academic medicine. Judgmental psychiatrists were in the minority, but their criticisms stung her. After the publication of *An Unquiet Mind*, a physician told Jamison at a Stockholm medical conference that "No Danish doctor would write what you wrote" (41), a comment not intended as a compliment. Unlike Oates and Didion, Jamison does not criticize all mental health professionals, only those who lack empathic understanding. She and her husband both question the received wisdom of psychiatry, and they offer insightful critiques of psychiatric theory and practice that have failed to withstand the test of time.

Oncology, no less than psychiatry, is imperfect. A combination of aggressive chemotherapy and radiation therapy allowed Wyatt to survive what otherwise would have been fatal Hodgkin's disease in 1973, when he was thirty-three. At sixty, he received a bone marrow transplant and more chemotherapy to treat his newly diagnosed Burkitt's lymphoma. He then developed terminal lung cancer. Wyatt is the first to acknowledge that medical science gave him an additional thirty years of life but could not save him in the end. The radiation therapy that cured his Hodgkin's disease was responsible for the "seeds of death" that produced Burkitt's lymphoma in 1999 and then inoperable lung cancer. Wyatt is more accepting of the imperfection of medicine than Jamison is. "Richard lived longer than initially expected because of the remarkable scientific times in which we live. He died because there are limits to knowledge. We knew these limits well—we saw them every day in studying and treating schizophrenia and depressive illnesses—and we were generally philosophical about them, Richard more so than I" (81–82).

Love is also imperfect. Jamison never idealizes her husband or their marriage. "Richard's acceptance of me was deep, but it was not entire. At times he was enraged when I was ill; at others, he was bewildered or coolly distant" (24–25). Their love for each other was the greatest gift in their lives, but it was never flawless. "I cannot remember a time in the years we had together that I was bored," she writes. "Nearly out the door on more than one occasion, certainly. But bored, never" (12). His droll wit defused her rage.

A Love Story

Nothing Was the Same is a love story. "He had always thought of me as an intense star," Jamison writes, and in a 1985 letter he refers to her "solar flares" and "black holes" (105). If she is a star, he is the galaxy in which she is centered. She then quotes lines from Byron's *Don Juan*, which she had used in dedicating *Touched with Fire* to Wyatt: "To those who, by the dint of glass and vapour, / Discover stars, and sail in the wind's eye" (105). Part 1 of the memoir, "Assured by Love," describes the ways in which Jamison and Wyatt coped with manic-depressive illness and cancer. Part 2, "Last Champagne," re-creates their love. She uses astrological imagery in two of the three chapters in this section: "Raining Stars" and "Joy Be the Starlight."

Of the five widowhood memoirs in my study—*A Widow's Story*, *Wrongful Death*, *Evenings at Five*, *The Year of Magical Thinking*, and *Nothing Was the Same*—Jamison's is the most unabashedly romantic and heartfelt. She describes their passion for each other, their growing understanding of each other despite vast temperamental and cultural differences, their support of each other's work, their devotion to each other in sickness and in health, and their undying gratitude to each other. Most poignant of all is the way in which approaching death deepens their intimacy and trust. Each helped the other to become more self-disclosing. Love was the transformative element in their lives, and though Wyatt did not believe in the "lasting influence of love" (102), she does, and the result is a deeply affecting story.

Wyatt expresses his love in many ways. He gives her many exquisite gifts, material expressions of love, but his greatest gifts to her are understanding and support. On several occasions, she takes him to her psychiatrist: "He respected my psychiatrist's clinical acumen, and I never heard him suggest a change in medication or treatment plan" (*Nothing Was the Same* 21). Wyatt urges her to write about her psychiatric history, convincing her that people who suffer from mood disorders need to hear stories about how others, including mental health professionals, have successfully dealt with their illness. He cheers her up when she hears or reads harsh criticisms of her work. His boundless faith in her never wavers. She finds herself conveying his optimistic and practical outlook when students ask her whether she is worried about becoming manic-depressive again. "Yes, of course I worry" (48) she tells them, adding, however, that progress is being made in the treatment of mood disorders. She is not afraid to use herself as a case study to educate others about her illness.

Jamison and Wyatt loved each other, and they also loved their own work. He shared her belief that the work that matters the most is that which "is done in the context of love and life and death" (166). He writes about her "self-confidence without arrogance" (134–135), an observation that describes himself as well. Both were stars in their fields, he in research on schizophrenia, she in research on mood disorders and creativity, but there seemed to be little or no competition between them. Each basked in the other's success. Neither felt compelled to subordinate his or her work for the other's. She calls attention to his many scientific awards, honors, and achievements, rejoicing when he is called by his colleagues a towering figure in schizophrenia research. She was unable to fulfill her teaching, writing, and lecturing responsibilities during the last years of his life, when she cared for him, but she implies he would have gladly done the same for her.

Gratitude

Wyatt regarded the nearly thirty years of extra life after his diagnosis of Hodgkin's disease as a "gift neither deserved nor undeserved, but an astonishing feat of medicine" (58). He did not believe it was "unjust" that the radiation therapy that had cured his Hodgkin's disease would be responsible for the lung cancer that eventually killed him decades later. Jamison expresses repeatedly their gratitude to the medical and nursing staff at Johns Hopkins, where they both taught and where he was treated. He was told when diagnosed with lung cancer that his life expectancy was six months; he lived an extra year, a year that was a "gift of science and the hard work of people who did everything they could to save Richard's life" (81). She expresses a thousand words of gratitude but knows that words cannot adequately repay their debt to others.

Wyatt encouraged Jamison to be open about her illness, but he himself was a private and reserved person, temperamentally averse to self-disclosure. She respects his privacy by remaining largely silent about his life before they met, admitting in her acknowledgments at the end of *Nothing Was the Same* that in "deference to privacy, I chose not to write about Richard's former wife and his children" (207). Unlike Oates, Jamison does not regard her husband's early life, before meeting her, as a mystery to be solved. A few hints of Wyatt's earlier life nevertheless appear. Early in the memoir, Jamison repeats his statement to her, at the beginning of their relationship, when he was forty-five and she thirty-eight, that he was "new to love" (12). Later she refers to his "unfortunate marriage" and "fraught relationships" (27). She mentions that when he thought he was going to succumb Hodgkin's disease, he tried to think of a way "to say good-bye to his three-year-old daughter and his twin sons, born only months earlier" (57). She implies that as a result of their relationship he became more demonstrative not only to her but also to his colleagues. Jamison's brother conveyed their family's condolences to Wyatt's children and his former wife at his funeral service.

Thanks to Jamison, Wyatt became more willing to write about his own illness. In 1985 he published *After Middle Age: A Physician's Guide to Staying Healthy While Growing Older.* He acknowledges the help of his "wife, Rollyn, [who] encouraged me to begin the project, helped with the research and writing, and provided an environment where I could work in tranquility." His words express gratitude for his wife's help but reveal nothing about marital love or happiness.

Wyatt never mentions in the chapter on "Cancer" his own experience with Hodgkin's disease. "Patients should be placed under the care of an oncologist (a physician who specializes in the treatment of cancer with drugs) or a radiotherapist (a physician who uses x-rays for treatment)," he writes matter-of-factly. "At times, both oncologist and radiotherapist will cooperate. In my experience, it is not easy to pick an oncologist" (254). This is the extent of his self-disclosure in the book. *After Middle Age* is useful but neither inspired nor inspiring. His advice in *After Middle Age* is always sober, helpful, and eminently sensible, but his words are seldom memorable. One statement in the section on "Death" may have helped him toward the end of his life. "Practically everyone has the regret, 'After I am dead I will miss what is going on.' Yes, but everyone has already missed a lot—the golden age of Greece, the Renaissance, knowing our ancestors. The richness and experience of present-life offers a great deal to those who participate. It is far more useful to relate to what is going on today than to dwell on the imponderables of the future" (302).

"Words to Live By"

Wyatt wrote *After Middle Age* largely before he met Jamison, when his entire affective world underwent a sea change. His article "Words to Live By," which appeared as the cover story in the Health section of the *Washington Post* on February 13, 2001, reveals a totally different type of prose style along with an irrepressible subjectivity missing from his scientific writings. Written in the form of a letter, "Words to Live By" captures better than any of Wyatt's other publications his sly humor, pragmatic sensibility, and tough-minded resilience. Addressed to a close friend and fellow physician who was newly diagnosed with cancer, the letter opens by urging "Jim" to avoid the temptation to be his own physician, citing the adage that a doctor who treats himself has a fool for a patient. Some of Wyatt's recommendations are clichés, as when he says, "Try not to sweat the big things," but other recommendations have practical value, as when he advises his friend to carry a purple surgeon's glove in his pocket in the event of nausea or vomiting from chemotherapy. "I had to use the glove only once, but it saved my wife's car from that indelible stink. Since you have had much less practice and therefore probably do not have my Olympic-quality aim, you might want something larger than a surgeon's glove. Think leaf bag."

Reading Wyatt's description of the ways in which chemotherapy plays havoc with the body, one thinks of the ancient Roman playwright Terence, who famously declared, "I am human; nothing human is alien to me." "Words to Live By" casts much light on *Nothing Was the Same*, including some of Jamison's caregiving responsibilities about which she remains generally silent in her memoir. He writes lightheartedly about the indignities of illness and, what is often worse, the tortures of chemotherapy. Admitting that he began to hate the foods he loved before his illness, he confesses that he "almost drove my wife to murder demanding that my food be prepared in specific ways and then rejecting it. Nor is this something that suddenly goes away. Fortunately, it appears to be in women's genes to be patient with us." He also advises his friend to subscribe to an extra movie channel. "In the early hours of the morning, you can never be sure what will pop up on cable TV, but the porn flicks went to waste—I, at least, lost any libido I might have had left." This is another subject about which Jamison remains discreetly silent in her memoir. He tells his friend to have several Fleet enema bottles around the house, to avoid becoming constipated. "Just don't leave them in the living room or where the dog can get at them."

Written only a year before his death, "Words to Live By" reflects Wyatt's deadpan wit, courage amid adversity, unquenchable love for life, and recognition of the importance of reaching out to others. He shares his experience battling three different types of cancer, the last of which he knows is treatable but not curable, and he is not afraid to admit that the treatment may feel worse than the disease. "Words to Live By" offers an inside account of battling cancer by a man who is a physician himself and who knows the right questions to ask. Organized and methodical, he urges his friend to set his finances in order for his wife, which he has already done for Jamison. He advises his friend to read the Harry Potter books, which Jamison tells us he did near the end of his life. He is also thrifty, recommending that his friend have a supply of sleeping pills on hand, preferably Valium, because it has been around the longest and is also "cheap." At the end of the letter, he remains hopeful but not in denial about the seriousness of his illness.

Jamison refers to a short book her husband was writing early in 2000, *Cancer Tales*, about his experience with lymphoma and lung cancer. She quotes the dedication page of the manuscript: "It was straightforward and very Richard. 'To Kay,' it read. 'Without whom I would not be'" (*Nothing Was the Same* 103). Wyatt apparently never finished the book; there is no listing of it in the Library of Congress. But writing the end-of-life memoir, like writing "Words to Live By," enabled him to summarize the knowledge he had gained from terminal illness and use that knowledge to benefit others. He was a mentor in life and in death, gladly teaching and being taught.

Paying Back Debts

Wyatt received many tributes from colleagues near the end of his life who honored his scientific achievements. These testimonies helped convince him that he had made a difference. He wanted to give to others what he himself had received:

> Many people think about death every day. Call me shallow—many have—but it is a rare day when I concern myself with my own death. Long ago, I decided that if I paid my debts I would not worry about death. As I was growing up, it occurred to me that I had been very fortunate—I had been given a great deal and owed a large debt. I had been healthy, born and raised in the United States, was well-educated, privileged to go to medical school and finish my training. By the time I was thirty-three years old and developed Hodgkin's disease, I believed I had performed a sufficient number of good deeds that I had paid back my debts—I might even be even. Being successfully treated for Hodgkin's left me in the hole again. So I spent the next few years getting myself on the right side of the ledger. Certainly there were many times I did things that hurt others or committed sins of omission, but by my accounting, I stayed ahead and feel I am still ahead. For me, not being in debt means I do not have to be concerned about death. (84–85).

Wyatt does not come across as shallow here (or anywhere else in his writings), though his approach to avoiding death anxiety may not work for everyone, as Jamison dryly observes: "Richard's views on death were not my own—death to me is unimaginable and horrifying—but he gave me an enviable slant on it" (85).

Wyatt's approach to life recalls that of another Richard, the titular protagonist of Ben Franklin's *Poor Richard's Almanac*, which is filled with pithy sayings. Franklin referred to the proverbs as the "harangue of a wise old man to the people attending an auction" (2). Franklin's Richard Saunders lives in a world strikingly different from Richard Wyatt's, but the latter would agree with many of the former's observations. " 'But dost thou love life? then do not squander time, for that's the stuff life is made of,' as Poor Richard says" (9). So, too, would Wyatt believe Poor Richard's statement that we may give advice but not conduct: "They that won't be counselled can't be helped" (31). Dr. Wyatt would surely agree with several of Poor Richard's enlightened medical insights: "Physicians, after having for ages contended that the sick should not be indulged with fresh air, have at length discovered that it may do them good" (115). Wyatt would assent to Poor Richard's awareness of the fleetingness of time. "Alas! art is long and life is short. My friends would comfort me with the idea of a name, they say, I shall leave behind me, and they tell me I have lived long enough to nature and to glory. But what will fame be to an ephemera who no longer exists?" (127–128). Wyatt and Jamison, writers both, would chuckle in agreement at Poor Richard's address to the "courteous reader": "I have heard that nothing gives an author so great pleasure as to find his works respectfully quoted by other learned authors" (5). Wyatt would also endorse the following proverbs attributed to Franklin: "What is serving God? 'Tis doing Good to Man"; "If you would not be forgotten As soon as you are dead and rotten, Either write things worth reading, Or do things worth the writing"; and "What you seem to be, be really."

Wyatt has few regrets at the end of his life apart from the regret that he has run out of time. He remains stoical, aware of the futility of raging against the dying of the light. Jamison remarks that he regrets not living to see a cure for schizophrenia. "There was no good answer to his regrets except to say that the pursuit of new knowledge is reward in its own right and that knowledge begets new knowledge" (116). When she reassures him of the importance of his own discoveries, he responds tentatively with the word *perhaps*, which captures his modesty.

Wyatt's Death

Jamison is present when her husband dies, but she chooses not to dramatize his death. They both anticipate the end, though they cannot know in advance when it will finally occur. One morning Wyatt wakes up gasping for air, and they drive immediately to George Washington University Hospital, where he undergoes emergency surgery to insert a chest tube that will allow him to breathe following two collapsed lungs. She is forced to leave him when visiting hours end, and he says to her, "I love you, sweetheart." A doctor from the intensive care unit telephones her at four o'clock the next morning with the news that Wyatt's health is deteriorating quickly. She remarks tersely that the drive to back to the hospital is a "nightmare," much as it was for Oates. She describes her husband's "bloated face" but gives few other details. She states early in the story that moods are contagious, spreading from one person to another like an infection. "It is rare for even an experienced clinician to remain unaffected by a manic or depressed patient" (18). Perhaps for this reason, she is reluctant to portray her husband's final death throes. Wyatt's death does not conjure up the image of a Final Examination that appears in Godwin's *The Good Husband*, but Jamison has shown how he has been taking stock of his life. Haunted by her last image of him, she has no intention to haunt the reader. To use Oates's words in "The Widows," Jamison "went down into the grave" with her husband, but she does not want the reader to accompany her.

Nevertheless, one may infer some of the horror Jamison experienced during his final moments. She learns, shortly after his death, that their fourteen-year-old basset hound, Pumpkin, has liver cancer, and a vet advises her to have the dog put down. "She just went, in peace, in every way different from the grotesque machinations attendant to Richard's death" (160). She tells us, in passing, about these grotesque machinations, but she spares the reader from actually seeing them. Pumpkin's death was "quiet, dignified." Her husband's death was not.

"Each disease is a distinctive process—it carries its own particular kind of destructive work within a framework of highly specific patterns." So writes Sherwin B. Nuland in his graphic study *How We Die*. "When we are familiar with the patterns of the illness that afflicts us, we disarm its imaginings" (143). Cancer is an insidious disease; Nuland personifies it as a form of *malevolence*. "Its cells behave like the members of a barbarian horde run amok—leaderless and undirected, but with a single-minded purpose: to plunder everything within reach" (207). Cancer is born with a "death wish," he adds grimly (210). Siddhartha Mukherjee is only slightly less metaphorical in *The Emperor of all Maladies*, a "biography" of cancer. "Cancer is not a concentration camp, but it shares the quality of annihilation: it negates the possibility of life outside and beyond itself; it subsumes all living. The daily life of a patient becomes so intensely preoccupied with his or her illness that the world fades away. Every last morsel of energy is spent tending the disease" (398).

Jamison does not show us the malevolence of cancer, the homicidal riot of devastation it wreaks on her husband's body. Nor does she describe the cancer patient's inexorable withdrawal from the world. She doesn't deny that these changes occur, but they remain a part of the story she has no desire to narrate.

There is no evidence in *Nothing Was the Same* to suggest that Wyatt experienced the sequence of emotions that Elisabeth Kübler-Ross calls the stage theory of dying, namely, denial, anger, depression, bargaining, and acceptance, a theory few contemporary thanatologists take seriously. Jamison talks about his "directness in dealing with death and his incapacity to deny the inevitable" (111). She implies that by accepting his illness, Wyatt was able, in Nuland's words, to disarm its imaginings. His death was not dignified, but he was treated with great dignity by everyone who cared for him. Few would say that Wyatt experienced a "good death" unless we accept Nuland's redefinition of the term. "The dignity that we seek in dying must be found in the dignity with which we have lived our lives. *Ars moriendi* is *ars vivendi*: The art of dying is the art of living. The honesty and grace of the years of life that are ending is the real measure of how we die" (268).

"Thank You for Such Happiness"

Of all the widows' memoirs, *Nothing Was the Same* conveys the deepest sense of gratitude. Jamison is grateful to the many people who have helped her and her husband, grateful for the medical advances that prolonged their lives, grateful for the opportunity to teach at a world-class university, grateful for life itself. She is grateful, most of all, to her husband, who has loved her despite—or perhaps because of—her illness. His acceptance make possible her self-acceptance. Her gratitude extends, in a most unlikely way, to her own illness. She asks herself, in the epilogue to *An Unquiet Mind*, whether she would choose to have manic-depressive disease. The answer would be a "simple no" if she knew lithium was not effective for her; but because it is, she is grateful for the intensity of emotions and euphoric visions she has been allowed to experience.

Wyatt cannot control how, when, and where he dies, but he has the foresight to offer Jamison a gift that proves to be lifesaving, or at least sanity saving. When he is close to death, his body kept alive by a respirator, she makes the "difficult but peculiarly straightforward" decision to take him off life support. She knows he would have wanted her to do this. The more agonizing decision is whether to stay with him in the hospital, which would mean missing a night of sleep. "To spend our final night apart seemed monstrous," she confesses. "Yet it was Richard's gift to me that I thought that night as Richard would have thought, not as others would think or as I would once have thought. I thought of sleep, of practical things. You cannot afford to lose sleep, he had said to me so often, in so many places: You are staying up too late; you are pushing it. You will get manic. Take something. Get some sleep." The decision feels like an act of betrayal to her, one of the few times in the memoir in which she engages in scathing self-blame, but she knows she has made the right choice to leave the hospital, one that was "rational in a way that Richard was; it was preserving" (10–11). The most moving moment in the story occurs when he is taken off life support. "He was alive, but scarcely and not for long. I had no idea what to say to him other than to repeat, again and again, 'Thank you for such happiness'" (121).

Caregiving

We don't see prolonged caregiving in *A Widow's Story, Wrongful Death, Evenings at Five,* or *The Year of Magical Thinking,* but we do in *Nothing Was the Same.* Caring for a terminally ill spouse who is wasting away from cancer is a heartrending experience, but Jamison emphasizes the opportunity to reciprocate her husband's care for her. She doesn't mention John Bayley's trilogy of spousal loss memoirs, *Elegy for Iris, Iris and Her Friends,* and *Widower's House,* but both writers portray caregiving as a sacred duty. Dying from cancer, as Wyatt did, and slowly losing one's identity to Alzheimer's disease, as Iris Murdoch did, pose different challenges to the caregiver. They also pose different challenges to spousal loss memoirists. Cancer ravages Wyatt's body, which, after two days in the ICU, becomes "unrecognizable" (119). Jamison doesn't elaborate. By contrast, Bayley describes the imperceptible loss of memory in a great novelist whose entire life was devoted to the acute study of human nature. Both forms of death are heartbreaking in different ways. And both are exhausting for the caregiver.

Jamison is one of the few memoirists who understands that caring for a dying spouse is a gift. Wyatt had reached out to her when she was vulnerable, and now she has the pleasure of reaching out to him with her "calmer" self. "For so long, for so many years, I had needed him, leaned upon his love and judgment. Through him, I had rediscovered some semblance of my true North, and now he drew upon his gift to me. There was fairness in all of this" (93). Not everyone would see the fairness of caring for a dying spouse as a way of reciprocating love and devotion. And not everyone would have the eloquence to express caregiving in this way. Jamison writes about love and loss with acute insight and elegiac intensity. She cites many creative writers in *Nothing Was the Same*, and the highest literary tribute one can pay to her is that her own language is as masterful as theirs.

Jamison is grief stricken by her husband's death but never breaks down. There are only a few moments when she experiences magical thinking. One day she opens a psychiatric journal, sees an article on schizophrenia written by her husband, and feels her heart racing. "I have to show this to him, I thought. If his name is on the article he must still be alive. Then I saw the superscript next to his name and traced it to the footnote at the bottom of the page. 'Deceased,' it read. Yes, of course. Deceased. Later that night I woke up, aware that I had forgotten to take my lithium. Richard would have asked if I had taken it, I thought. Richard is dead, I snapped to myself. Enough. Get over it" (190). Unlike *A Widow's Story* and *The Year of Magical Thinking*, *Nothing Was the Same* does not reveal the same emphasis on magical thinking, the irrational belief that death can be undone by performing certain rituals or uttering certain words. But like Didion, Jamison repeats certain sentences again and again. "I want my husband back" appears frequently, like a mantra or chant. She knows he is gone, and she appears more accepting of death than Oates, Gilbert, or Didion.

Nothing Was the Same is less wrenching to read than *A Widow's Story*, *Wrongful Death*, or *The Year of Magical Thinking*, largely because it does not brood to the same degree on dark emotions. There are only three moments when Jamison tortures herself over her husband's death. The first occurs when she "betrays" him by spending their last night apart, though she knows he would have wanted her to do this. The second occurs when she looks down at his coffin during burial and torments herself because she doesn't know his final thoughts. The only way she can stop her mind from racing is by reading *The Book of Common Prayer*, which she finds comforting. The third occurs when she finally accepts the reality of his death. "I had no choice but to bow to a kind of end to love, but it was a treason to go on with the drift of things" (187). This feeling of treason, or existential guilt, never proves crushing: she notes its presence and then moves on. Apart from these moments, she does not punish herself. Like Oates and Gilbert, she has a large support system of colleagues and friends to help her, and there is never a moment when she seriously gives up on life or wishes she were dead. Is she devastated by her husband's death? Yes. Suicidal? No.

"Mourning and Melancholia"

Recovery proves slower for Jamison than she imagines. Just as everyone responds differently to spousal loss, so does everyone experience active bereavement for a different length of time. The first anniversary of loss is significant, but it doesn't necessarily hasten the end of grief. She doesn't wish to emulate those who spend the rest of their lives in mourning: "I had no interest in sewing my own shroud" (*Nothing Was the Same* 186). She knows it will take time to return to life and that she will need to develop a new relationship with her deceased husband. Now that he is gone, she must find a way to keep him alive in her heart and learn how to continue her life without forgetting him or dwelling on him to the exclusion of others. She is prepared to make this change but doesn't yet know how to do it.

Jamison is reluctant to burden others with her grief, and she accuses herself of not telling the truth to friends and colleagues. "My years of dissembling when depressed, of persuading others that I was fine when I was not, turned out to be useful in navigating the no-man's-land between my grief and others' queries and concerns" (149). She seems to be too hard on herself here, if only because it is exhausting to describe in abundant detail the heaviness of one's heart after a crushing loss. It's not dissembling to say that one is coping as best as one can. Her friends and colleagues may have accurately interpreted her "fine" as merely "okay," which was truthful. There is another reason why it is easier to answer the question "How are you?" with the one-word answer "fine" or "okay." Many people in Jamison's situation discover that the dying or their caregivers are expected to cheer up those who inquire into their health or state of mind. Sometimes it is simply too difficult to play the role of therapist to a well-wisher. Thus, "fine" or "okay."

The advice that Jamison took most to heart about love and loss came from a poet-friend who spoke paradoxically of the futility of advice. Nevertheless, one learns much about the landscapes of bereavement from reading *Nothing Was the Same*. Perhaps because she has experienced suicidal depression earlier in her life and has worked hard to avoid becoming mentally ill again, she insists that mood disorders and spousal loss produce different kinds of grief. "I did not get depressed after Richard died. Nor did I go mad. I was distraught, but it was not the desperation of clinical depression" (168).

Jamison conveys these insights in part 3 of *Nothing Was the Same* in the chapter titled "Mourning and Melancholia," an allusion to one of Freud's most influential essays. Her chapter title is curious in that she never speaks kindly of psychoanalysis. She generally reveals a thorough mistrust if not hostility to psychoanalysis, objecting to its sweeping theories, ideological rigidity, and opposition to psychopharmacology for the treatment of mood disorders and schizophrenia. She is incredulous when she comes across a copy of Anna Freud's *The Ego and the Mechanisms of Defense* in his study. She can't believe he bought the book. "What was it doing on Richard's bookshelf? He was a die-hard psychopharmacologist and biological psychiatrist" (132). She is "oddly reassured" to see that there were no margin notes or underlined phrases, suggesting, perhaps, that he didn't read the book. A few pages later, she tells us that it was "always disconcerting" to hear her husband express a psychoanalytic thought, "usually a lingering remnant of his Harvard residency; it meant, among other things, that he was unlikely to change his mind" (137).

Despite these criticisms of psychoanalysis, Jamison is open-minded enough to agree with several of Freud's prescient observations in his essay. "Mourning, as Freud made clear, is a natural part of life, not a pathological state. 'Although grief involves grave departures from the normal attitude to life,' he wrote, 'it never occurs to us to regard it as a morbid conclusion and hand the mourner over to medical treatment. We rest assured that after a lapse of time it will be overcome'" (180). Oates, we recall, criticizes Freud's "heavy-footed and wrong headed 'interpretations,'" believing he understood "mourning well enough but hasn't a clue to melancholia" (*Journal* 221), but Jamison agrees with his belief that mourning and depression have much in common, though she emphasizes the differences more than the similarities.

Differences between Depression and Grief

These differences make *Nothing Was the Same* essential reading for anyone who is interested in widowhood memoirs and the dynamics of bereavement. These differences also distinguish Jamison's story from others. "Mourning and Melancholia" is the shortest chapter in *Nothing Was the Same* but the most dazzling, filled with luminous observations not readily found in other memoirs. "Grief may bear resemblance to depression, but it is a distant kinship" (170). Some of her insights are expressed aphoristically, as when she remarks that death is the solution to pain in depression but the cause of pain in grief. Time proves dangerous to a person who is depressed but restorative to one who is in grief. Jamison loses many of her dreams after her husband's death but not the ability to dream. The love of her life is gone but not her love for life. Her life is changed irrevocably but not her personal or professional identity. She sleeps fitfully after her husband's death, but she is spared the deadly insomnia that ravaged her years earlier. She fears growing mad again, but her psychiatrist reassures her that she is not becoming depressed or manic. She fears the absence of a life but not life itself. Despite the evocative title of her memoir, there is much in her life at the end of the story that resembles her life before her husband's death.

Jamison sees a more positive value in grief than does Oates, Gilbert, Godwin, or Didion. "Grief transforms the nature of how death is experienced. There is wisdom in the pain attached to grief; it is not irredeemable suffering" (*Nothing Was the Same* 177). Grief instructs, she reminds us: "It teaches that one must invent a way back to life" (182). She accepts, to a certain degree, Freud's assertion in "Mourning and Melancholia" that the living must give up their connection with the dead. She quotes lines from Robert Bridges's "Poem," which she had read aloud to her husband, about not letting go of a dying love, adding, "And then I let him go, for a while" (154).

The Healing Power of Words

Jamison doesn't cite Gilbert's *Death's Door*, but she turns to the literature of bereavement for wisdom and serenity. The grief arising from mourning, unlike that associated with melancholia, renders her able to "take solace from those who had written so well about loss and suffering" (175). She reads Douglas Dunn's *Elegies*, Graham Greene's *The End of the Affair*, Lewis Grassic Gibbon's *Sunset Song*, William Bradford's *Of Plymouth Plantation*, and poetry written by Edward Thomas, Louis MacNeice, Thomas Hardy, and Robert Frost. In one of the most memorable passages in *Nothing Was the Same*, she singles out Tennyson's monumental *In Memoriam* as providing her with great solace. "To read *In Memoriam* was to throw a summer wreath over an unclimbable fence in impassable weather. I could see life on the other side: the way over the fence would be hard, but the wreath gave me something to keep sight of, something toward which to move. Tennyson saw me through dark times. Words made a difference" (178). She also learns from Byron. "Many years earlier, after I had nearly died from my attempt to kill myself, I wrote out lines from Byron that I have kept since for courage: 'Yet, see, he mastereth himself, and makes / His torture tributary to his will.' Having been so ill in my mind did not allow me an easier or faster way through grief, but it did give me some way of seeing grief for what it is: a human thing" (181).

Literature is so much a part of Jamison's world that it helps her when she must take leave of her husband in the ICU. Looking at his body after he is taken off life support, she remembers Hazel, the leader of a band of rabbits in *Watership Down*, a book she and Wyatt loved to read together. Richard Adams's best-selling novel describes a group of rabbits who must find a new home after their own has been destroyed. "When Hazel died, he simply left his body on the edge of a ditch and then ran off free of his tiredness, through the woods and into a field of primrose" (*Nothing Was the Same* 122). Hazel's fairness and self-assurance, Jamison remarks, have always reminded her of Wyatt. Thinking of Hazel's "light taking-leave-of-life" comforts her when she finds herself saying good-bye to her husband.

Literature literally accompanies Jamison to her husband's grave. One day she takes Isak Dinesen's *Out of Africa*, a book her husband loved, to the cemetery. "Reading at Richard's grave on Christmas morning, I thought: I am where I ought to be" (193). She doesn't use the word *bibliotherapy*, which is perhaps too clinical for her, but she implies that reading literature was one of her most valued death rituals. Suffering reaffirms the healing nature of words, the power of the consolation of language.

A Grief Observed

Jamison quotes only one line from C. S. Lewis's *A Grief Observed*, likening grief to a "winding valley where any bend may reveal a totally new landscape" (*Nothing Was the Same* 170). There are many similarities between the widowhood memoirs. Jamison and Lewis both find consolation and meaning in penning stories of love and loss. There is nothing sentimental about their understanding of consolation. "It is not that consolation is always possible during grief," Jamison writes; "it is not. It is, rather, that consolation is possible" (178). Both authors are helped by writing and hope that their own writing will help others. Jamison would agree with many of Lewis's observations, including his wry qualifications: "By writing it all down (all?—no: one thought in a hundred) I believe I get a little outside it" (Lewis 10). Jamison doesn't share Lewis's muscular Christianity, nor did she go through a religious crisis after her husband's death, but she would agree with his skepticism about reunion in the next world pictured in earthly terms, an idea he knows is unscriptural: "There's not a word of it in the Bible. And it rings false. We *know* it couldn't be like that. Reality never repeats" (25). Jamison writes ironically about her Episcopalian upbringing, referring to being one of the "Frozen Chosen" (34), but she derives comfort from her religion and, like Lewis, regards doubt as an essential aspect of faith.

There are other commonalities between *A Grief Observed* and *Nothing Was the Same*, including their belief, in Lewis's words, that bereavement "is a universal and integral part of our experience of love. It follows marriage as normally as marriage follows courtship or as autumn follows summer" (Lewis 50). Jamison would agree with his rejection of perpetual mourning characteristic of the Victorian era. Both realize that grief must end sooner or later; as Jamison notes curtly, "Grief was beginning to wear out its welcome" (190). Perhaps her strongest agreement with Lewis lies in his recognition that "passionate grief does not link us with the dead but cuts us off from them" (54). The more joy there can be in the marriage between the living and the dead, both Lewis and Jamison remind us, the better.

Creating a Posterity Self

Reading helps Jamison in many ways, including convincing her that she was loved. She never questions her love for her husband, but one day she worries that he might not have loved her as much as she loved him. She goes through his file cabinets filled with the cards and letters she had sent him, all of which he preserved, like a treasure trove. "I was touched by the fact that he had kept these things and somehow relieved that he had concrete evidence of how much I loved him" (*Nothing Was the Same* 133). She sees the notes he had kept about her illness—chartings of her moods and medications, lithium research papers, and photocopies from books about mania. She comes across a letter she had written to him with a paragraph bracketed in red ink: "Thursday is the anniversary of my almost having killed myself." The saved cards, letters, and notes about her illness confirm her importance to him. Quoting extensively from these writings conveys Jamison's desire to re-create their marriage for her readers. She knows that words are not a substitute for palpable life; nevertheless, words can remind us of presence-in-absence. "They preserve differently than one might choose, but they do preserve" (196).

Reading condolence letters also helps Jamison, as it does Oates in *A Widow's Story*. Just as Wyatt feels comforted when his colleagues honor him for his scientific contributions, so does Jamison feel cheered by the outpouring of support she receives from friends and acquaintances. The cards and letters bring him back momentarily to life. It is painful to read these writings, but she remains grateful for them.

Jamison brings her husband's words back to life, posthumously, by assisting in the 2005 publication of the third edition of *Wyatt's Practical Psychiatric Practice*, cowritten with Robert H. Chew. She writes in the foreword that her husband was an excellent doctor and that he "worked hard to put his own clinical and research expertise into a practical format that might help other doctors." Jamison herself works hard to create her husband's posterity self, compiling a body of published words that becomes his legacy. By facilitating the publication of a new edition of his textbook and calling attention to his work, she does everything possible to ensure he is not forgotten. She quotes the neurosurgeon Henry Cushing's belief that what one achieves in one's work does not die. If true, her husband's work will not die—nor will her own.

"Your Work Is Important"

Jamison's major way of keeping her deceased husband with her while simultaneously moving on with her life is through writing, first *Exuberance*, then *Nothing Was the Same*. It is a testament to the importance of writing for both of them that they spent their last day at home together reading and writing. He worked on a foreword for a colleague's book, and she read to him what she wrote the day before in *Exuberance*. She quotes from Robert Louis Stevenson's essay on youth and old age where he compares the "headlong course of our years to a swift torrent in which man is carried away" (*Nothing Was the Same* 115). Hearing this passage, Wyatt must have reflected on his own youth and old age—though he wasn't very old when he died. Dying in character, he spent his last conscious days reading and writing. After his death, Jamison recalls his statement to her, on their last Valentine's Day together: "Your work is important. It will help you when you are missing me. It will draw us close." She agrees, adding that writing and teaching "take one through sadness, countervail it" (164).

Exuberance must have seemed an incongruous subject for Jamison to write about during her husband's dying and death, but in retrospect it was exactly what she needed to do. In writing about exuberant people, she writes about herself. This is evident when, while working on the book, she reaches for one of her research folders and comes across an e-mail her husband had sent to a biologist studying elephants in Kenya. " 'Kay is away today,' he had written, 'but has not been very patiently awaiting your response. Not being patient is a fairly common trait, I think, among exuberant people. Which she is' " (188). Writing about exuberance allows her to reflect on love and joy, reminding her of all that life has to offer. Writing about exuberance keeps her in touch with the past and points her toward the future. *Exuberance* serves as a bridge spanning the nearly twenty-year relationship with Wyatt and a future in which a new love may appear.

Exuberance is not an emotion one commonly experiences during bereavement, but Jamison knows as an act of faith that exuberance will return after grief subsides. Writing about exuberance while her husband was alive gave her "purpose" and both of them "heart." It seemed "absurd" to continue writing the book after his death, but she persists despite misgivings. "Exuberant by nature, I now found it hard to enter into the lives of my subjects, harder still to write about them. I had been weaving a tale for Richard's mornings and nights, brewing a physic to keep death away. It hadn't worked. He was dead. It seemed another of my chagrining enthusiasms" (*Nothing Was the Same* 198–199). She is wrong about this last observation. When at last grief begins to ease, she realizes that "writing about joy seemed a more comprehensible, and indeed a quite wonderful, thing to do" (198–199). Her decision to focus in the last chapter of *Exuberance* on the restless optimism of the American pioneers has autobiographical significance. She is one of those restless pioneers.

"A Love for Life"

No experience adequately prepares one for the death of a spouse, but Jamison's history of manic-depressive illness gives her a resilience that might have otherwise been lacking. "Indeed, my close acquaintance with madness turned out to be a deft tutor for my passage through grief" (*Nothing Was the Same* 179). Mental illness does not kill her; instead, it makes her stronger. In grief, she becomes more like herself. After rereading her husband's letters, she wonders, "Will any man love me this way again?" (135). Near the end of the story, she expresses the hope that "at some point, unannounced, a love for life would emerge," adding that "Richard had taught me not to lower my expectations of life in the presence of difficulty and not to squander love" (181). These are the only hints that she may fall in love again. We learn from the one-page author's biography at the beginning of the book that in 2010, eight years after Richard Wyatt's death, Jamison married Thomas Traill, a cardiologist and professor of medicine at Johns Hopkins. Traill is one of the dedicatees of the memoir, suggesting her gratitude for his encouragement and support in writing a book about her deceased husband.

"Great teachers," Jamison writes in *Exuberance*, "infect others with their delight in ideas, and such joy . . . alerts and intensifies the brain, making it a more teeming and generative place" (227). Great writers similarly infect others with their delight. *Nothing Was the Same* has the power to generate hope in readers, showing how they can survive crushing loss and find new meaning in life. Writing both books enables Jamison to find her way back to life, as her husband had predicted.

Conclusion

Mourning Sickness

What conclusions can we reach about the experience of widowhood as described by Joyce Carol Oates, Sandra Gilbert, Gail Godwin, Joan Didion, and Kay Redfield Jamison? They are obviously not representative of *all* widows, because most women who have lost their spouses do not write about their experiences. Nor are their experiences necessarily representative of other women writers. Few widows pen spousal loss memoirs. Writing in 1989, DiGiulio states that there are "never fewer than five widows for each widower throughout the balance of the life span" (131). Oddly enough, for reasons that are not apparent, more widowers write spousal loss memoirs than widows. Of the five spousal loss memoirists I wrote about in *Companionship in Grief,* only one, Didion, was a widow.

For Oates, Gilbert, and Godwin, the loss of their spouses remains the most cataclysmic experience in their lives. This was true of Didion until the death of her only child less than two years later. The death of Jamison's spouse was also the most life-transforming event, though not the lowest point in her life, which occurred years earlier when she nearly succeeded in committing suicide.

All five writers portray grief as a wave that crashes into the widow, threatening to carry her away in its violent current. Oates and Didion write about being *deranged* by grief. *A Widow's Story* depicts widowhood as a time when sleep or death is preferable to life. Nothing in Oates's earlier life had prepared her for her husband's death, and the loss was staggering. So, too, is Didion's world shattered by her husband's death, and just when she believes that the nightmare of widowhood has ended in *The Year of Magical Thinking,* her daughter unexpectedly dies. *Blue Nights* confirms Edgar's statement in *King Lear* that "The worst is not / So long as we can say 'This is the worst.'" Sandra Gilbert is grief stricken throughout

Wrongful Death and appears on the verge of collapse. Gail Godwin grieves throughout *Evenings at Five*, and though her memoir lacks the *Sturm und Drang* of *A Widow's Story*, her largely autobiographical protagonist, Christina, struggles at the end to break a dangerous dependency on alcohol. Jamison is crushed by her husband's death: *Nothing Was the Same* demonstrates that life has changed for her in nearly every way.

The Landscapes of Bereavement

No one can be adequately prepared for the shock of widowhood, even when a spouse's death is protracted rather than sudden, but reading widowhood memoirs is one of the best ways to understand how others have experienced this life-changing event. Without being didactic or "professorial," Oates, Gilbert, Godwin, Didion, and Jamison have written compelling widows' stories that help us to understand the shock and horror of spousal loss. They offer us insights into love and loss and show us how they endured the unendurable.

Each of the writers would acknowledge, however, that no author can write a story that is universal of widowhood. Every story of widowhood is different, just as every widow is different. The five spousal loss memoirists reveal many differences in their portrayal of love and loss. They differ, perhaps most dramatically, in their portrayal of the landscapes of bereavement. They differ in the ways in which they experience the physical and psychological symptoms of loss and bereavement, including heightened vulnerability to depression and suicide. They differ in the degree to which their religious or spiritual faith offers consolation and comfort during bereavement. They differ in their judgment of whether psychotherapy and psychopharmacology are helpful or harmful for grief-stricken widows. They differ in the degree of guilt and self-blame they experience as a result of their spouses' deaths. They differ in the ways in which death affects their understanding of and attachment to their deceased spouses. They differ in the degree to which they are willing to expose their loved ones' lives to public scrutiny. And they differ in the ways in which they reveal—or conceal—falling in love again after spousal loss.

These differences allow us to see a larger portrait of widowhood and bereavement than would be possible from a single story. Widowhood turns out to be, not surprisingly, the most anguished years of their lives, the time when many of their lifelong assumptions are shattered and when life as they have experienced it seems to end. As DiGiulio observes, "widowhood is a powerful role that makes one powerless" (57).

Morning/Mourning Sickness

All five women were grief stricken, yet their devastation did not prevent them from writing about widowhood. They all needed time to remain in their "nest," the Oatsian metaphor that conjures up the place of refuge to which the writers retreated during this bleak period in their lives. The nest allowed them to regain their strength, physically and psychologically, and prepared them for the daunting challenge of writing about their grief. The nest was also the site of their creativity. They experienced in their nest what may be described as *mourning sickness*, a state of bereavement that gave birth to their stories of love and loss.

Artistic creativity has long been associated with childbirth, and there are intriguing parallels between mourning sickness and morning sickness. The old theory of morning sickness, also called nausea and vomiting in pregnancy (NVP), which occurs in the first trimester in up to 80 percent of pregnancies, was that it is a regrettable result of significant hormonal changes during early pregnancy. This theory assumed that morning sickness has a negative impact on intrauterine growth and health in later life, largely as a result of undernutrition. The new theory of morning sickness suggests that it has an adaptive function, protecting the fetus from toxins. Randolph M. Nesse and George C. Williams point out in their 1996 book *Why We Get Sick* that "women who have no pregnancy nausea are more likely to miscarry or to bear children with birth defects" (89). Nesse and Williams also emphasize the correlation between "toxin concentrations and the tastes and odors that cause revulsion." In a 2006 cross-cultural study, Gillian V. Pepper and S. Craig Roberts note that NVP is negatively associated with cereal consumption and positively associated with sugars/sweeteners, oil crops (used with fried food), alcohol, and meat, a pattern that is consistent with gestational food aversion studies and NVP rates in traditional societies. From an evolutionary point of view, morning sickness has a beneficial effect on both mother and fetus, heightening the mother's immune system, which is usually suppressed during pregnancy, and protecting the fetus from pathogens.

So, too, does mourning sickness have an adaptive function. Spousal loss is the most life-changing event one is likely to experience, and it produces all the dark emotions imaginable: shock, sadness, anger, emptiness, depression, guilt, and self-blame. Mourning sickness also produces physical and psychological suffering, including gastrointestinal symptoms, loss of appetite, insomnia or excessive sleep, and a lowered immune system leading to illnesses like shingles. Mourning sickness may feel pathological, but it is an inevitable part of loss. Grief changes over time, and it usually lessens, as does mourning sickness, though the change may be imperceptibly slow.

Mourning sickness feels like it is never ending, interminable, in part because many people fear that if their grief ends, they will lose touch with their lost loved ones. The end of mourning sickness may thus represent for some people a betrayal of the dead. Mourning sickness may feel like homesickness, the distress caused by intense yearning for one's home and family.

Like morning sickness, mourning sickness can be mild or intense, but it is generally not so severe that it results in derangement. Oates, Gilbert, Godwin, Didion, and Jamison struggled to concentrate on their work in the days and months following the deaths of their spouses; sooner or later, they all resumed writing. There were days when they felt deranged by grief, but none of them broke down permanently. The wave of grief at first seemed overwhelming, but it gradually subsided, allowing the mourner to regain strength. The intensity and duration of the wave varied from writer to writer, predictable only in its unpredictability.

Morning sickness generally ends after three months, but mourning sickness can last much longer. The first phase of mourning sickness seems to end after a year—the year of magical thinking. The one-year anniversary of a person's death is noteworthy not only because of its symbolic value but also because the mourner has cycled through the major events of the deceased spouse's life, including birth and death. *A Widow's Story* and *The Year of Magical Thinking* both may be viewed as "anniversary reactions," the culmination of intense sadness and loneliness that mark the anniversary of a loved one's death.

Just as morning sickness protects both the fetus and the mother, so does mourning sickness allow the bereft to return slowly to life. One need not accept Oates's bias against psychiatry to agree with her that the "psyche is its own therapist" (*Journal* 49). One of the most striking ways in which the psyche is its own healer is through writing. Oates, Gilbert, Godwin, Didion, and Jamison all affirm the healing nature of writing. The writing cure does not bring back the dead, but it allows them to spring to life on the printed page, where readers can understand and appreciate them. Simon Critchley's statement in *The Book of Dead Philosophers* applies to all people who are brought to life through writing: "wherever a philosopher is read, he or she is not dead. If you want to communicate with the dead, then read a book" (243).

Or write a book. Chekhov's observation in his short story "Lights" affirms the need to leave a record of one's life for posterity. "You know, when a man of melancholy disposition is on his own by the sea, or contemplates any scenery that impresses him with its grandeur, his sadness is always combined with a conviction that he'll live and die in obscurity, and his automatic reaction is to reach for a pencil and hasten to write his name in the first place that comes handy" (208). This insight remains true whether one is writing about one's own mortality or a loved one's.

Mourning sickness is the impulse behind many fictional and nonfictional stories of love and loss. Mourning sickness demonstrates, in Oates's words, the writer's woundedness, the ability to transmute suffering into "something rich and strange and new and beautiful." Again to use Oates's term, mourning sickness is the impulse behind the memoir of crisis. Indeed, mourning sickness is the defining characteristic of widow—and widower—memoirs.

Oates, Gilbert, Godwin, Didion, and Jamison probably did not write their spousal loss memoirs *primarily* to heal themselves. Each turned instinctively to writing for other reasons: to honor a beloved spouse who is no longer alive, to bear witness to life's greatest tragedy, to create a posterity self for her deceased companion, to write/right a wrong. These reasons affirm the absent other, not the self. The need to heal oneself through writing may not have been a major or even a conscious motive behind the creation of spousal loss memoirs, but healing was an inevitable consequence of writing about loss. Phrased differently, each widow would have written her story even if it felt like she was banging her head against a wall during the act of writing. No one can deny that writing about spousal loss is wrenching, but the writer invariably felt better afterward—not simply because she no longer had a headache but also because she realized she had produced something priceless. All five memoirists would agree that writing about loss is less painful than *not* writing about loss.

Penning a spousal loss memoir allowed each widow to recreate her assumptive world, to find a meaning to her loss, to establish a new relationship with her lost loved one, to maintain a connection with her community of readers, to consider the possibility of falling in love again, and to construct a new post-widowhood identity that turns out to be remarkably consistent with her pre-widowhood identity. The motives behind widowhood stories strengthen the writer's will to live.

Exposure

Why does writing about mourning sickness lead to healing? George A. Bonanno does not directly raise this question in *The Other Side of Sadness*, but his insights into grief help us understand the resolution of mourning sickness. A professor of clinical psychology at Columbia University's Teacher's College, Bonanno offers a new paradigm on bereavement that affirms the surprising resilience of most people who experience loss. For those who experience "prolonged grief," that is, grief that remains severe after the passage of six months, Bonanno singles out one psychological treatment that has proven effective: *exposure*, which, he notes, is also effective for those suffering from post-traumatic stress disorder. "Exposure involves having patients confront those aspects of the event that they most dread. For trauma, the patient gradually relives the traumatic experience in the safety of the therapist's office and with the therapist's guidance. With time, the patient becomes able to tolerate the memories of the trauma and learns to control his or her fearful reactions to those memories" (110). Bonanno cites a Dutch clinician who emphasizes the role of narration in exposure therapy: "the therapist asks patients to tell their story about the loss, what happened when their loved one died and how they experienced the death. As the story unfolds, the areas that are most distressing usually stand out" (11).

This is precisely what we see in widows' stories. Writing about the death of one's spouse is a powerful example of exposure. The memoirist must think about every aspect of her spouse's life and death. She writes about her spouse's distress and her own. She re-creates in concrete detail the experiences of dying and death. She can choose to show her beloved's dying and death in graphic, piercing detail or summarize his passing. The former is dramatically effective; the latter encourages reflection. The widow writes from her own point of view while at the same time trying to imagine her spouse's viewpoint. The writer relives the traumatic and nontraumatic details and tries to find the right words to convey these details to the reader. If the details are too painful to remember today, she can try again tomorrow—or the next day. Or years later. The writer retains control over every aspect of the story: when and where to write, what to include and exclude, which emotions to emphasize and deemphasize. The writer supplies her own interpretation of the loss, including the way in which the passing of time has altered her story. The writer retains her agency: she writes the story, though there may be times when she feels the story writes her. Unless one is a Mozart, who was miraculously able to create a composition fully formed in his head, a writer must revise a story repeatedly to "get it right." Each revision of a traumatic incident represents another "exposure" to something painful or frightening.

The main difference between the clinical use of exposure for the treatment of grief and the literary use of exposure for art is that the latter occurs not in a therapist's office but in the writer's office, bedroom, or nest. It is difficult for patients and writers alike to confront traumatic experiences. The empty page can be terrifying to writers, and they inevitably worry that their creations may be stillborn or deformed. But for those who can work through the anxiety of writing, including the ever-present fear of rejection, writing is a way to comprehend the incomprehensible. However distressing mourning sickness may be, it is for the artist a catalyst for creativity. Illness may also be a catalyst for God's creation of the universe, at least according to the poet Heinrich Heine, who imagines God as saying: "Illness was no doubt the final cause of the whole urge to create. By creating, I could recover; by creating, I became healthy." Freud admired these lines so much that he quotes them in his 1914 essay "On Narcissism: An Introduction" (85).

Exposure implies something that is not only hidden but also shameful. "The very etymology of the word *shame*," Jeffrey Kauffman recognizes, "leads to the word *hidden*. Often it is taboo to speak of shame. And, beyond taboos against recognizing shame, shame and taboo have very close ties. The power of taboos to prohibit *is*, indeed shame" (vii). We shouldn't be surprised, then, to realize the close ties between shame and death, both of which result in silence.

"Exposure" is an evocative word, one that captures the writer's challenge to disclose and expose traumatic loss. Exposing a loved one's dying and death requires writers to bare their deepest feelings and thoughts about love and loss, including shock, sadness, fear, anger, confusion, guilt, and self-blame. In the process, they disclose their raw wounds, vulnerability, and shattered assumptions. Writers must determine how much of their loved ones' lives they are willing to expose, a decision that may sometimes be problematic, as we saw in Joan Didion's *Blue Nights*.

For all of its newness, exposure therapy is based on the principles of verbal therapy that psychoanalysts, psychiatrists, and psychologists have practiced for more than a century. Painful or traumatic memories are recalled and reconstructed in a safe, empathic setting and worked through until they are less terrifying. Memory is a palimpsest undergoing constant transformation, and while the past cannot be changed, our understanding of it can be, in effect modifying our view of the past. The self-exposure

206 / Writing Widowhood

that occurs during the talking cure or writing cure is controlled, deliberate, and intentional. Writers have the time to reflect on every aspect of the story they wish to tell. If the incident cannot be contained by language, writers can pause and seek guidance elsewhere—from a relative or friend, a "grief book," or an editor. The process of revision ensures that writers can modify their self-exposures or eliminate them entirely if they are not willing or ready to share them with readers. Before submitting the story for publication, the writer usually asks others to read the manuscript, seeking their advice and points of view. The writer submits the story for publication only when she is psychologically ready. By then, mourning sickness is likely to have subsided. If not, the writer can start all over again, writing another fictional or nonfictional book about bereavement. Some widows, like Oates, write fictional stories about widowhood; others, like Gilbert, write poems about widowhood and scholarly books on "death's door." Mourning sickness may lead to lifelong literary or scholarly activity.

Writing a book generally takes longer, in most cases, much longer, than the nine months it takes for a woman to have a baby. Mourning sickness is usually more protracted than morning sickness. The gestation of a book allows the writer to reflect on the complexity of love and loss and maintain a connection with the lost loved one. Oates, Gilbert, Godwin, Didion, and Jamison all succeed, in varying degrees, in bringing their spouses verbally back to life so that they can be alive to readers. The writers perform acts of textual resurrection, communion with the dead. Far from "decathexing" from their lost loves ones—withdrawing from them, as Freud theorizes in "Mourning and Melancholia"—the writers remain connected to their deceased spouses. The widows thus maintain a "continuing bond" with them—a bond that helps the writers maintain a connection with their past even as they live in the present and prepare for the future.

A writer's continuing bond with the deceased may be seen in Julian Barnes's *Levels of Life*, a grief memoir published in 2013 about the death of his wife, Pat Kavanagh, who died in 2008 at the age of sixty-eight from brain cancer. "Every love story is a potential grief story," Barnes declares. "If not at first, then later. If not for one, then for the other. Sometimes, for both" (39). A fiercely private writer, Barnes offers few details about his wife's life or death; her name never even appears in the story. *Levels of Life* is filled with insights on love and loss, including the distinction between grief and mourning. "Grief is vertical– and vertiginous—while mourning is horizontal. Grief makes your stomach turn, snatches the breath from you, cuts off the blood supply to the brain; mourning blows you in a new direction" (95–96). Barnes rejects traditional forms of consolation, including

Nietzsche's statement that whatever doesn't kill us makes us stronger, but near the end of his emotionally restrained memoir he affirms the paradox of grief: "If I have survived what is now four years of her absence, it is because I have had four years of her presence. And her active continuance disproves what I earlier pessimistically asserted. Grief can, after all, in some ways, turn out to be a moral space" (112). In his 1985 book *Flaubert's Parrot*, Barnes remarks that the "deaths of writers aren't special deaths; they just happen to be described deaths" (189). This may be true, but description confers significance and specialness to all deaths.

Spousal loss memoirists demonstrate what thanatologists Margaret Stroebe and Henk Schut call a "dual process" model of bereavement, in which the bereaved oscillate between holding onto and letting go of their attachments. The widows alternate between a "loss-oriented" coping mechanism, in which they maintain a relationship with the deceased by writing about them, and a "restoration-oriented" coping mechanism, in which they focus on the responsibilities of living in the here and now and, in some cases, on forming new love interests (215–216). That is, one can be simultaneously bereft and not bereft when remembering and writing about a lost spouse.

Memoir of a Debulked Woman

Widowhood memoirs resemble end-of-life memoirs in many ways. Both types of memoirists describe either a loved one's death or their own impending deaths. Both memoirists are part of the tradition of memento mori. Both reveal mourning sickness. Both create harrowing stories in which they reveal their fears of mortality and reflect on end-of-life issues. Both practice the art of "exposure," in which they explore the dynamics of shame while confronting what they most dread. Both often raise the question of suicide or, if they are dying, physician-assisted death. Both depict the writer's woundedness along with the physical and psychological changes that take place during dying and death. Both engage in self-blame as they meditate on what they could have done differently to avert or delay their loved ones' or their own deaths. Both record the discomfort of those who don't know how to react to dying or death. Both forge a posterity self for lost loved ones or themselves. And both types of memoirists share with the reader what they have learned from their engagement with dying and death. Susan Gubar's *Memoir of a Debulked Woman*, published in 2012, has much in common with widowhood memoirs, and because she refers several times to Gail Godwin, Joan Didion, and Sandra Gilbert, and because Joyce Carol Oates comments on Gubar's own book, it may be appropriate to end with her story.

Gubar was diagnosed with advanced metastatic ovarian cancer—a redundancy because most ovarian cancer has spread by the time it is detected—on November 5, 2008, when she was sixty-three. She soon underwent radical surgery referred to as "debulking," the "surgical removal of a part of malignant growth that cannot be totally excised" (4). Her own debulking resulted in the removal of her uterus, ovaries, fallopian tubes, appendix, and seven inches of her intestines. After three rounds of debilitating chemotherapy, she developed a life-threatening infection in her colon that required additional abdominal surgery, including an ileostomy. The result of this horrendous treatment is that in 2009 Gubar was forced to retire from Indiana University, where she had been teaching since 1973. The prognosis is grim, but she is still able to read and write.

And write she does, under impossible conditions. As wrenching as *A Widow's Story* is, *Memoir of a Debulked Woman* is even more so, largely because of its rending descriptions of the cumulative effect of virulent cancer, aggressive chemotherapy, and radical surgery. Gubar struggles to shatter the taboo of silence surrounding ovarian cancer, the deadliest of all gynecological cancers. And yet she is sensitive to her readers. Honesty compels her to acknowledge that her story will not be reassuring to those who may find themselves confronting the same gloomy diagnosis. She asks herself in the foreword, "How can I justify a disquieting account that may only heighten anxieties in such an understandably distraught population?" She knows that emotions are contagious and that her book will alarm if not terrify certain readers. "For those who have reason to believe or need to believe that their cancer is curable, please remember that this book is not about you" (xii). And so while writers in general want their readers to identify with their stories, Gubar cautions readers not to identify too closely, lest they lose all hope.

But all is not lost, for even if Gubar knows that her cancer is treatable but not curable—that, in fact, she has been given a death sentence—her keen intelligence, mordant humor, and fierce determination never fail her. She is always thinking like a writer, realizing opportunistically that her illness has given her a subject for a new book project. She admits that her collaborative work on women's literature with Sandra Gilbert "had dwindled into producing edited anthologies that were voluminous and useful but certainly not pioneering in the now established field of gender studies." Having recently completed a book on Judas Iscariot, she was looking without much success for another scholarly project. "Here was a new topic arriving with a vengeance as well as an urgency, one that would teach me (I assumed) a great deal about women, about myself, about my family and friends, and about betrayal, but in a radically new and fearsome context" (11–12).

No Poetic Justice

Reading *Judas: A Biography* (2009) after reading *Memoir of a Debulked Woman*, one is struck by a terrible irony. Gubar's description of Judas's "filthy ends" foreshadows by only a few months her own ghastly situation. Early commentators emphasized Judas's "stinky deformity, bloating, exploding excrement, bloody intestines, and hemorrhages," a startlingly accurate description of her post-surgical life. "Curiously feminized by all these bodily outpourings, in poems and in paintings a leaky Judas frequently holds a sack that presumably contains the thirty pieces of silver. Given his physical seepages, though, it begins to look weirdly like a uterus or a colostomy bag." In a classic instance of poetic justice, Gubar adds, "the thief who secretly concealed, connived, and coveted is flagrantly and filthily turned inside out" (*Judas* 110). No such poetic justice explains her own physical deterioration.

There are many daunting challenges of conveying physical pain to readers. Elaine Scarry observes in *The Body in Pain* that physical suffering cannot be adequately expressed through language. "Physical pain is not only resistant to language but also actively destroys language, deconstructing it into the pre-language of cries and groans. To hear those cries is to witness the shattering of language" (172). Another challenge of conveying the suffering implicit in end-of-life or disability narratives, Ann Jurecic suggests, is "how to make readers receptive to stories of pain" (44). It is the same challenge confronted by spousal loss memoirists: How much pain is a memoirist willing to inflict upon the reader?

Gubar acknowledges early in her memoir that probably the greatest challenge in writing about advanced ovarian cancer is "telling the truth about the experiences of the female body," a subject that fills her with dread and loathing because of the gruesome consequences of the disease and treatment. She understandably wishes to spare her two grown daughters and husband, Donald J. Gray, a retired English professor at Indiana. But writing about the truth of the body is necessary to overcome what her daughter Molly calls the " 'cultural dishonesty' about medical side effects and end-of-life issues" (32).

Exposing Shame

To write the truth about the body means to expose the shame surrounding those organs of the body that, even when functioning perfectly, are hidden from view and discussion. Reading women's illness narratives and cancer memoirs, Gubar discovers that there is almost no mention of what is euphemistically called "plumbing problems," especially those that deal with the "defections of the body through defecation" (122). Wondering why this silence exists even among women who find themselves in her own situation, she then asks, in her best professorial voice, "Is this reticence a reaction against the age-old identification of women with waste that dates back to the time of the church father Tertullian, who defined woman as a 'temple built over a sewer?'" (122).

Gubar has spent decades writing cutting-edge scholarly books, but in *Memoir of a Debulked Woman* she exposes another part of her personality, a woman who excels in caustic humor, Jewish wry. She often sounds like a more intellectual version of Gilda Radner, the zany comedienne on *Saturday Night Live* who died of ovarian cancer in 1989 at the age of forty-two, and whose line, "It's always something," became the title of her autobiography. Many of the funniest passages in Gubar's story occur during excruciating procedures that leave her moaning, as when she describes a physician who inserts a six-foot plastic tube to drain an abscess in her sutured colon. "The radiologist inserted the thick tube into the center of my right buttock," she tells us and then, wordsmith that she is, plays upon the various colloquialisms used to name this part of the body: "in the Midwest, 'the butt'; in New York, 'the tush'; in the South, 'the bottom'; in fancy French, 'the derrière'; in pseudo-science, 'the gluteus maximus', on the street, 'the ass'; in Don's jokey repetition of the nurse's word, 'the bee-hind'" (134–135). She can't help adding, after describing the procedures that only heighten her torment, that she has become, quite literally, "one pain in the ass" (136).

Like a stand-up comedienne, Gubar finds humor when describing an abscess in her pelvis, which excludes her from a new clinical trial. "Infected fluids in the pelvic abscess had found a way to pool under the bruised skin on my aching bottom. How? Everyone has heard of an infected toe or a sinus infection, but an infected *tush*? Would I need a tushectomy? The idea might be funny, if the experience were not so horribly painful" (249).

Losing control over her bowels is horrifying to Gubar but not so shameful that she cannot laugh at the situation. An "ostomy," she remarks, "literalizes the statement, I am at loose ends" (156). Her husband is a source of great comfort to her, cheering her up with the statement that "Nobody had a more miserable bottom" in the country. "While clasping my hand, he recalls a grade-school joke that cracks me up, the one about the lady who backed into a propeller: 'Dis-assed-her!' " (163). Scatology fascinates her. Legend has it, she recounts, that a donkey defecated on the stage during a production of the opera *Cavalleria Rusticana*. "The eminent conductor, Sir Thomas Beecham, stopped the performance, turned to the audience, and announced, 'Ladies and gentlemen, a moment's reverent silence, please. We are in the presence of a superior being: a critic' " (199). One of the ironies of Gubar's use of the anecdote is that she, too, is a superior being, a critic in the best sense of the word; she marshals her formidable literary skills to comment on and critique the stupefying events of her posthumous existence. The effect of these anecdotes and others is to help her smile about situations that would otherwise make her scream.

Gubar knows that shame is one of the most complex emotions. The psychoanalyst Leon Wurmser has identified three separate meanings in the word: (1) shame is the "*fear* of disgrace," the "*anxiety* about the danger that we might be looked at with contempt for having dishonored ourselves"; (2) shame is the "*affect of contempt*" directed against the self; (3) and shame "is also almost the antithesis" of the second meaning, an "overall *character* trait preventing any such disgraceful exposure," as in discretion or tact (67–68). We see all three meanings of the word shame in *Memoir of a Debulked Woman*. Gubar expresses her shame over what has happened to her and exposes the dark emotions surrounding the "tyranny of the body." Her inability to speak about this shame propelled her obsessive reading and writing. She knows that she must overcome her shame if she is to tell the truth of one of the most gruesome illnesses affecting women, but she is prepared to do this. She thus uses writing as a countershame technique.

Gubar's physicians did not recommend writing as part of her treatment plan, but there is no doubt in her mind that it has been essential to her health. "The composition of this narrative kept me sane during a hard time," she admits in the foreword. "It let me come to terms with my attitudes toward death, with my ideas about the resonant role played by the arts as we live with awareness of death, and also with my family history and the loves of my life." Gubar's words could have as easily been spoken by Oates, Gilbert, Godwin, Didion, and Jamison to describe how the composition of *their* narratives kept them sane during a hard time.

"Never Have Memoirs and Novels Meant More to Me"

Writing *Memoir of a Debulked Woman* enabled Gubar to begin to make sense of the catastrophic events that have befallen on her. Shifting from third to first person, she observes that the "rapidity of the surgery has left her in a stunned state so she can explain quite calmly, for instance, that she has advanced ovarian cancer, yet it has not fully sunk in. Thus, for me the writing becomes an effort to catalog the physical and mental states through which I am passing, with the hope of then comprehending their significance" (77). She finds herself reading everything she can about ovarian cancer, including accounts written by women who eventually succumbed to the dreaded disease. "Isn't that why we read memoirs and novels—to glimpse other people's or characters' experiences not to supplant our own but to grapple with how our feelings might be or become how we might be or become beings other than who we are?" However ominous the prognosis is, she finds herself compelled to read other women's stories. "Never have memoirs and novels meant more to me than during these difficult times" (161–162). Reading accounts of ovarian cancer created a life-saving bond for her that remained strong despite the knowledge that most of the authors died of the disease. "Reading and writing about cancer cast a lifeline between me and people whose honesty about mortal encounters mitigated my fearful loneliness and thereby steadied me" (262). Oates, we recall, similarly use the word *lifeline* to describe how writing allows her to deal with her own grief. Indeed, writing was a lifeline for *all five* spousal loss memoirists.

Throughout her memoir, Gubar expresses gratitude to the many relatives and friends who have helped her, including her family and friends. The last word of *Memoir of a Debulked Woman* is "thankful," suggestive of her recognition of the importance of gratitude and other positive emotions, gratitude that is as deep as Jamison's in *Nothing Was the Same*.

Gubar mentions reading Reynolds Price's *A Whole New Life*, a riveting account of surviving spinal cancer that almost always proves fatal. He, too, felt compelled to read anything that might help him survive his ordeal. "But nothing turned up in my own library," he admits ruefully, "apart from short stretches of the Bible, or in all the would-be helpful books that friends sent to me on every subject from crystals and macrobiotic cooking through cheerful wheelchair tours of Europe and the rules for a last will and testament" (180). After many years of intractable pain and permanent paralysis from the waist down, he experienced an improbable recovery, and once he was able to contemplate the "far side of catastrophe," he began to write about his experience.

Gubar also turns to fiction to see how novelists have imagined ovarian cancer. "The heroine in Gail Godwin's *The Good Husband* pictures her ovarian cancer as a 'gargoyle' munching on her internal organs" (68). A few pages later Gubar recognizes that there is "no chance that I will be able to pluck from the diagnosis an opportunity to compose 'a little obituary of my soul history,' like Magda in *The Good Husband*. The gross details of case history, not the spiritual configurations of soul histoty [sic], would absorb all my attention" (74). The typographical error here unintentionally confirms that Gubar's attentions lie elsewhere. Imagining that she will probably die by wasting away, as many women do from ovarian cancer, she returns near the end of her memoir to *The Good Husband*, musing over the heroine's last thoughts. Godwin's jaundiced and catheterized character feels the "thrumming"of pain" (225). Few people in Gubar's situation would have the fortitude to read a novel like *The Good Husband* or study for Magda's Final Examination, but she finds solace in Godwin's depth of compassion for her dying character.

Gubar also quotes from *The Year of Magical Thinking*. "Writing about her grief, Joan Didion realizes 'how open we are to the persistent message that we can avert death. And to its punitive correlative, the message that if death catches us we have only ourselves to blame" (222). Many of Gubar's relatives and friends remain in denial that her cancer is treatable but not curable. " 'Mazel Tov!' is the subject heading of my childhood friend Evie's e-mail in which she congratulates me on averting death" (222). Earlier in the story Gubar cites an example of her own "magical thinking": her hope that "I have cancer so my two girls will not" (107).

Gubar's references to *The Year of Magical Thinking* suggest an unexpected link between widowhood and end-of-life memoirs. As Virginia Blum observed to me, Gubar's memoir is "charting the loss of her body as she knows it: even the title of her memoir, 'debulked woman,' points to the centrality of the body." Spousal loss memoirists trace the loss of their beloved companions' bodies; Gubar traces the loss of her own.

Not surprisingly, Gubar mentions Margaret Edson's award-winning play *Wit*, about a cerebral English professor who, dying of ovarian cancer, learns compassion and humility from one of the nurses who treats her. Moved by the play, Gubar nevertheless deletes it from the syllabus of her fall graduate class on twentieth-century women's literature, not wishing to call attention to her own medical situation. Ironically, though she doesn't highlight this bibliographical detail, she uses the edition of *Wit* that appears in the *Norton Anthology of Literature by Women*, edited by Gilbert and Gubar—an example of how a perceptive editorial decision foreshadows art's uncanny ability to speak with perhaps too much relevance to the editor's life.

Memoir of a Debulked Woman is not as self-blaming or as self-lacerating as *A Widow's Story* or *Wrongful Death*, but Gubar can't help pointing out several disquieting ironies that may have contributed to her ovarian cancer. She observes in the chapter called "Ovariana" that although ovarian cancer is largely asymptomatic until it has spread, which is the reason it is so lethal, there were early warning signs that she chose not to heed, including severe bouts of constipation and diarrhea that often sent her rushing into restaurant bathrooms or making emergency stops at gas station restrooms. In the late 1970s, when she and Gilbert published *The Madwoman in the Attic*, she began experiencing gastrointestinal problems that compelled her gynecologist to recommend a radical hysterectomy. She admits that her denial of gynecological symptoms and feminist misgivings over gynecological practices will probably result in her death, but she doesn't torture herself over this. Writing a truthful account of her illness "will provide recompense for my earlier reticence" (56).

Gubar completed *Memoir of a Debulked Woman* in December 2010, a few months before the publication of *A Widow's Story*, but they are alike in many ways. Like Oates, Gubar scolds herself for being "clueless" (86) and an "ingrate" (159) about medical matters. Like Oates, she sees the tragedy and absurdity of her situation, ending a chapter with a line from a Billy Wilder film, "the situation is hopeless but not serious" (234). Like Oates, she brings a lifetime of university teaching and scholarship to her writing, along with a growing antipathy to "academic jargon" (155). This mistrust, however, does not prevent her from delighting in wordplay, as when she coins the onomatopoetic expression "cockamamie conundrums," or when she points out, frustrated by her ninety-three-year-old mother's belief that her daughter is merely going through a hysterectomy, rather than debulking surgery, that the word "mother" dwells inside the word "chemotherapy" (11). Gubar's gratitude to her physicians doesn't prevent her from critiquing what she calls "loconocology," or "lo-*con*-ocology," the "double binds into which current protocols put medical practitioners of cancer and their patients" (240). Like Oates, she finds herself annoyed when she is forced to hold court to a "succession of voyeurs" (82), though she knows that her irritation or pique "is no doubt misdirected at guests" (83). Like Oates, she finds the "breezy parlance" (158) of self-help books off-putting—though she continues to read them. Like Oates (and Gilbert and Didion), she uses literary quotations as refrains, repeating a line from Salmon Rushdie's *Midnight Children*: "What can't be cured must be endured" (146, 160). Like Oates, she suffers from "blasts of self-doubt" (171), finds herself engulfed by self-pity, and falls into the "brink of depression" (194), from which it is hard to emerge.

Again like Oates, Gubar falls "half in love" with what John Keats calls "easeful death" (105). She cannot help from ruminating over suicide, a subject that has a long, traumatic history for her, mainly because two of her grandparents and her father took their own lives. "Parents who kill themselves make the act imaginable for their children, as I know too well" (177). Though she sympathizes with those who in irremediable pain choose to end their lives, she loves her children too much to burden them with the guilt that is part of the unintended legacy of suicide. Nevertheless, the horror of wasting away terrifies her, along with the fear of depleting the strength of her daughters and husband, and she admits candidly that she doesn't know whether she will be able to stay the course. "My family has been riddled with too many suicides—so many that one fears a sort of contagion, with each suicide breeding another" (221). Suffering has taught her the "pedagogy of pain" (145), which she is anxious to teach to others. Unable to find any nonfictional first-person accounts of women who die from ovarian cancer, she can only conclude that "Perhaps one cannot approach the idea of one's own death until it ripens" (225).

Gubar never mentions that she flew to California after Elliot Gilbert's death to be with her coauthor, but she does point out that Sandra Gilbert flew to Indiana to be with her. "My collaborator has determined to brave a series of Arctic freezes as well as her own health problems and grief over the death of her partner so as to visit me" (139). She describes her spirits quickening when she looks at her grandson, who is named after "Sandra's unforgettably vibrant and so long dead husband" (216). Unlike the Gilberts' close marriage, Gubar's first marriage ended in divorce, and she remains silent about the failed relationship except to say that she was inconsolable when her ex-husband left her. She pays loving tribute to her second husband, who cared for his dying first wife and now, an octogenarian, is cheerfully taking care of his second wife.

Thoughts of her collaboration with Sandra Gilbert, producing landmark books that will withstand the test of time, compel Gubar to write about her most recent book, *Judas: A Biography*, which received a "snide" review by Joan Acocella in the *New Yorker*. "Her trouncing of me—I am an 'amateur' who spouts 'shocking nonsense,' a 'Neo-Freudian' or 'postmodern' justice-seeker—did spawn a host of pathetic revenge fantasies (not unlike the ones I entertained about the interventional radiologists)" (216–217). It is painful enough for a writer to read a negative review, but it is even more painful when one is dying and confronts a bruised posterity self.

Ending a Memoir—and a Life

How does one end a memoir about one's impending death? Gubar is not sure, partly because she doesn't know how much time she has left, and partly because the story of her posthumous life is filled with surprises. Just when she decides to forgo further treatment and prepare herself stoically for the end, she changes her mind and opts for additional abdominal surgery, knowing that it comes with its own complications. She understands that death cannot be scripted. She rejects ending her memoir on a note of serenity, for she hardly feels peaceful about the gruesome deaths of most ovarian cancer patients. She then ponders the endings of other dying cancer narrations, "assuring readers that cancer teaches us to appreciate the precariousness of the present moment" (255). These endings ring hollow to her. Crafting an ending for her memoir is almost as problematic as choosing an ending for her life. She never explicitly discusses the idea of dying in character, but this is the question that preoccupies her. Earlier in the story she cites a statement by Marie de Hennezel, a French psychologist who worked with the terminally ill: "the person who can say to someone else '*I am going to die*' does not become the victim of death but, rather, the protagonist in his or her own dying" (30). This would be for Gubar an example of dying in character.

Gubar would agree with Anatole Broyard's statement in his end-of-life memoir, *Intoxicated by My Illness*, and which I use as the epigraph to *Dying in Character*: "The British psychoanalyst D. W. Winnicott began an autobiography that he never finished. The first paragraph simply says, 'I died.' In the fifth paragraph he writes, 'Let me see. What was happening when I died? My prayer had been answered. I was alive when I died. That was all I had asked and I had got it.' Though he never finished his book, he gave the best reason to write in the world for writing one, and that's why I want to write mine—to make sure I'll be alive when I die" (29–30).

Gubar would also agree with Hilary Mantel's observation in her memoir *Giving Up the Ghost* about the importance of putting pen to paper after major illness—in Mantel's case, struggling with endometriosis that was for years misdiagnosed as psychiatric illness. "I have been so mauled by medical procedures, so sabotaged and made over, so thin and so fat, that sometimes I feel that each morning it is necessary to write myself into being—even if the writing is aimless doodling that no one will ever read, or the diary that no one can see till I am dead" (200). What Gubar and Mantel write, however, is neither aimless doodling nor unread diaries but moving memoirs that many readers will find unforgettable.

Gubar ends *Memoir of a Debulked Woman* by affirming the value of writing her story. "Two years and one month after diagnosis, it is finished, and Don can begin editing, as he has edited all of my writing, and I delight in the prospect of our ensuing conversations. So this is, after all, a happy ending, the happiest ending I can now imagine" (263). Writing cannot stave off death, but she is determined to keep writing to the end. In an interview with Robin Wilson published in the *Chronicle of Higher Education*, Gubar states that she has started a new book, a fictional account of how the sick die. "It sounds ghoulish," she confesses. "But 'since that's what I'm facing next, I think it has something to tell me'" (April 27, 2012).

There's nothing ghoulish writing about impending death, either of one's spouse or oneself, particularly if such writing "might sustain a degree of acceptance comparable to what meditation instills in others" (13). No one reading *Memoir of a Debulked Woman* will feel that Gubar becomes complicit in her illness. Nor does she give up on life. She would agree with Reynolds Price's statement near the end of *his* memoir: "I strongly sense that the illness itself either unleashed a creature within me that had been restrained and let him run at his own hungry will; or it planted a whole new creature in place of the old" (190–191). Like Price, she has become a new person, transformed by her illness into a woman in a race with death and silence. And yet, as we have seen with Oates, Gilbert, Godwin, Didion, and Jamison, she re-creates her new identity in a way that is consistent with her old identity, revealing inner sameness and continuity. Or, as Roger Rosenblatt observes, people in grief become more like themselves. Floyd Skloot makes a similar observation in his memoir *In the Shadow of Memory*, a first-person account of living with brain damage: "As people age, they often become distilled versions of themselves. They present a purer self, a stripped-down form of the person they had been before. Perhaps smaller physically, but intensified rather than diminished. This is especially true when the elderly live alone, freed from the corrective of companionship. A concentration of character occurs, a refinement through longevity, and their essence is laid bare" (224–225).

Gubar remains, to the end, a "narrative junkie" (119), for which her readers will be grateful. She asks herself, in the middle of her book: "Can I learn to deepen compassion by realizing that my distress is shared, that there are many other people all over the world feeling pain worse than mine?" (138). The answer is never in doubt.

Gubar continues to be a narrative junkie, and, happily, there is no end in sight. In her article "Living with Cancer: Difficult Choices," published in the *The New York Times* on August 7, 2014, she refers to Eve Ensler's 2013 memoir *In the Body of the World*, a meditation on the pain of living with uterine cancer. "Cancer patients and physicians should engage in serious conversations," Gubar advises her readers. She knows these conversations are fraught with urgency and anxiety.

In a comment quoted on the book jacket, Joyce Carol Oates describes *Memoir of a Debulked Woman* as an "extraordinary testament to the human spirit," a "rare mixture of honesty, eloquence, humor, and passionate curiosity about the truth." Oates's comment is true not only of Gubar's memoir but also of her own, *A Widow's Story*, as well as of Sandra Gilbert's *Wrongful Death*, Gail Godwin's *Evenings at Five*, Joan Didion's *The Year of Magical Thinking* and *Blue Nights*, and Kay Redfield Jamison's *Nothing Was the Same*. These authors penned stories that demonstrate resilience, grit, and creativity. All of the writers grew through their grief and found their lives transformed positively as well as negatively. All write with stunning clarity and candor. All perform acts of textual resurrection, celebrating their lives with lost loved ones who remain alive to readers. Mourning sickness inspired these memoirists to forge a bond between author and reader that will survive death.

Works Cited

Barker, Wendy, and Sandra M. Gilbert, eds. *The House Is Made of Poetry: The Art of Ruth Stone.* Carbondale: Southern Illinois University Press, 1996.

Barnes, Julian. *Flaubert's Parrot.* New York: McGraw-Hill, 1985.

———. *Levels of Life.* New York: Knopf, 2013.

Bauby, Jean-Dominique. *The Diving Bell and the Butterfly: A Memoir of Life in Death.* Translated by Jeremy Leggatt. New York: Vintage, 1977.

Bayley, John. *Elegy for Iris.* New York: Picador, 1999.

———. *Iris and Her Friends: A Memoir of Memory and Desire.* New York: Norton, 2000.

———. *Widower's House: A Study in Bereavement, or How Margot and Mella Forced Me to Flee My Home.* New York: Norton, 2001.

Berman, Jeffrey. *Companionship in Grief: Love and Loss in the Memoirs of C. S. Lewis, John Bayley, Donald Hall, Joan Didion, and Calvin Trillin.* Amherst: University of Massachusetts Press, 2010.

———. *Dying in Character: Memoirs on the End of Life.* Amherst: University of Massachusetts Press, 2013.

———. *Surviving Literary Suicide.* Amherst: University of Massachusetts Press, 1999.

Bonanno, George A. *The Other Side of Sadness: What the New Science of Bereavement Tells Us about Life after Loss.* New York: Basic Books, 2009.

Brothers, Joyce. *Widowed.* New York: Ballantine, 1992.

Broyard, Anatole. *Intoxicated by My Illness and Other Writings on Life and Death.* Compiled and edited by Alexandra Broyard, foreword by Oliver Sacks. New York: Columbine, 1992.

Caine, Lynn. *Being a Widow.* New York: Penguin, 1988.

———. *Widow.* New York: William Morrow, 1974.

"Charles G. Gross Award for Distinguished Scientific Contributions." *American Psychologist* 60 (2005): 753–763.

Chekhov, Anton. "Lights." In *Stories 1888–1889.* Vol. 4 of *The Oxford Chekhov,* translated and edited by Ronald Hingley. Oxford: Oxford University Press, 1980.

Couser, G. Thomas. *Memoir: An Introduction*. New York: Oxford University Press, 2011.

———. *Vulnerable Subjects: Ethics and Life Writing*. Ithaca: Cornell University Press, 2004.

Critchley, Simon. *The Book of Dead Philosophers*. New York: Vintage, 2009.

Csikszentmihalyi, Mihaly. *Creativity*. New York: HarperCollins, 1996.

Didion, Joan. *Blue Nights*. New York: Knopf, 2011.

———. *A Book of Common Prayer*. New York: Simon and Schuster, 1977.

———. *Play It as It Lays*. New York: Farrar, Straus & Giroux, 1970.

———. *Slouching towards Bethlehem*. New York: Farrar, Straus & Giroux, 1968.

———. *We Tell Ourselves Stories in Order to Live: Collected Nonfiction*. Introduction by John Leonard. New York: Everyman's Library, 2006.

———. *The White Album*. New York: Simon and Schuster, 1979.

———. "Why I Write." In *Joan Didion: Essays & Conversations*, edited by Ellen G. Friedman, 5–10. Princeton: Ontario Review, 1984.

———. *The Year of Magical Thinking*. New York: Knopf, 2005.

———. *The Year of Magical Thinking: The Play*. New York: Vintage, 2007.

DiGiulio, Robert C. *Beyond Widowhood: From Bereavement to Emergence and Hope*. New York: Free Press, 1989.

Doka, Kenneth J. *Disenfranchised Grief: Recognizing Hidden Sorrow*. New York: Lexington Books, 1989.

Dolby, Sandra K. *Self-Help Books: Why American Keep Reading Them*. Urbana: University of Illinois Press, 2005.

Dunne, John Gregory. *Dutch Shea, Jr.* New York: Linden Press/Simon & Schuster, 1982.

———. *Harp*. New York: Simon and Schuster, 1989.

———. *Quintana & Friends*. New York: Dutton, 1978.

Eliot, George. *Middlemarch*. London: Zodiac Press, 1967.

Ensler, Eve. *In the Body of the World: A Memoir of Cancer and Connection*. New York: Metropolitan Books, 2013.

Erikson, Erik H. *Identity: Youth and Crisis*. New York: Norton, 1968.

Forster, E. M. *Howard's End*. New York: Buccaneer Books, n.d.

Frank, Arthur W. *The Wounded Storyteller: Body, Illness, and Ethics*. Chicago: University of Chicago Press, 1995.

Franklin, Benjamin. *Poor Richard's Almanac*. New York: David McKay, 1963.

Freud, Sigmund. "Beyond the Pleasure Principle." In *The Standard Edition of the Complete Psychological Works of Sigmund Freud*. Vol. 18, translated and edited by James Strachey. London: Hogarth Press, 1955.

———. "Mourning and Melancholia." In *The Standard Edition of the Complete Psychological Works of Sigmund Freud*. Vol. 14, translated and edited by James Strachey, 239–258. London: Hogarth Press, 1957.

———. "On Narcissism: An Introduction." In *The Standard Edition of the Complete Psychological Works of Sigmund Freud*. Vol. 14, translated and edited by James Strachey, 69–102. London: Hogarth Press, 1957.

———. "Totem and Taboo." In *The Standard Edition of the Complete Psychological Works of Sigmund Freud.* Vol. 14, translated and edited by James Strachey. London: The Hogarth Press, 1953.

Gabbard, Glen O. "Review of *Borderline Personality Disorder: A Clinical Guide,* by John G. Gunderson." *New England Journal of Medicine* 345 (2001): 1003.

Gilbert, Elliot L. *The Good Kipling: Studies in the Short Novel.* Oberlin: Ohio University Press, 1971.

———. *"O Beloved Kids": Rudyard Kipling's Letters to His Children.* London: Weidenfeld and Nicolson, 1983.

———, ed. *The World of Mystery Fiction.* San Diego: University Extension, University of California Press, 1978.

———. *The World of Mystery Fiction: A Guide.* San Diego: University Extension, University of California Press, 1978.

Gilbert, Roger. "Experiencing Otherness: Ruth Stone's Art of Inference." In *The House Is Made of Poetry: The Art of Ruth Stone,* edited by Wendy Barker and Sandra M. Gilbert, 140–150. Carbondale: Southern Illinois University Press, 1996.

Gilbert, Sandra M. *Acts of Attention: The Poems of D. H. Lawrence.* Ithaca: Cornell University Press, 1972.

———. *Aftermath: Poems.* New York: Norton, 2011.

———. *Blood Pressure.* New York: Norton, 1988.

———. *Death's Door: Modern Dying and the Ways We Grieve.* New York: Norton, 2006.

———. "Definitions of Love: Ruth Stone's Feminist Caritas." In *The House Is Made of Poetry: The Art of Ruth Stone,* edited by Wendy Barker and Sandra M. Gilbert, 194–206. Carbondale: Southern Illinois University Press, 1996.

———. *Emily's Bread.* New York: Norton, 1984.

———. *Ghost Volcano: Poems.* New York: Norton, 1997.

———. *In the Fourth World: Poems.* Tuscaloosa: University of Alabama Press, 1979.

———, ed. *Inventions of Farewell: A Book of Elegies.* New York: Norton, 2001.

———. *Kissing the Bread: New and Selected Poems, 1969–1999.* New York: Norton, 2000.

———. *On Burning Ground: Thirty Years of Thinking about Poetry.* Ann Arbor: University of Michigan Press, 2009.

———. *Rereading Women: Thirty Years of Exploring Our Literary Traditions.* New York: Norton, 2011.

———. *Wrongful Death: A Memoir.* New York: Norton, 1995.

Gilbert, Sandra M., and Susan Gubar. *The Madwoman in the Attic: The Woman Writer and the Nineteenth-Century Literary Imagination.* New Haven: Yale University Press, 1979.

———. *Masterpiece Theater: An Academic Melodrama.* New Brunswick: Rutgers University Press, 1995.

———. *No Man's Land: The Place of the Woman Writer in the Twentieth Century.* 3 vols. New Haven: Yale University Press, 1988–1994.

———, eds. *The Norton Anthology of Literature by Women: The Tradition in English.* New York: Norton, 1985.

———, eds. *Shakespeare's Sisters: Feminist Essays on Women Poets.* Bloomington: Indiana University Press, 1979.

Godwin, Gail. *Dream Children.* New York: Knopf, 1976.

———. *Evenings at Five: A Novel and Five New Stories.* Illustrations by Frances Halsband. New York: Ballantine, 2004.

———. *Evensong.* New York: Ballantine, 2000.

———. *Father Melancholy's Daughter.* New York: Avon, 1992.

———. *The Good Husband.* New York: Ballantine, 1994.

———. *Heart: A Natural History of the Heart-Filled Life.* New York: Perennial, 2002.

———. "Losing Ground." In *In the Fullness of Time: 32 Women on Life after 50*, edited by Emily W. Upham and Linda Gravenson, 89–100. New York: Atria, 2010.

———. *The Making of a Writer: Journals, 1961–1963.* Edited by Rob Neufeld. New York: Random House, 2006.

———. *The Making of a Writer: Journals, 1963–1969.* Vol. 2. Edited by Rob Neufeld. New York: Random House, 2011.

———. *Mr. Bedford and the Muses.* New York: Viking, 1983.

———. *The Odd Woman.* New York: Knopf, 1974.

———. *The Perfectionists.* New York: Ballantine, 1995.

———. *A Southern Family.* New York: Morrow, 1987.

———. *Violet Clay.* New York: Knopf, 1978.

Goodwin, Frederick K., and Kay Redfield Jamison. *Manic Depressive Illness.* New York: Oxford University Press, 1990.

Gross, Charles G. *Brain, Vision, Memory: Tales in the History of Neuroscience.* Cambridge: MIT Press, 1998.

———. *A Hole in the Head: More Tales in the History of Neuroscience.* Cambridge: MIT Press, 2009.

Gross, Charles G., and H. Philip Zeigler, eds. *Readings in Physiological Psychology.* New York: Harper & Row, 1969.

Gubar, Susan. *Judas: A Biography.* New York: Norton, 2009.

———. "Living with Cancer: Difficult Choices." *New York Times*, August 7, 2014.

———. *Memoir of a Debulked Woman: Enduring Ovarian Cancer.* New York: Norton, 2012.

Gunderson, John G. *Borderline Personality Disorder: A Clinical Guide.* Washington, DC: American Psychiatric Association, 2001.

Gunther, John. *Death Be Not Proud.* 1949. Reprint, New York: Perennial, 1998.

Hall, Donald. *The Best Day the Worst Day: Life with Jane Kenyon.* Boston: Houghton Mifflin, 2005.

———. *Unpacking the Boxes: A Memoir of Life in Poetry.* Boston: Houghton Mifflin, 2008.

Herman, Ellen. *Kinship by Design: A History of Adoption in the Modern United States*. Chicago: University of Chicago Press, 2008.

Holmes, Thomas, and Richard Rahe. "The Social Readjustment Rating Scale." *Journal of Psychosomatic Research* 11 (1967): 213–218.

Horowitz, Mardi, Nancy Wilner, Charles Marmor, and Janice Krupnik. "Pathological Grief and the Activation of Latent Self-Images." *American Journal of Psychiatry* 137 (1980): 1157–1162.

Jamison, Kay Redfield. *Exuberance: The Passion for Life*. New York: Knopf, 2004.

———. *Night Falls Fast: Understanding Suicide*. New York: Knopf, 1999.

———. *Nothing Was the Same: A Memoir*. 2009. Reprint, New York: Vintage, 2011.

———. *Touched with Fire: Manic-Depressive Illness and the Artistic Temperament*. New York: Free Press, 1993.

———. *An Unquiet Mind: A Memoir of Moods and Madness*. New York: Knopf, 1995.

Janoff-Bulman, Ronnie. *Shattered Assumptions: Towards a New Psychology of Trauma*. New York: Free Press, 1992.

Johnson, Greg. *Invisible Writer: A Biography of Joyce Carol Oates*. New York: Plume, 1999.

Jurecic, Ann. *Illness as Narrative*. Pittsburgh: University of Pittsburgh Press, 2012.

Kafka, Franz. *Letters to Friends, Family, and Editors*. Translated by Richard Winston and Clara Winston. New York: Schocken, 1977.

Kauffman, Jeffrey, ed. *The Shame of Death, Grief, and Trauma*. New York: Routledge, 2010.

Keats, John. *Selected Poems and Letters*. Cambridge, MA: Riverside Press, 1959.

Klass, Dennis, Phyllis R. Silverman, and Steven L. Nickman, eds. *Continuing Bonds: New Understandings of Grief*. Washington, DC: Taylor and Francis, 1996.

Konigsberg, Ruth Davis. *The Truth about Grief: The Myth of Its Five Stages and the New Science of Loss*. New York: Simon & Schuster, 2011.

Krementz, Jill. *How It Feels to Be Adopted*. New York: Knopf, 1982.

Kuehl, Linda. "Interview with Joan Didion." In *Writers at Work: The Paris Review Interviews*, edited by George Plimpton, introduction by Francine du Plessix Gray, 342–357. New York: Viking Press, 1981.

Lewis, C. S. *A Grief Observed*. 1963. Reprint, San Francisco: Harper San Francisco, 1994.

Mantel, Hilary. *Giving Up the Ghost*. New York: Picador, 2004.

Maslin, Janet. "The Shock of Losing a Spouse." *New York Times*, February 13, 2011.

McCready, Louise. "Joyce Carol Oates on *A Widow's Story*." *Huffpost Books*, February 16, 2011. http://www.huffingtonpost.com/Louise-Mccready/joyce-carol-oates-on-a-wi_b_824237.html.

McGrath, Charles. "Joyce Carol Oates Updates Her *Widow's Story*." *New York Times*, May 10, 2011.

Menninger, Karl. *Man against Himself.* New York: Harcourt, Brace & World, 1938.

Mukherjee, Siddhartha. *The Emperor of All Maladies: A Biography of Cancer.* New York: Scribner, 2010.

Nasar, Sylvia. *A Beautiful Mind: A Biography of John Forbes Nash, Jr.* New York: Simon & Schuster, 1998.

Nesse, Randolph M., and George C. Williams. *Why We Get Sick: The New Science of Darwinian Medicine.* New York: Vintage, 1996.

Nuland, Sherwin B. *How We Die: Reflections on Life's Final Chapter.* New York: Vintage Books, 1995.

Nutt, Amy Ellis. "Joyce Carol Oates: Princeton's 'Dark Lady of Fiction' Comes Shining." *The Star-Ledger,* March 15, 2010.

Oates, Joyce Carol. *Conversations 1979–2006.* Edited by Greg Johnson. Princeton: Ontario Review Press, 2006.

———. *Conversations with Joyce Carol Oates.* Edited by Lee Milazzo. Jackson: University Press of Mississippi, 1989.

———. *In Rough Country: Essays and Reviews.* New York: Ecco, 2010.

———. *The Journal of Joyce Carol Oates, 1973–1982.* Edited by Greg Johnson. New York: Ecco, 2007.

———. "Letter." *New York Review of Books.* May 26, 2011.

———. *Little Bird of Heaven.* New York: Ecco, 2010.

———. *Night-Side: Eighteen Tales.* New York: Vanguard, 1977.

———. *The Profane Art: Essays and Reviews.* New York: Dutton, 1983.

———. *Sourland.* New York: Ecco, 2010.

———. *The Tattooed Girl.* New York: Ecco, 2003.

———. *them.* New York: Fawcett, 1970.

———. *Uncensored: Views & (Re)views.* New York: Ecco, 2005.

———. *A Widow's Story.* New York: Ecco, 2011.

———. *Where I've Been, and Where I'm Going: Essays, Reviews, and Prose.* New York: Plume, 1999.

———. *With Shuddering Fall.* New York: Vanguard, 1964.

Oates, Joyce Carol, and Meghan O'Rourke. "Why We Write about Grief." *New York Times,* February 26, 2011.

Parkes, Colin Murray. "'What Becomes of Redundant World Models?' A Contribution to the Study of Adaptation to Change." *British Journal of Medical Psychology* 48 (1975): 131–137.

Pausch, Jai. *Dream New Dreams: Reimagining My Life After Loss.* New York: Crown, 2012.

Pausch, Randy. *The Last Lecture.* With Jeffrey Zaslow. New York: Hyperion, 2008.

Pepper, Gillian V., and S. Craig Roberts. "Rates of Nausea and Vomiting in Pregnancy and Dietary Characteristics across Populations." *Proceedings of the Royal Society B* 273 (2006): 2675–2679.

Price, Reynolds. *A Whole New Life: An Illness and a Healing.* New York: Scribner, 2003.

Rando, Therese. *How to Go on Living When Someone You Love Dies*. New York: Bantam, 1988.

Rosenberg, Elinor B. *The Adoption Life Cycle: The Children and Their Families through the Years*. New York: Free Press, 1992.

Rosenblatt, Roger. *Kayak Morning: Reflections on Love, Grief, and Small Boats*. New York: HarperCollins, 2011.

———. *Making Toast: A Family Story*. New York: Ecco, 2010.

Scarry, Elaine. *The Body in Pain: The Making and Unmaking of the World*. New York: Oxford University Press, 1985.

Seinfeld, Jeffrey. "Loss, Belonging, Identity, and the Dynamics of an Adoptee's Identification with Her Birth Mother." In *Understanding Adoption: Clinical Work with Adults, Children, and Parents*, edited by Kathleen Hushion, Susan B. Sherman, and Diana Siskind, 181–196. Lanham, MD: Jason Aronson, 2006.

Silverman, Phyllis R. *Widow to Widow: How the Bereaved Help One Another*. 2nd ed. New York: Brunner-Routledge, 2004.

Skloot, Floyd. *In the Shadow of Memory*. Lincoln: University of Nebraska Press, 2004.

Smith, Raymond J. *Charles Churchill*. Boston: Twayne, 1977.

Solomon, Robert C. *In Defense of Sentimentality*. New York: Oxford University Press, 2004.

Starer, Robert. *Continuo: A Life in Music*. New York: Random House, 1987.

———. *The Music Teacher*. Woodstock, NY: Overlook Press, 1997.

Stewart, Garrett. *Death Sentences: Styles of Dying in British Fiction*. Cambridge: Harvard University Press, 1984.

Stone, Ruth. *Who Is the Widow's Muse?* Cambridge, MA: Yellow Moon Press, 1991.

Stroebe, Margaret, and Henk Schut. "The Dual Process Model of Coping with Bereavement: Rationale and Description." *Death Studies* 23 (1999): 197–224.

Styron, Alexandra. *Reading My Father*. New York: Scribner, 2011.

Styron, William. *Darkness Visible: A Memoir of Madness*. New York: Random House, 1990.

Tanner, Laura A. *Lost Bodies: Inhabiting the Borders of Life and Death*. Ithaca: Cornell University Press, 2006.

Underwood, Doug. *Chronicling Trauma: Journalists and Writers on Violence and Loss*. Urbana: University of Illinois Press, 2011.

Westerlund, Kerstin. *Escaping the Castle of Patriarchy: Patterns of Development in the Novels of Gail Godwin*. Stockholm: Uppsala, 1990.

Wilson, Craig. "Joyce Carol Oates' Pilgrimage of Widowhood." *USA Today*, February 14, 2011.

Wilson, Robin. "Susan Gubar's Closing Chapters." *Chronicle of Higher Education*, April 27, 2012.

Worden, J. William. *Grief Counseling and Grief Therapy: A Handbook for the Mental Health Practitioner*. 3rd ed. New York: Springer, 2002.

Wurmser, Leon. "Shame: The Veiled Companion of Narcissism." In *The Many Faces of Shame*, edited by Donald L. Nathanson, 64–92. New York: Guilford Press, 1987.

Wyatt, Richard J. *After Middle Age: A Physician's Guide to Staying Healthy While Growing Older*. New York: McGraw-Hill, 1985.

———. "Words to Live By." *Washington Post*, Health Section, February 13, 2001.

———, and Robert H. Chew. *Wyatt's Practical Psychiatric Practice: Forms and Protocols for Clinical Use*. 3rd ed. Washington, DC: American Psychiatric Publishing, 2005.

Index